Snacks & Beverages

Kitchen Hints

- If you over-salt soup or vegetables, add cut raw potatoes and discard once they have cooked and absorbed the salt. A teaspoon each of cider vinegar and sugar added to salty soup or vegetables will also remedy the situation.
- If you over-sweetened a dish, add salt.
- Pale gravy may be browned by adding a bit of instant coffee straight from the jar...no bitter taste either.
- Drop a lettuce leaf into a pot of homemade soup to absorb excess grease on top.
- Ice cubes will also eliminate the fat from soup and stew. Just drop a few into the pot and stir; the fat will cling to the cubes; discard the cubes before they melt.
- If fresh vegetables are wilted or blemished, pick off the brown edges, sprinkle with cool water, wrap in paper towel and refrigerate for an hour or so.
- Perk up soggy lettuce by adding lemon juice to a bowl of cold water and soak for an hour in the refrigerator.
- Lettuce and celery keep longer if you store them in paper bags instead of cellophane.
- Soupy whipped cream can be saved by adding an egg white, chilling thoroughly, and then beating it again for a fluffy surprise!
- A few drops of lemon juice added to whipping cream helps it whip faster and better.
- Brown sugar won't harden if an apple slice is placed in the container. But if your brown sugar is already brick-hard, put your cheese-grater to work and grate what you need.
- No more tears when peeling onions if placed in the deep freeze for 4-5 minutes first.
- Scalding tomatoes, peaches or pears in boiling water before peeling makes it easier on you and the fruit – skins slip right off.
- To hasten the ripening of garden tomatoes or avocados, put them in a brown paper bag, close the bag and leave at room temperature for a few days.
- When pan frying, always heat the pan before adding the butter or oil.
- A little salt sprinkled into the frying pan will prevent spattering.
- Meat loaf will not stick if you place a slice of bacon on the bottom of the pan.
- Vinegar brought to a boil in a new frying pan will prevent foods from sticking.
- Muffins will slide right out of tin pans if the hot pan is first placed on a wet towel.
- No sticking to the pan when you scald milk if you first rinse the pan in cold water.
- A few teaspoons of sugar and cinnamon slowly burned on top of the stove will hide unpleasant cooking odors and make your family think you've been baking all day.
- A lump of butter or a few teaspoons of cooking oil added to water when boiling rice, noodles, spaghetti or potatoes will prevent boiling over.
- A few drops of lemon juice added to simmering rice will keep the grains separate.
- A dip of the spoon or cup into hot water before measuring shortening or butter will cause the fat to slip out easily without sticking to the spoon.
- Before measuring honey or syrup, oil the cup with cooking oil and rinse in hot water.
- A dampened paper towel or terry cloth brushed downward on a cob of corn will remove every strand of corn silk.
- To determine whether an egg is fresh, immerse it in a pan of cool, salted water. If it sinks, it is fresh; if it rises to the surface, throw it away.
- To determine whether an egg is hard-boiled, spin it. If it spins it is hard boiled. If it wobbles and will not spin it is raw.
- Egg shells remove easier from hard-boiled eggs if quickly rinsed in cold water first.
- For fluffier omelets, add a pinch of cornstarch before beating.
- Keep bacon slices from sticking together; roll the package into a tube shape and secure with rubber bands.
- Cheese won't harden if you butter the exposed edges before storing.
- Thaw fish in milk; the milk draws out the frozen taste and gives a fresh-caught flavor.

Avalon Hix
770-998-1419

EWGA FOUNDATION

Presents

Recipes for Success – On and Off the Course

A selection of recipes and golf games
from members, staff, partners
and friends of the EWGA

Acknowledgements

The EWGA Foundation is dedicated to enriching the lives of women through the game of golf. *"Recipes for Success – On and Off the Course"* is our first cookbook fundraiser. Proceeds from sales will be used to further our efforts to support women in need, develop education programs and cultivate leadership development opportunities, enabling more women and future generations to enjoy the benefits of golf for their personal, professional and emotional well-being.

Our sincere thanks to everyone who contributed recipes, artwork, ideas, time and talent to this project. We also thank those who are supporting the EWGA Foundation through the purchase of our cookbook. We could not have done this without you!

We hope the recipes in this cookbook will enrich your life and the lives of your loved ones. Bon Appétit!

Margaret E. Downey

Margaret E. Downey
EWGA Foundation Board President
Jacksonville, FL Chapter

EWGA Foundation Cookbook Committee

Kathy Thomas, Co-Chair & Former EWGA Board Member
Kansas City Metro & Tucson-Old Pueblo, AZ Chapter
Angie Niehoff, Co-Chair & Former EWGA Foundation Board President
Palm Beach County, FL Chapter
Nona Footz, EWGA Board Member & Foundation Fundraising Chair
Fairfield County, CT Chapter
Judy Dickinson, Former EWGA Foundation Board Member
Palm Beach County, FL Chapter
Jo-Ann C. Dixon, EWGA Board Member
Northern New Jersey Chapter
Margaret Downey, EWGA Foundation Board President
Jacksonville, FL Chapter
Sheri Harvey
Genesee County, MI Chapter
Kristen Skivington, Foundation Fundraising Committee
Genesee County, MI Chapter
Susan Naugle, EWGA Director of Marketing
Palm Beach County, FL Chapter
Molly Taylor, EWGA Foundation Intern

Cookbook cover and divider designs created by
Sheri Harvey, EWGA Genesee County, MI Chapter
Shar Graphics, Lapeer, MI
www.shargraphics.com

Having played golf for only a few years, freelance graphic designer Sheri Harvey joined the EWGA Genesee County, MI Chapter in 2010 and quickly got involved. Shortly after joining the Chapter, she qualified to participate on the scramble team that competed in EWGA's Upper Midwest Championship Semi-finals and was recently selected to serve on her Chapter's Board of Directors.

Thank you Sheri for our beautiful cover!

Table of Contents

Appetizers, Snacks & Beverages 1

Soups & Salads 33

Vegetables 61

Pasta, Rice & Potatoes 75

Meat & Poultry 91

Seafood...141

Breads & Rolls 155

Desserts...171

Games For The Course......................... 213

FAVORITE RECIPES
FROM MY COOKBOOK

Recipe Name	Page Number

Copyright © 2011

Printed By
Cookbook Publishers, Inc.
P.O. Box 15920
Lenexa, Kansas 66285-5920

A product of utypeitonline *software.*

Appetizers, Snacks & Beverages

Crab Triangles

1 stick butter, softened (do not microwave!)
1 jar Old English cheese
1½ tsp. mayonnaise
½ tsp. all seasoned salt
½ tsp. garlic powder
7 oz. white lump crab meat
6 English muffins, sliced in half

Blend all ingredients (except muffins). Spread mixture on muffins. Bake at 350° until heated through or broil. Cut in fours when ready to serve. Makes 48 triangles.

Cindy McGeever
Greater Philadelphia, PA Chapter
Nancy Oliver Founder's Award Winner and
Former Association Board President

"I never thought of myself as a pioneer. We were just a bunch of stubborn women who loved golf and figured we could make it happen."
-Marlene Hagge

Marinated Shrimp

1 lb. shrimp, cooked and peeled
3 yellow onions, thinly sliced
1 lemon, sliced
½ c. apple cider vinegar
¼ c. water
1 tsp. salt
1 tsp. sugar
¼ tsp. ground ginger
½ tsp. whole black peppercorns
½ tsp. dry mustard
1 bay leaf
¼ c. lemon juice
½ c. canola oil
Tabasco sauce to taste

Fill bowl with alternating layers of shrimp, lemon and onions. In a saucepan, combine vinegar, water, salt, sugar, ginger, peppercorns, mustard and bay leaf. Bring to a boil. Cover and simmer 5 minutes. Cool. Strain. Add lemon juice, oil and Tabasco sauce. Pour over shrimp. Cover and refrigerate 24 hours, stirring occasionally. Drain before serving. Makes 1 quart. Serves 8. This is a great way to serve shrimp for a cocktail party!

Lisa Van Divender
Cincinnati, OH Chapter

Shrimp Butter

2 (5 oz.) cans deveined shrimp, drained
1½ sticks butter, softened
4 Tbsp. mayonnaise
1 Tbsp. minced onion flakes
2 Tbsp. lemon juice
1 (8 oz.) pkg. cream cheese, softened

Mix all ingredients with an electric beater or mixer. Beat until light and fluffy. Serve with crackers or vegetables. Keep chilled until serving.

Le Ann Finger, PGA, LPGA
Palm Beach County, FL Chapter
National Promotions Specialist, PGA of America

Jalapeno Shrimp Wraps With Bacon

24 large shrimp
3 jalapeno peppers
12 thick cut bacon slices, halved (center cut smoked preferred)

3 Tbsp. olive oil
¼ tsp. salt
¼ tsp. black pepper

Preheat oven to 425°. Boil shrimp, drain and rinse. Peel shrimp, remove tail, and devein. Cut shrimp on the spine (similar to butterflied) with enough room to insert jalapeno slice. Cut peppers in rings, enough for 24 pieces. Snip one side for inserting into shrimp. Toss together shrimp, olive oil, salt, and pepper in a bowl. Set aside. Insert jalapeno slice into spine of shrimp. Wrap ½ slice of bacon around shrimp and close. Lay in glass baking dish (if preferred, you can secure with a toothpick). Repeat procedure with remaining bacon slices, shrimp, and jalapeno pieces. Place in oven (middle rack) for 20 minutes until golden brown. Serve with toothpicks and optional dipping sauce (creamy peppercorn sauce).

Terri D. Pearce
Metro Detroit, MI Chapter
Association and Foundation Board Member

Brook's Shrimp Shooters

1½ lb. cooked shrimp
⅔ c. extra virgin olive oil
½ c. white balsamic vinegar
1 Tbsp. chopped fresh cilantro

2 Tbsp. grated lemon rind
1 tsp. salt
1 tsp. freshly ground pepper
1 tsp. hot sauce

Combine all ingredients and marinate for a couple of hours before serving. (If done ahead of time and refrigerated, allow enough time for it to come to room temperature before serving so olive oil warms up.) If using frozen shrimp, remove tails. I add a little juice from the lemon as well.

Jo-Ann Dixon
Northern New Jersey Chapter
Association and Foundation Board Member

Jalapeno Smoked Oyster Appetizer

1 can smoked oysters
8 oz. cream cheese
1 can pickled jalapenos
1 box Triscuits (regular)

Open can of smoked oysters and drain. Place oysters on paper towel and pat off oil. Open can of pickled jalapenos and drain. Cut off stem. Cut whole jalapenos in half lengthwise to make a boat. Devein and remove seeds. Rinse peppers and place on paper towel and pat dry. Open package of cream cheese and using a butter knife, apply ⅔ to 1 tablespoon of cream cheese to the jalapeno boat. Top with an oyster and serve with Triscuits crackers, or any other preferred cracker or hors d'oeuvre toasted bread slices. These different flavors are wonderful together. There's nothing quite like it. Smokin' Hot Cheese! Enjoy!!!

Elizabeth Rinehold
Santa Barbara, CA Chapter

Mouth-Watering Meatballs

1 lb. uncooked ground sausage
1 lb. uncooked ground ham
1 c. finely ground graham cracker
1 egg
¼ c. milk
1 (10 oz.) can tomato soup
1 c. brown sugar
¼ tsp. dry ground mustard

Preheat oven to 325°. In a large bowl, knead together the sausage, ham, graham crackers, egg, and milk until evenly distributed. In a separate bowl, mix tomato soup, brown sugar, and mustard together, stirring until any lumps are gone. In a 9x13 inch glass baking dish, use the meat mixture to make walnut-sized meatballs and place uniformly in baking dish. Using a small serving spoon, gently pour sauce over meatballs, ensuring all meatballs are evenly coated. Bake 45 minutes, or until sauce begins to brown. Let cool 5 minutes before serving. Enjoy!

Pam Brammann
Quad Cities, IA Chapter

Sweet Cranberry Crockpot Meatballs

1 (4 lb.) bag frozen beef meatballs
2 (16 oz.) cans whole berry cranberry sauce
2 (10 oz.) cans condensed tomato soup

Place frozen meatballs in bottom of crockpot. Pour cranberry sauce and tomato soup over meatballs. Simmer 5 to 6 hours on low, stirring occasionally. Enjoy after your round of golf...easy and delicious!

Jen Smith
Omaha, NE Chapter

Sweet & Sour Meatballs

3 to 5 lb. frozen cocktail meatballs
32 oz. grape jelly
2 jars chili sauce

In a crockpot, combine the grape jelly, chili sauce, and meatballs. Cook on low for 4 to 6 hours.

Kristie M. Carter
Central New York (Syracuse) Chapter

"We look at history. We have a challenge ahead of ourselves. You only get a chance so many times. That's all I need to get going."
-Annika Sorenstam

Meatballs

1 c. milk
3 c. fine dry bread crumbs
1 lb. ground beef
¼ lb. ground pork
¼ lb. ground veal
1 egg slightly beaten
4 Tbsp. minced onions
4 Tbsp. minced green bell pepper
¾ tsp. salt
¼ tsp. each pepper and nutmeg
2 Tbsp. each butter and oil
1 (16 oz.) can tomatoes
1 (12 oz.) can tomato paste
½ c. light brown sugar
½ c. light corn syrup

Pour milk over 1 cup of the bread crumbs and let it absorb. Combine meats with crumb mixture. Add egg, onion, peppers, salt and nutmeg. Mix thoroughly and form into small balls. Heat half of the butter and oil in a large skillet. Brown meatballs while adding the remainder of the butter and the oil as needed. Beat tomatoes to a consistent liquefied state and then add to tomato paste, brown sugar, corn syrup, and remainder of the dried bread crumbs. Mix all ingredients well and place on medium high and gradually add previously cooked meatballs to mixture. Remove once thoroughly heated and serve. Serves 10 to 12.

Judy Dickinson, LPGA
EWGA Leadership Award Winner
Former Foundation Board Member

Sausage In Puff Pastry

1 lb. Italian sausage links
1 sheet Pepperidge Farm Puff Pastry, thawed

Remove casings from the sausage. Place sausage links end to end on ⅓ of the pastry sheet at a time. Wrap pastry around sausage links and slice into silver dollar sized pieces (about ½ inch thick). Repeat with the rest of the sausage and pastry. Place on cookie sheet and bake in 425° oven for approximately 10 minutes, until pastry is brown and sausage cooked through. Cool and freeze in freezer bags for future entertaining. To serve, remove from freezer and warm in oven at 350° for 10 minutes. Serve with spicy mustard or BBQ sauce for dipping.

Angie Niehoff
Palm Beach County, FL Chapter
Former Foundation Board President and Association Board Member

Sausage Crescent Wrap

1 lb. breakfast sausage
4 oz. cream cheese
1 roll crescent pastry sheet
   (similar to crescent rolls but
   without perforations)

In frying pan, break breakfast sausage up into small pieces and brown. Remove cooked sausage from pan and place on paper towel covered plate. Pat off grease with additional paper towels. Return sausage to pan. Add cream cheese to cooked sausage and stir until cheese is completely melted. Unroll pastry sheet onto baking sheet. Make sure there are no holes or perforations. Place entire sausage and cheese mixture in the middle of the sheet leaving only a little bit of space on each short end of the sheet for folding. Fold in ends of roll and then the sides, making sure there are no breaks. Bake (seam side up) at 350° until golden brown, about 12 minutes. Slice and serve.

Barb Oswald
Metro Detroit, MI Chapter

"Do your best, one shot at a time and then move on. Remember that golf is just a game."

-Nancy Lopez

Caramelized Sweet Onion And Goat Cheese Tartlets

3 Tbsp. melted butter (plus extra for greasing pan - can also use PAM)
2 c. butter cracker crumbs (like Ritz or Townhouse)
1½ Tbsp. olive oil
1 large Vidalia onion, diced
¾ tsp. chopped fresh thyme
Salt and pepper to taste
1 (5 oz.) log Goat cheese (room temperature)
2 large eggs, lightly beaten
½ c. heavy cream or half and half
¼ tsp. cayenne pepper

Preheat oven to 425°. Combine cracker crumbs and butter in a medium bowl; stir to incorporate. Spoon mixture into lightly buttered 12 cup silicon muffin pan (or use a pie plate). Firmly press the mixture evenly over the bottom and ¾ up the sides of the pan. Place in preheated oven, about 8 minutes, until just golden brown. Set aside to cool. Reduce oven to 350°. Heat a medium saute pan with olive oil. Add the chopped onion, then reduce the heat to medium-low. Cook, stirring often, until golden brown and caramelized, about 45 minutes. Stir in the thyme, salt, and pepper and cook 2 to 3 minutes more. Cool. Divide the cooled onions between the tartlets (or over the pie plate with crumbs), spreading evenly. Combine the Goat cheese, eggs, cream and cayenne pepper into the bowl of a food processor. Process until creamy and well blended. Pour the mixture over the onions. Bake at 350° until light golden brown and somewhat firm, about 40 minutes. Cool for 10 minutes, then serve hot, warm, or at room temperature with fresh herb salad.

Susan Caruso
Long Island, NY Chapter

Gorgonzola Torte

6 oz. crumbled Gorgonzola
   cheese (Blue cheese)
½ lb. unsalted butter, softened
½ lb. cream cheese, softened
2 garlic cloves, finely chopped

1 small shallot, finely chopped
2 Tbsp. chives or fresh parsley,
   chopped
Salt and pepper to taste
1 jar orange fig preserves

Combine butter, cream cheese, shallot, garlic, salt, and pepper in a food processor until smooth. Add crumbled Gorgonzola to processor using the pulse button until mixed. Line a small container with plastic film, pour in cheese mixture, and press down. Refrigerate overnight. Turn onto plate and top with orange fig preserves and serve with crackers and fruit.

Penelope 'Penny' Rahman
Palm Beach County, FL Chapter

Shoa Mai Dumplings

Filling:

1 lb. chicken breast or mild
   tasting fish
1 Tbsp. shallots, minced
3 garlic cloves, minced
2 scallions, finely minced
½ c. jicama, finely minced

1 Tbsp. Chinese rice wine
2 tsp. fresh ginger, minced
Kosher salt to taste
30 to 35 wonton or egg roll
   wrappers

Dipping Sauce:

2 Tbsp. soy sauce
¼ c. rice vinegar

1 tsp. sesame oil

Puree chicken or fish in food processor. Transfer chicken or fish to bowl and stir in rest of filing ingredients. Put a scant tablespoon of filing in center of round wrapper. Bring wrapper up on four sides and press to form loose four lobed cloverleaf. Arrange dumplings ½ inch apart in oiled steamer tray or on cabbage leaf in a bamboo steamer. Stem over medium high heat for 12 to 15 minutes. Remove and let stand for 5 minutes covered. Garnish with cilantro and serve with dipping sauce.

Barbara Bettman
Miami, FL Chapter

Ikra (Ukrainian Eggplant Appetizer)

2¼ lb. eggplant, whole and unpeeled
4 large tomatoes, diced
2 to 3 medium onions, diced
1 to 2 Tbsp. oil
Juice of ½ lemon
1 to 3 garlic cloves, minced
Salt and pepper to taste
1 tsp. sugar
2 to 3 Tbsp. chopped flat leaf parsley

Bake or roast the eggplant at 400° for about an hour. If roasting make slits in skin. Cool the eggplant, remove skin, and process in a food processor for a few minutes or finely chop the eggplant manually. Saute the onions in oil until wilted; add minced garlic and saute for a minute, then add the tomatoes. Add the eggplant, mixing well, and saute for 15 minutes. Add lemon juice, salt, pepper, and sugar. Mix and remove from heat, adding the parsley. Cool the Ikra and refrigerate. Serve with crackers or toasted bread, or as a side dish.

Lucy Doroshenko Slobidsky
Omaha, NE and Tampa Bay, FL Chapters

Stuffed Belgian Endive Appetizer

1 (2 oz.) pkg. fresh basil, stems removed
1 medium tomato, cut in chunks
1 handful cashews or walnuts
1 to 2 garlic cloves
Lemon juice, salt and pepper
Belgian endive

Put all ingredients (except endive) in food processor and "let her rip!" Recommend adding the basil first as it fills up the food processor; when almost chopped add the remaining ingredients. Allow to rest for at least 1 hour. Fill endive leaves and enjoy.

Shelley French
Seattle, WA Chapter
Nancy Oliver Founder's Award Winner

Spanekopita

16 oz. Ricotta cheese
½ c. Romano cheese
½ lb. Feta cheese, crumbled
8 eggs, beaten
2 Tbsp. oil
1 c. butter, melted
½ c. chopped fresh parsley
1 bunch green onions, finely chopped
3 lb. fresh spinach, steamed and chopped (or 4 pkgs. frozen, chopped spinach)
Salt and pepper to taste
1 lb. phyllo

Prepare filling as follows: add Ricotta and Romano cheese to crumbled Feta cheese and blend. Blend in beaten eggs, oil, and 4 tablespoons melted butter. Stir in onions and parsley, then add spinach (drain as much water as possible). Phyllo must be worked with quickly, so have everything prepared and ready to go before you begin. Unroll phyllo and have a damp towel ready to cover, should it begin to dry out. Work quickly and there should not be any problems. Use a pan about the size of a phyllo sheet, approximately 15x24x3 inch pan. Brush sides and bottom of pan with melted butter. Next, place 3 layers of phyllo, folding over any excess; brush with butter. Place 3 more sheets and brush with butter. Continue to brush phyllo 3 layers at a time until half the pound is used. Pour filling onto phyllo and spread evenly. Continue placing remaining phyllo, 3 layers at a time, brushing with butter between each set until phyllo is used. With a sharp knife score the top layers of phyllo into squares or triangles. Place in preheated oven, 350° for 45 minutes. Tops should be golden. Remove; cool until it can be handled. Cut through the layers and remove from the pan.

Tyra Jarvis
Sacramento, CA Chapter
Nancy Oliver Founder's Award Winner and
Former Association Board President

Persian Melon With Prosciutto, Mint, And Balsamic Reduction

Main Recipe:

1 Persian melon (may use cantaloupe if Persian unavailable)	4 oz. prosciutto, thinly sliced 1 pomegranate 15 fresh mint leaves

Peel pomegranate, and separate the red arils (seeds) from the white membrane, set aside. Cut Persian melon into wedges, remove outer rind and inside seeds. Place each wedge on individual small serving plate. Sprinkle with chiffonaded, thinly sliced Prosciutto. Drizzle with balsamic vinegar reduction. Sprinkle with chiffonaded fresh mint. Sprinkle with some of the pomegranate arils. Serve.

Balsamic Reduction:

1 (8 oz.) bottle balsamic vinegar   ½ tsp. refined sugar

To make a reduction takes a watchful eye and a few very simple instructions. Pour bottle of vinegar in a stock pot. Try to use one with sloping sides as the liquid will begin to boil faster as well as reduce at a quickened pace. Turn the heat to high and wait for the vinegar to begin to boil. Reduce the temperature of the burner to medium. Add sugar to the pot and stir until the sugar is dissolved. Continue simmering, uncovered, until 75% of the vinegar has evaporated. Remove vinegar from the heat and allow it to cool. The reduction is done if it is thickened to the consistency of syrup. To make thicker, heat again and reduce it further.

Linda Lemon-Steiner
Manatee, FL Chapter

Chicken Wings

1 pkg. chicken wings
1 stick butter
Worcestershire sauce to taste
Garlic salt to taste
Hickory smoked salt to taste
Cayenne pepper to taste
2 capfuls dry vermouth

Microwave chicken wings for 5 to 10 minutes until partially cooked. In saucepan, melt butter and add Worcestershire sauce, cayenne pepper, garlic salt, and hickory smoked salt to taste. Add dry Vermouth. Start grill and place chicken wings on. Baste with butter sauce and sprinkle with garlic salt and hickory smoked salt. Turn frequently, basting each time you turn. Sprinkle with garlic salt and hickory smoked salt after first turn. Remove when cooked through, about 15 to 20 minutes. Serve warm or cold. Can be used on larger pieces of chicken for dinner.

Mary Jo Burke
Naples, FL and Minnesota Metro Chapters

Toasted Rye Rounds

1 c. grated Parmesan cheese
1 c. mayonnaise
2 Tbsp. finely minced onion
1 Tbsp. horseradish
Worcestershire sauce (a dash or two)
1 loaf party rye bread

Mix together cheese, mayonnaise, onion, horseradish, and Worcestershire and spread on slices of party rye bread. Toast until golden brown and bubbly. Enjoy!

Patricia L. Joyce
Palm Beach County, FL Chapter
EWGA Managing Director, Strategic Initiatives

Chutney Topped Cream Cheese

1 (8 oz.) pkg. cream cheese, softened
1 tsp. powdered curry
Chutney for topping

Add powdered curry to softened cream cheese and mix well. Reshape or form into a log or rectangle and refrigerate overnight. Take out and cover top with chutney. Can also be made with light cream cheese. Serve with crackers.

Nancy Matus
Palm Beach County, FL Chapter
EWGA Event Manager

Vegetable Pizza

2 (8 oz.) pkgs. refrigerated crescent rolls
2 (8 oz.) pkgs. cream cheese, softened
1 c. mayonnaise
1 Tbsp. chopped onion
1 Tbsp. chopped dill
1 c. chopped fresh broccoli
1 c. chopped tomatoes
1 c. chopped red and yellow bell pepper
1 c. chopped cauliflower
1 c. shredded carrots
1 c. chopped tomatoes (drained and put on pizza last so it does not get soggy)
1 c. shredded Cheddar cheese

Preheat oven to 375°. Roll out the crescent roll dough onto a 9x13 inch baking sheet, and pinch together edges to form the pizza crust. Bake crust for 12 minutes in the preheated oven. Once finished cooking, remove crust from oven and let cool 15 minutes without removing it from the baking sheet. In a small mixing bowl, combine cream cheese, mayonnaise, onion, and dill. Spread the mixture over the cooled crust. Arrange broccoli, tomato, bell pepper, cauliflower, shredded carrots, and Cheddar cheese over the cream cheese layer. Chill for one hour, slice and serve.

Lori Cook North
Naples, FL Chapter
Nancy Oliver Founder's Award Winner and
Former Association Board Member

Veggie Pizza

2 cans crescent rolls
16 oz. cream cheese (room temperature)
¾ c. mayonnaise or Miracle Whip
1 pkg. Hidden Valley ranch dip (dry mix)
1 c. chopped broccoli
1 c. chopped cauliflower
1 c. chopped green pepper
1 c. grated carrot
½ c. chopped onion
1 c. (or more) grated Cheddar cheese

Flatten crescent rolls and spread on cookie sheet (12x18 inch cookie sheet with sides or 2 smaller sheets) coated with Pam. Bake at 375° for 12 to 15 minutes. Cool completely. Cream mayonnaise, cream cheese, and ranch dip dry mix together. Spread over cooled crust (to the edge). Combine chopped vegetables in a bowl and spread evenly over creamed cheese layer, pressing vegetables in. Sprinkle Cheddar cheese on top, lightly pressing down. Chill. Cut into squares. Do not make too far in advance because it will get soggy.

Judy Hillhouse
Charlotte, NC Chapter

Small Pizza For Lunch

2 pieces pita bread (100% whole wheat)
2 Tbsp. sundried tomato sauce
1 tomato, chopped
¼ red onion, chopped
½ red and green bell pepper, chopped
2 small mushrooms, chopped
¼ lb. sharp Cheddar cheese
¼ lb. cooked shrimp (or any cooked meat)
¼ lb. Mozzarella cheese

Place 2 pieces of pita bread on a baking sheet. Spread sundried tomato sauce on bread. Top with all of the chopped vegetables. Add Cheddar cheese. Next, top with shrimp or cooked meat, and spread Mozzarella cheese over all ingredients. Broil about 5 to 8 minutes. Cut each pizza into 4 pieces and serve hot. Serves 2.

Stephanie Sook Kang
Portland, OR Chapter

Appetizers, Snacks & Beverages

Baked Chestnuts

1 lb. lean bacon, cooked
2 cans water chestnuts, drained
1 c. catsup
1 c. sugar
2 Tbsp. Worcestershire sauce

Wrap bacon around water chestnut, secure with toothpick. Place in foil lined pan. Bake at 350° for 45 minutes. Mix catsup, sugar and Worcestershire sauce and pour over chestnuts. Bake for an additional 30 minutes. Can be made the day before and stored in refrigerator, reheat before serving.

Ellen Brothers
Genesee County, MI Chapter

Curried Fruit

1 can pear halves
1 can apricots
1 can pineapple chunks
1 can peaches
1 small bottle cherries
½ c. salted almonds
⅓ c. butter, melted
¾ c. brown sugar
3 tsp. curry powder

Mix butter, brown sugar, and curry powder. Drain all fruit and place in oblong casserole dish. Pour brown sugar mixture over fruit. Bake at 325° for 1 hour. Excellent as a side with turkey or pork. Serves 8.

Nune Richards
San Diego, CA Chapter

Mexican Caviar/Avocado Salad

4 oz. sliced black olives, drained
4 oz. chopped green chilies, drained
3 tomatoes, chopped
4 green onions, chopped
1 tsp. garlic salt (or 2 fresh garlic cloves, minced)
4 Tbsp. olive oil
1½ Tbsp. red wine vinegar
¼ tsp. pepper
1 tsp. salt
3 avocados, peeled and chopped

Combine all ingredients and chill overnight. Can drain if needed before serving. Serve as an appetizer with corn chips or as a salad. A fabulous and refreshing dish with home grown tomatoes!

Chris Ferguson
Kansas City Metro Chapter

Cowboy Caviar

Dressing:

1 Tbsp. olive oil
1 Tbsp. red wine vinegar
1/4 tsp. Tabasco
Salt and pepper to taste

Combine all ingredients and mix well. Set aside.

Cowboy Caviar:

1 (15 oz.) can black eyed peas or black beans, drained and rinsed
1 (15 oz.) can white corn drained and rinsed or 1 c. frozen white corn
1/2 c. green onion (scallions), chopped
1/2 c. black olives, chopped
1 jalapeno, seeded and chopped (or substitute a 2 oz. can chopped mild green chilies)
1 medium tomato, chopped
1 avocado, chopped
1 c. chopped fresh cilantro

Mix together beans and corn, green onions, olives, and chopped jalapeno. Stir in dressing. Just before serving add avocado, tomato, and cilantro. Serve with corn tortilla chips.

BJ Hansen
Salt Lake City, UT Chapter

Hummus

4 c. garbanzo beans (chickpeas), drained
2 Tbsp. tahini paste
1/3 c. warm water
2 Tbsp. extra virgin olive oil
2 lemons, fresh squeezed juice
1 garlic clove, minced
1/4 c. chopped cilantro
Pinch of cayenne
2 tsp. ground cumin
1 1/2 tsp. salt

Combine chickpeas, tahini, warm water, olive oil and juice of 1 lemon in a food processor. Process until smooth and creamy. Add garlic, salt, cumin, cayenne and cilantro and process to blend. Taste and correct seasonings. Add more lemon juice. Refrigerate until ready to serve.

Barbara Bettman
Miami, FL Chapter

Appetizers, Snacks & Beverages

Lemon And Garlic Hummus

1 can chickpeas
Zest and juice of 1 lemon
4 to 5 sprigs thyme
¼ c. olive oil (eyeball it)
Coarse salt and pepper to taste
Couple dashes hot sauce
1 garlic clove

Mix all ingredients in food processor. Serve with pita chips or bread, celery sticks, red pepper and cherry tomatoes. Enjoy!

Alice Osur
Northern New Jersey Chapter

Rachael Ray's Red Pepper Hummus

2 (15 oz.) cans chickpeas (garbanzo beans), drained
1 (6 oz.) jar roasted red peppers, drained
½ lemon, juiced
2 garlic cloves
4 stems fresh rosemary, leaves stripped from stems
Coarse salt and fresh pepper to taste
2 Tbsp. extra virgin olive oil, drizzled in

Combine all ingredients in food processor until well blended. Drizzle in the olive oil. Enjoy!

Alice Osur
Northern New Jersey Chapter

Beer Cheese

8 oz. cream cheese
2 c. shredded Cheddar cheese
1 pkg. Hidden Valley Ranch dry dressing mix
1 can beer

Mix together softened cream cheese, Cheddar cheese and ranch dressing mix packet. Add beer (about ½ can) until consistency becomes creamy. Serve with pretzels for dipping.

Ellen Brothers
Genesee County, MI Chapter

Dilly Dip

2 c. sour cream
1 c. Hellmann's mayonnaise
2 Tbsp. dill weed
2 Tbsp. parsley flakes
2 Tbsp. onion flakes
1¼ tsp. seasoned salt

Mix well and serve with a variety of vegetables. Best prepared a day in advance for full flavor.

Ellen Brothers
Genesee County, MI Chapter

Swiss-Bacon Dip

1 c. grated Swiss cheese
8 oz. cream cheese, softened
½ c. mayonnaise
4 to 8 slices crispy bacon, crumbled
2 tsp. minced chives (optional)

Preheat oven to 400°. Combine cheeses and mayonnaise and then fold in bacon and chives (optional). Place in a small baking dish and bake until golden and bubbly. Serve with garlic pita chips or, for a nice twist, rosemary crackers.

Kelly Grant
Atlanta, GA Chapter

Quick Cheesy Ro-Tel Dip

2 (1 lb.) rolls of Jimmy Dean's sausage (1 hot and 1 mild)
2 (8 oz.) bricks Philadelphia cream cheese
2 (6 oz.) cans Ro-Tel tomatoes with chilies (1 hot and 1 mild)

Brown sausage and drain off fat. Add the two bricks of cream cheese and two cans of Ro-Tel. Stir to mix thoroughly and heat through. Serve warm as a dip. Best with Fritos over other types of corn chips.

BJ Hansen
Salt Lake City, UT Chapter

Buffalo Chicken Dip

2 c. chopped, cooked chicken breasts
2 (8 oz.) pkg. cream cheese, softened
1 c. mild or sharp shredded Cheddar cheese
½ c. Blue cheese dressing
½ c. ranch dressing
4 to 6 oz. Frank's hot sauce

Mix all ingredients together. Place in oven proof serving dish. Bake at 350° for 45 minutes. Serve with Tostitos Scoops, regular Tostitos, Fritos, or crackers. This recipe will easily serve 6 to 8 people. Preparation time is about 10 to 15 minutes.

Susan Shaeffer
Naples, FL Chapter

Zesty Buffalo Chicken Dip

2 (10 oz.) cans white meat chicken
2 (8 oz.) pkgs. cream cheese, softened
1½ c. ranch dressing
½ to 1 c. red hot sauce (Frank's)
1 c. shredded Cheddar cheese
Club crackers

Melt softened cream cheese, red hot sauce and ranch dressing over the stove at medium heat until very hot. Gently add flaked canned chicken. Cook over medium heat, stirring until blended and hot. Pour mixture into a non-stick casserole dish. Top with shredded Cheddar cheese. Bake at about 350° for 20 to 30 minutes, or until bubbly. Serve with Club crackers.

Lisa Dugan
Pittsburgh, PA Chapter

Chicken Wing Dip

6 to 10 oz. Frank's Hot Sauce
1 c. Blue cheese dressing
  (Marie's works best)
2 (8 oz.) bricks cream cheese
1 c. chopped celery
8 oz. shredded Cheddar Monterey Jack cheese
3 cooked chicken breasts (or 1 roasted chicken), shredded

Put cream cheese, Blue cheese, Frank's Hot Sauce and celery in sauce pan on stove to melt. Simmer, don't boil. Mix in ½ bag cheese. Mix in chicken. Stir. Put in a casserole dish and sprinkle with the rest of the cheese. Bake at 350° for 20 to 30 minutes. Serve with tortilla chips, celery stalks, pita chips, etc.

Rebecca Kravitz
Palm Beach County, FL Chapter
EWGA Marketing Projects Coordinator

Fiesta Veggie Dip

1 (4 oz.) can chopped green chilies
1 (11 oz.) can shoe peg (white) corn, drained
1 small red or green pepper (or combination of both), chopped
3 green onions, finely chopped
1 (4 to 6 oz.) can sliced black olives, drained
2 (8 oz.) blocks cream cheese, softened
1 pkg. Hidden Valley Fiesta Ranch dip mix (powdered)

Blend cream cheese and mix in the rest of the ingredients. Chill and serve with tortilla chips or Fritos.

Sue Martin
Quad Cities, IA Chapter

Blue Inlet Wild Roasted Red Pepper "Love" Dip

4 large roasted red peppers
1 c. whole walnuts

1½ c. Feta cheese
Agave nectar or honey to taste

To make roasted peppers, roll red peppers in olive oil and roast at 400° until skin blisters. Remove skin and let sit until peppers come to room temperature. Remove core and seeds. Place in food processor. Add walnuts, Feta cheese and sweetener. Blend until mixture is chunky, not smooth. Serve with pita chips.

Katherine Roberts
Founder and President, Yoga for Golfers

Reuben Dip

1 (8 oz.) can sauerkraut
8 oz. cream cheese

8 oz. corned beef
1 (8 oz.) pkg. Swiss cheese

Heat all ingredients in a small crock pot. Stir to mix. Serve on rye or pumpernickel cocktail bread or crackers.

Darlene 'Babe' Lamb
Kansas City Metro Chapter

Dried Beef & Dill Pickle Spread

1½ c. dill pickles, chopped (use whole kosher dills)
6 oz. dried beef (3 of the 2 oz. pkgs. of Buddig)
8 oz. cream cheese, softened (light is okay)
2 Tbsp. sour cream (light is okay)
½ c. chopped onion
⅛ tsp. garlic powder (or more to taste)

Chop dill pickles into pieces slightly larger than pickle relish, about ¼ inch. Measure 1½ cups and set aside. Use a knife to cut dried beef into pieces, about ½ inch. Set aside. Combine cream cheese, sour cream, onion and garlic powder. Process until smooth. Scrape into large bowl and stir in dill pickles and dried beef. Chill until ready to serve. Serve with Ritz crackers or dip chips. I do not recommend putting pickles and beef in the processor because this dip needs the chunky texture.

Paula Dean
Quad-Cities, IA Chapter
Nancy Oliver Founder's Award Winner
and Former Association Board President

Chipped Beef Tailgate Dip

8 oz. cream cheese, softened
2 Tbsp. milk
½ c. sour cream
½ onion, chopped or 2 Tbsp. onion flakes
½ tsp. garlic salt
¼ tsp. pepper
1 small (approx. 8 oz.) jar chipped beef
2 Tbsp. butter, melted
½ c. pecans, chopped
Bag of Fritos (Scoops) for dipping

Preheat oven to 350°. Take the softened cream cheese and mix with milk. Add sour cream, onion, garlic salt, and pepper and mix together. Take the jar of chipped beef and tear the beef into smaller pieces and add to mixture; place into 8 or 9 inch square baking dish. In a separate bowl, take the pecan pieces and add butter, then mix together. Spread the pecan pieces on top of the mixture in the baking dish and bake 20 minutes at 350°. Serve warm with Frito chips.

Susan Naugle
Palm Beach County, FL Chapter
EWGA Director of Marketing

My Granny's Favorite Clam Dip

1 garlic clove
8 oz. cream cheese
2 tsp. lemon juice
1½ tsp. Worcestershire sauce
¼ tsp. salt
Pepper
1 (7 oz.) can minced clams, well drained
4 Tbsp. clam broth

Rub a mixing bowl with a garlic clove which has been cut in half. Then place cream cheese in the bowl and cream it with a spoon until smooth. Blend in lemon juice, Worcestershire sauce, salt, dash of pepper and minced clams (well drained). Gradually add clam broth. This can be made hours before serving and refrigerated. If it thickens, add another tablespoon of clam broth. Serve this dip with raw vegetables (such as carrots, mushrooms, cauliflower, and broccoli) and potato chips.

Cindy Davis
Portland, OR Chapter
President, Nike Golf and EWGA Leadership Award Winner

Chip And A Putt Appetizer

2 (11 oz.) cans Mexican corn with peppers
2 (4 to 6 oz.) cans sliced black olives, drained
4 (15 oz.) cans black-eyed peas, drained
1 medium to large onion
1 each of green, yellow, orange, and red bell peppers
Scallions to taste
Sliced jalapenos to taste
1 jar picante sauce
1 small bottle zesty or robust Italian dressing
Lime flavored Tostitos

Drain liquid from corn, olives, and black-eyed peas. Cut all vegetables into bite-size pieces. Mix all ingredients together and refrigerate overnight. Serve with tortilla chips. Recipe makes a very large batch, so leftovers can be frozen. You can omit or add any ingredients. Variations include kidney beans, garbanzo beans, hot sauce, cilantro, or cumin.

Sharon Hall
Minnesota Metro Chapter

Black Bean Salsa

2 cans black beans, drained and rinsed
1 can diced tomatoes, drained
1 can white and yellow corn, drained
1 (4 oz.) can green chilies, drained
1 bunch green onions, chopped
2/3 c. lime juice
1 Tbsp. olive oil
2 Tbsp. cumin

Mix all ingredients. Chill. Serve with tortilla chips.

Karen McIntosh
Genesee County, MI Chapter

Black Bean Salsa

1 (15 oz.) can black beans, drained
2 plum tomatoes, seeded and chopped
1/4 white onion, finely chopped
1 jalapeno pepper, seeded and finely chopped
1 garlic clove, finely chopped
1 lime, juice only
1 Tbsp. salt (kosher preferred)
Chopped cilantro leaves
1 bag Tostitos Scoops

Combine beans, tomatoes, onions, pepper, garlic, lime juice, salt, and cilantro in a bowl. Mix together thoroughly and serve with Scoops. As an option, add a little bit of Cholula hot sauce for extra flavor and kick.

Stephanie Jennings, PGA
Palm Beach County, FL Chapter
EWGA Director of Golf Programs

Katherine's Blue Inlet Wild Salsa

2 fresh jalapenos and/or pickled jalapenos to taste (remove seeds)
4 avocados
4 mangos
1 to 2 grapefruits to taste (or 1 to 2 blood oranges)
Pomegranate seeds and juice to taste
Red onion, finely chopped (do not add too much onion or it will be too strong)
Juice of 2 to 3 limes (or to taste)
Cilantro to taste
Salt and pepper to taste

Dice avocados and mangos into large pieces. Gently toss all prepared ingredients together. Serve with tortilla or pita chips (or try with cucumber slices to save calories). Makes a beautiful accompaniment to grilled fish. Make sure all of the fruit is nice and ripe!

Katherine Roberts
Founder and President, Yoga for Golfers

Easy Sassy Salsa

2 (14 oz.) cans fire roasted tomatoes
2 approx. chipotle peppers (in adobe sauce)
½ white onion, chopped and rinsed
¼ c. cilantro, chopped
½ lime, juice only
Salt to taste

Put all ingredients in a food processor and process until well combined. Serve with tortilla chips. Use only one pepper for less spicy salsa. Remaining peppers can be frozen for future use.

Renee Birklund
Canton, OH Chapter

Appetizers, Snacks & Beverages

Jezebel Sauce

1 (5 oz.) jar prepared horseradish
1 (1.12 oz.) can dry mustard
1 (18 oz.) jar pineapple or apricot preserves
1 (18 oz.) jar apple jelly
1 to 2 Tbsp. coarsely ground pepper

Mix horseradish and dry mustard. Combine with remaining ingredients. Refrigerate. Makes 4 cups and will keep in fridge for years! Serve over cream cheese for a quick appetizer for an after golf cocktail party. Also good on ham or pork.

Bobbie Corbett
Eastern Shore, MD Chapter

KPJ's Back Nine Energy Squares

½ c. butter or butter substitute, room temperature
½ c. light brown sugar
1 c. whole wheat flour
Dash of salt
1 c. rolled oats
¾ c. fruit-only seedless jam (raspberry is my favorite)

Preheat oven to 350°. Grease an 8 inch square pan, line it with aluminum foil, and then grease the foil. Combine all the ingredients except the jam. Press 2 cups of mixture into bottom of pan. Spread the jam within ¼ inch of the edge. Sprinkle remaining crumb mixture over the top and lightly press it into the jam. Bake 35 to 40 minutes and allow to cool on wire rack before cutting. Cut into squares. Freeze squares the night before your round and then remove from freezer the day of your round. The squares will be thawed by the back nine.

Karen Palacios-Jansen, LPGA
2008 LPGA National Teacher of the Year

Crunchy Orange Spice Snack Mix

1 (6 oz.) pkg. Bugles original flavor snacks
1 (12 oz.) can cashews (or cashew, almond, and pecan mix)
2 egg whites
2 Tbsp. orange juice
1⅓ c. sugar
2 tsp. ground cinnamon
1 c. dried cranberries or cherries

Preheat oven to 275°. Grease 15½ x 10½ x 1 inch jellyroll pan. Mix snacks and nuts in a large bowl. Beat egg whites, orange juice, sugar, and cinnamon in small bowl using a wire whisk or hand beater until foamy. Pour over snack mixture, stir until evenly coated, and spread in pan. Bake uncovered 35 minutes, stirring every 15 minutes. Stir in cranberries. Bake another 10 to 15 minutes or until light brown and crisp. Cool completely. Store in airtight container.

Darlene 'Babe' Lamb
Kansas City Metro Chapter

Sugared Wine Nuts

1½ c. sugar
½ c. cream sherry or Kahlua
½ tsp. cinnamon
1 Tbsp. white corn syrup
½ tsp. salt
2 to 3 c. nuts (pecan or walnuts)

Combine sugar, sherry, cinnamon, corn syrup and salt in a pan. Cook to soft ball stage. Remove from heat and add nuts, stir until creamy. Turn out on baking sheet lined with foil. Separate the nuts and allow to cool. Break into pieces. I used Kahlua instead of sherry and the recipe turned out delicious! Great snack for the holidays.

Kay Pierson
Cincinnati, OH Chapter

Mississippi Spiced Pecans

1 lb. pecan halves
1 Tbsp. packed dark brown sugar
1½ tsp. kosher salt
1 tsp. chopped fresh thyme
1 tsp. chopped fresh rosemary
½ tsp. freshly ground pepper
½ tsp. cayenne pepper
2 Tbsp. extra virgin olive oil

Preheat oven to 350°. Spread pecans on a large baking sheet. Roast until fragrant, about 12 minutes. Watch carefully so they do not burn. Combine brown sugar, salt, thyme, rosemary, pepper and cayenne (to taste) in a small bowl. Transfer the roasted pecans to a large bowl, drizzle with oil and toss well to coat completely. Sprinkle with the spice mixture and toss again. Serve warm or let cool completely and store in an airtight container for up to 2 weeks.

Jo-Ann Dixon
Northern New Jersey Chapter
Association and Foundation Board Member

19th Hole Root-Beer Martini

1¼ oz. root beer vodka
¾ oz. Kahlua
1 scoop vanilla ice cream
Splash of Coke
Ice cubes

Throw all ingredients into a blender and blend until smooth. Fill your favorite golf themed martini glass and enjoy!

Karen Alesch
Fox Cities/Green Bay, WI Chapter
EWGA Women Who Lead Award Winner

Bear Catcher Drink

1 part honey liqueur
2 parts vodka
Dash of sweet and sour mix
Splash of cranberry juice
Lemon flavored seltzer water
Ice cubes

You must like honey for this drink. I suggest a 16 ounce cup or glass, but any size will do. Mix 1 part honey liqueur (Baerenjaeger or similar) and 2 parts vodka over ice in a glass. Add a dash of sweet and sour, a splash of cranberry juice and seltzer water. Stir it up and it is ready to serve. Be careful - it is very tasty!

Kerstin Koenig
Miami, FL Chapter

Spiced Apple Cider

2 qt. apple cider
1 qt. cranberry juice cocktail
2 c. orange juice (not concentrate)
¾ c. sugar
3 cinnamon sticks, broken
1 tsp. cloves

Mix cider, cranberry juice, and orange juice in a large percolator. In the basket, mix sugar and spices. Percolate. Dump basket when perking stops.

Paula Dean
Quad-Cities, IA Chapter
Nancy Oliver Founder's Award Winner and Former Association Board President

Lite Iced Coffee Beverage

1 Tbsp. chocolate Carnation Instant Breakfast mix
1 Tbsp. instant coffee
2 to 3 packets Splenda
2 oz. hot water
5 oz. cold water
2 oz. fat free milk
1 Tbsp. fat-free liquid coffee creamer
Lots of ice

For each 16 ounce serving, combine breakfast mix, coffee, Splenda and hot water in 16 ounce glass. Add cold water, milk and coffee creamer. Stir. Fill cup with ice. You can top with lite whipped cream if desired.

Karen McIntosh
Genesee County, MI Chapter

Irish Cream

1¾ c. Irish whiskey
1 (14 oz.) can sweetened condensed milk
1 c. whipping cream
4 eggs
2 Tbsp. chocolate syrup
2 tsp. instant coffee
1 tsp. vanilla extract
½ tsp. almond extract

In a blender, combine all ingredients; blend until smooth. Store covered in the refrigerator. Will last about 1 month.

Terrie Marshall
Portland, OR Chapter

Kahlua (Get Your Bottles Ready!)

1 c. instant coffee
1 qt. water
1 qt. water mixed with 6 c. sugar
1 c. corn syrup
2 oz. vanilla extract
1 fifth grain alcohol

Boil 1 quart of water and add coffee, let mixture cool. Boil water and sugar mixture for about 5 to 6 minutes. Add corn syrup, let cool. Combine mixtures. Add vanilla. Add grain alcohol and mix well.

Terrie Marshall
Portland, OR Chapter

PB & J Martini

1 oz. raspberry vodka
1 oz. hazelnut liqueur (Frangelica)
1 oz. purple grape juice

Fill cocktail shaker with ice cubes. Add all ingredients and shake vigorously. Strain into a chilled martini glass and garnish with a grape or two.

Ava (A.J.) Bessette
Albuquerque, NM and Brevard County/Space Coast, FL Chapters

Raspberry Liqueur

5 c. raspberries
1⅓ c. sugar
1 qt. vodka, Canadian whiskey, or scotch

Put raspberries in 4 quart container. Pour sugar over and add vodka, whiskey, scotch, or whatever you have (no sloe gin). Cover and let soak for three weeks. Filter out with cheese cloth. Pour into bottles and add a couple of raspberries. Cap until needed.

Gretchen Stelter and George Kuehn Sr.
Genesee County, MI Chapter

Slush

9 c. water
1 c. sugar
1 tea bag
¼ c. hot water
1 large can frozen orange juice concentrate
1 large can frozen lemon or lime juice concentrate
2 c. vodka

Add sugar to water and bring to a boil to dissolve sugar in 4 quart pan. Put tea bag in ¼ cup hot water. Add orange juice, lemon juice, vodka, and tea to pan. Mix thoroughly. Fill 2 large Cool Whip containers with mixture. Place in freezer until it turns to slush. Spoon into glasses to serve. Makes about 3 quarts.

Gretchen Stelter and Ruth Stelter
Genesee County, MI Chapter

Vodka Shake

3 oranges, cut into slices
2 lemons, cut into slices
1 (8 oz.) jar maraschino cherries
½ c. grenadine
⅓ c. sugar
2 c. vodka of your choice

Fill large tea jar or glass jar with ice cubes. Add in all ingredients and wrap jar with wet kitchen towel. Shake until towel freezes to jar. Pass the jar, shake, and drink. Warning: goes down way too easy. This recipe is in memory of my mother Alice. She and her golf buddies enjoyed this treat after a hot and humid day of golf.

Darlene 'Babe' Lamb
Kansas City Metro Chapter

Bunkers & Rough

Soups & Salads

A HANDY SPICE AND HERB GUIDE

ALLSPICE- a pea-sized fruit that grows in Mexico, Jamaica, Central and South America. Its delicate flavor resembles a blend of cloves, cinnamon, and nutmeg. USES: (Whole) Pickles, meats, boiled fish, gravies; (Ground) Puddings, relishes, fruit preserves, baking.

BASIL- the dried leaves and stems of an herb grown in the United States and North Mediterranean area. Has an aromatic, leafy flavor. USES: For flavoring tomato dishes and tomato paste, turtle soup; also use in cooked peas, squash, snap beans; sprinkle chopped over lamb chops and poultry.

BAY LEAVES- the dried leaves of an evergreen grown in the eastern Mediterranean countries. Has a sweet, herbaceous floral spice note. USES: For pickling, stews, for spicing sauces and soup. Also use with a variety of meats and fish.

CARAWAY- the seed of a plant grown in the Netherlands. Flavor that combines the tastes of anise and dill. USES: For the cordial Kummel, baking breads; often added to sauerkraut, noodles, cheese spreads. Also adds zest to French fried potatoes, liver, canned asparagus.

CURRY POWDER- a ground blend of ginger, turmeric, fenugreek seed, as many as 16 to 20 spices. USES: For all Indian curry recipes such as lamb, chicken, and rice, eggs, vegetables, and curry puffs.

DILL- the small, dark seed of the dill plant grown in India, having a clean, aromatic taste. USES: Dill is a predominant seasoning in pickling recipes; also adds pleasing flavor to sauerkraut, potato salad, cooked macaroni, and green apple pie.

MACE- the dried covering around the nutmeg seed. Its flavor is similar to nutmeg, but with a fragrant, delicate difference. USES: (Whole) For pickling, fish, fish sauce, stewed fruit. (Ground) Delicious in baked goods, pastries, and doughnuts, adds unusual flavor to chocolate desserts.

MARJORAM- an herb of the mint family, grown in France and Chile. Has a minty-sweet flavor. USES: In beverages, jellies, and to flavor soups, stews, fish, sauces. Also excellent to sprinkle on lamb while roasting.

MSG (MONOSODIUM GLUTAMATE)- a vegetable protein derivative for raising the effectiveness of natural food flavors. USES: Small amounts, adjusted to individual taste, can be added to steaks, roasts, chops, seafoods, stews, soups, chowder, chop suey, and cooked vegetables.

OREGANO- a plant of the mint family and a species of marjoram of which the dried leaves are used to make an herb seasoning. USES: An excellent flavoring for any tomato dish, especially pizza, chili con carne, and Italian specialties.

PAPRIKA- a mild, sweet red pepper growing in Spain, Central Europe, and the United States. Slightly aromatic and prized for brilliant red color. USES: A colorful garnish for pale foods, and for seasoning Chicken Paprika, Hungarian Goulash, salad dressings.

POPPY- the seed of a flower grown in Holland. Has a rich fragrance and crunchy, nut-like flavor. USES: Excellent as a topping for breads, rolls, and cookies. Also delicious in buttered noodles.

ROSEMARY- an herb (like a curved pine needle) grown in France, Spain, and Portugal, and having a sweet fresh taste. USES: In lamb dishes, in soups, stews, and to sprinkle on beef before roasting.

SAGE- the leaf of a shrub grown in Greece, Yugoslavia, and Albania. Flavor is camphoraceous and minty. USES: For meat and poultry stuffing, sausages, meat loaf, hamburgers, stews, and salads.

THYME- the leaves and stems of a shrub grown in France and Spain. Has a strong, distinctive flavor. USES: For poultry seasoning, croquettes, fricassees, and fish dishes. Also tasty on fresh sliced tomatoes.

TURMERIC- a root of the ginger family, grown in India, Haiti, Jamaica, and Peru, having a mild, ginger-pepper flavor. USES: As a flavoring and coloring in prepared mustard and in combination with mustard as a flavoring for meats, dressings, salads.

Copyright © 2011 by Cookbook Publishers, Inc.

Soups & Salads

Minestrone Soup

2 tsp. olive oil
1 medium yellow onion, chopped
2 garlic cloves
2 medium size carrots, peeled, halved lengthwise, and sliced thin
1 medium size all-purpose potato, peeled and cut into ½ inch cubes
1 medium size green or yellow squash (about ½ lb.), cut into ½ inch cubes
1 Tbsp. dried basil, crumbled
1 tsp. dried oregano, crumbled
2 large bay leaves
1 (28 oz.) can crushed low sodium tomatoes, with juice
6 c. chicken or vegetable stock
¼ lb. green beans, trimmed and cut into 1 inch pieces
4 oz. tiny shells or tubettini
1 can Great Northern white beans, drained and rinsed
Grated Parmesan cheese, if desired
3 Tbsp. minced parsley

In a large heavy kettle, heat olive oil over low heat for 1 minute; add the onions and cook, uncovered, for 5 minutes or until soft (translucent). Add the garlic and cook for 1 minute. Raise the heat to moderate and add the carrots, potato, squash, basil, oregano, and bay leaves. Cook, uncovered, 5 minutes longer, stirring occasionally. Add the tomatoes and stock and bring to a boil; adjust heat so the mixture bubbles gently and cook, uncovered, 20 minutes longer. Add the green beans, cover, and cook until the beans are tender but still crisp, about 10 minutes. Remove the bay leaves. Add the pasta and cook until tender. Add additional water, if necessary. Add the white beans. Cook 3 to 5 minutes longer, until heated through. Ladle into soup bowls and sprinkle with cheese and parsley.

Dorothy Rooney
Greater Philadelphia, PA Chapter

Soups & Salads

Confetti Soup

1 can cream corn
1 can whole kernel corn (yellow)
¼ c. carrot (orange)
¼ c. celery (green)
¼ c. red onion (purple)
¼ c. red and green bell pepper (red and green) or use pimentos for the red
Chopped green chili (optional, for a Southwestern flair)
⅛ c. fresh parsley (green)
1 c. chicken stock
1 to 2 c. Colby Jack cheese
1 Tbsp. flour
¾ c. milk
1 to 2 Tbsp. butter

In a large pot combine the cream corn and the whole kernel corn (drained) over low heat. Set aside liquid from corn to add later as needed. Dice carrots and steam before adding to the pot. Dice celery and onion and saute; add to pot. Dice peppers, saute separately, and add to pot. Chop parsley and add to pot. Melt butter in skillet, add flour, and mix until melted together. Add ¼ cup of milk. When hot, add remaining milk and 1 to 2 cups cheese. Cheese sauce should be thick but not too thick. Add chicken stock and/or liquid from the drained corn, as needed. Add cheese sauce to the Confetti Soup, salt and pepper to taste, then heat and serve. I usually have this for brunch with garlic toast, my favorite spinach salad, and a glass of zinfandel.

Paula Jenkins
Albuquerque, NM Chapter

"If you play poorly one day, forget it. If you play poorly the next time out, review your fundamentals of grip, stance, aim, and ball position."
-Harvey Penick

Soups & Salads

Onion Soup

6 large white onions (Vidalia if available)
1 stick of butter
1 bag of croutons or hard rye bread
1 (16 oz.) carton beef stock (my favorite is Rachael Ray Stock-in-a-Box)
1 pkg. fresh Mozzarella cheese, sliced
4 to 6 Ramekin bowls (I recommend Pier One - $2.50 each.)

Cut up the onions (run water while you do this and you will not cry). Put butter and onions in a large pot and caramelize over low heat for about an hour, stirring occasionally. When done add a little of the beef stock to loosen the drippings from the bottom of the pan. Divide onion mixture into the bowls and pour in the beef stock. Top with croutons and cover with generous slices of fresh mozzarella. Cook in 350° oven until the cheese bubbles and is brown around the edges. Enjoy...it's a meal with a slice of garlic bread!

Joan Cavanaugh
Fairfield County, CT Chapter
EWGA Businesswoman Award Winner and
Former Foundation Board President

"It is better to be prepared for an opportunity and not have one than to have an opportunity and not be prepared."
-Maya Angelou

Mango Gazpacho

2 large ripe mangoes, peeled, pitted, and chopped
1 small apple, peeled, seeded and chopped (optional)
1 medium celery stalk, chopped
1 small cucumber, peeled, seeded, and chopped
2 Tbsp. fresh lime juice
1 to 2 medium jalapenos, seeded and minced
1 Tbsp. red pepper
½ tsp. salt
¾ c. orange juice (fresh if possible)

Puree all ingredients in a blender, or I prefer using a large Cuisinart to avoid the fine chopping and mincing. You can refrigerate overnight or chill at least 1 hour ahead. Serve individual portions in fancy martini glasses and garnish with a fresh sprig of cilantro (optional). Very refreshing for a 1st course or sweet enough for dessert!!

Carol Baltzer
Manatee, FL Chapter

Simple Summer Fish Chowder

2 medium tomatoes
2 small ears corn, shucked
1 Tbsp. olive oil
1 large celery rib, chopped
1 large shallot, finely chopped
6 oz. cod or halibut fillet, cut into bite-sized pieces
1½ c. chicken broth
¼ c. fresh basil, finely chopped
⅛ tsp. pepper
Salt to taste

Make an 'X' with a knife in the bottom of the tomatoes. Place in a pot of boiling water for 30 seconds. Remove and slip off tomato skins. Core, seed, and coarsely chop tomatoes. Set aside. Using a paring knife, cut kernels off corn. Heat oil in a large pot. Add corn, celery, and shallot. Cook over medium-high heat for 5 minutes or until tender. Add fish. Cook 1 minute per side. Add tomatoes and chicken broth. Bring to a simmer. Stir in basil and pepper. Simmer for 5 minutes or until fish is cooked through and chowder is aromatic. Season with salt to taste. Serves 2. Recipe attributed to Bev Bennett.

Betsy Clark, LPGA
President, dbc Consulting

Soups & Salads

Cream Of Cauliflower-Crab Soup

½ lb. butter
½ c. finely chopped onions
1 c. finely chopped celery
1½ c. flour
2 c. half and half

2 medium heads cauliflower
1 Tbsp. crab or lobster base
½ lb. Swiss cheese, shredded
2 to 3 pkg. imitation crab

Cut cauliflower into florets, place in pan, and cover with water. Cook until slightly tender. Drain, separating the florets and water and saving both. Melt butter in a saute pan. Add the onions and celery and cook until tender. Add the flour to create a roux. Add half and half and water reserved from cooking the cauliflower. Stir until just about boiling. Add the shredded Swiss cheese and stir until cheese is melted. Dissolve the base into 8 ounces of additional water and add to above mixture. Add the cauliflower and crab. Season with salt, black pepper, and white pepper.

Diana Johnson
Naples, FL Chapter

Dot's Turkey Chili

2 lb. ground turkey
¼ c. olive oil
2 garlic cloves, crushed
2 lb. tomatoes, undrained
1 can tomato paste
3 Tbsp. chili powder
1 Tbsp. sugar
3 tsp. salt
1 tsp. pepper
½ tsp. paprika
2 bay leaves

1 Tbsp. cumin
1 Tbsp. dried basil
Dash cayenne (red) pepper
1 c. chopped onion
1 large red pepper, chopped
1 lb. carrots, chopped
1 lb. red or white kidney beans
1 lb. chick peas (garbanzo
    beans)
1 lb. black beans

Brown ground turkey in large pot; drain fat. Add olive oil, garlic, tomatoes, tomato paste, sugar, salt, pepper, paprika, bay leaves, cumin, basil, and cayenne pepper. Simmer covered for 2 to 3 hours (or in crockpot 6 to 8 hours on medium). Add remaining ingredients and simmer 3 more hours. Easiest to cook in crockpot. Can be topped with Cheddar or Monterey Jack cheese or served over rice or spaghetti squash.

Dorothy Rooney
Greater Philadelphia, PA Chapter

White Bean Chili

1 tsp. olive oil
2 c. chopped onion
1 (4 oz.) can chopped, peeled green chiles with liquid
3 (14 oz.) cans chicken broth
1 (48 oz.) jar white navy beans with liquid
1 lb. cooked boneless chicken breast, chopped
2 heaping tsp. cumin
2 tsp. oregano
2 Tbsp. garlic, minced
¼ tsp. cayenne pepper

Saute olive oil, onion and garlic. Stir in chiles with liquid. Add chicken broth, white beans with liquid and cooked chicken. Stir in cumin, oregano and cayenne pepper. Heat to boiling, turn down and simmer on low for at least 1 hour.

Karen McIntosh
Genesee County, MI Chapter

Taco Soup

1 lb. ground chicken
½ c. chopped onion
1 pkg. ranch salad dressing
1 pkg. taco seasoning
2 cans Mexican tomatoes
1 can black beans
1 can chili beans
1 (4 oz.) can chopped green chilies

Brown chicken and chopped onion. Add the rest of the ingredients and simmer for about 30 minutes. Serve soup with sour cream, shredded cheese, and whole grain chips. Yummy!

Sue Hendrix
St. Louis, MO Chapter

Tortilla Soup

3 or more chicken breasts, cooked and cubed
1 can navy beans
1 can black beans
2 cans white corn
2 cans chicken broth
2 cans diced tomatoes
1 can diced chilies
½ to 1 onion, chopped
1 red pepper, chopped
1 green pepper, chopped
Cumin to taste

Place all ingredients into a crock pot and set on low for 8 hours. Serve with shredded Cheddar cheese, sour cream, and tortilla chips.

Rita Kathryn Johnson
Long Island, NY Chapter

"Golf, more than most games, has a number of cliches, often successfully disguised as 'tips.' Watch out!"

-Kathy Whitworth

Soups & Salads

French Market Soup

- ¼ c. dry black beans
- ¼ c. dry navy beans
- ¼ c. dry red beans
- ¼ c. dry garbanzo beans
- ¼ c. dry pinto beans
- ¼ c. dry lentils
- ¼ c. dry barley
- ¼ c. dry black-eyed peas
- ¼ c. dry split peas
- ¼ c. dry baby lima beans
- 1 qt. stewed tomatoes
- 2 garlic cloves, minced
- 6 celery stalks, chopped
- 1 ham hock
- Thyme to taste
- 2 raw chicken breasts
- 2 medium onions, chopped
- 1 green pepper, chopped
- Salt and red pepper to taste
- Bay leaf
- ½ to 1 lb. smoked sausage
- Chopped parsley to taste

This recipe takes some planning. You cannot just run to the store and pick up the ingredients and have dinner ready in an hour. If you start the process on a Friday evening, you can have soup for a couple of long, cold weekend days. (Depending, of course, on how many people you are feeding). Wash 2½ cup dry bean mix and drain (the lentils and barley are very small. Make sure your strainer has small holes so these do not get rinsed down the drain). Add water to cover and 1 tablespoon salt. Soak overnight (It is important NOT TO SKIP this step. I know this from experience). Drain the salt water from the mixture (again, making sure not to lose the smaller ingredients) and add 3 quarts of fresh water, the ham hock, bay leaf, and thyme. Simmer covered for 3 hours. After 3 hours: add the tomatoes, onions, garlic, green pepper, celery, salt, and red pepper. Simmer 1½ hours uncovered. After 1½ hours: add the smoked sausage and raw chicken. Simmer until chicken is tender. Pull the chicken out, remove the bones and shred the meat (if you were using boneless chicken, just skip the part about removing the bones). Return the shredded chicken to the soup. This marvelous soup is now ready to eat. The recipe says to add chopped parsley to the entire mixture ten minutes before serving. I do not add the parsley to the stock pot ingredients but rather into the individual bowls after I have scooped the soup, OR I just put a bowl of chopped parsley on the table and allow my guests/family/free-loading friends to add their own. Makes enough soup to feed about 8 people. If the entire neighborhood shows up at your house, just keep adding more water to the stock pot until everyone is served.

Robin K. Anderson
Houston, TX Chapter
EWGA Businesswoman of the Year Award Winner

Soups & Salads

Chicken Soup Ala Alice Osur

1 package of chicken breasts, on bone
1 large can chicken broth, fat free or low fat and low sodium, like College Inn (or 4 to 6 regular size cans of chicken broth)
1 bunch of fresh dill
1 bunch of fresh parsley
1 bunch of carrots
2 to 3 large parsnips
1 large turnip
1 large onion
1 bunch of celery tops and a couple of stalks of celery

Take the skin off the chicken breast if you can't find the skinless ones on the bones. Clean all the veggies well. Put the broth in a large pot. Add the chicken on the bone. Cut up the clean veggies and add to soup. Add some kosher salt and pepper. Top it off with some extra water from the soup cans. Cover and cook for several hours (maybe 4 to 5). When the chicken is very soft, remove it to a bowl; cut it up and set aside to put back in the soup later. If you have an immersion blender, just puree all the veggies in the pot with the soup. If not, take out the veggies with a slotted spoon and puree them in a blender or a food processor and then place the pureed veggies back in the soup and mix well. Add the chicken back to the soup and add salt and pepper to taste before serving. Put cooked noodles, orzo, rice, matzo balls, dumplings, or kreplach in if you like. Enjoy!!!

Alice Osur
Northern New Jersey Chapter

"I manage my game really well. ... When I make a mistake I speak kindly to myself."

-Rosie Jones

Blueberry Salad

Salad:

2 c. hot water
2 (3 oz.) pkgs. grape jello
1 (20 oz.) can crushed
   pineapple, drained

1 (21 oz.) can blueberry pie filling

Mix jello in hot water until dissolved. Add crushed pineapple and blueberry pie filling. Place in salad bowl and chill until it is congealed.

Topping:

8 oz. cream cheese, softened
¼ c. sugar

¾ chopped pecans

Mix cream cheese and sugar. Spread on congealed salad. Top with pecans.

Linda Keaton
Huntsville, AL Chapter

Ann Liguori's Holiday Jello Delight

2 (3.4 oz.) pkgs. lemon jello
3 c. boiling water
1 c. crushed pineapple, drained
   (save juice for topping)
1½ c. mini marshmallows

3 bananas, cubed
1 egg
1½ Tbsp. flour
½ c. sugar
1 c. whipping cream, whipped

Dissolve jello in water and cool in a 9x13 inch pan. Mix in marshmallows, bananas, and crushed pineapple; cover and allow to gel. For topping, beat egg, flour, sugar, and 1 cup reserved pineapple juice (add cold water if needed to make up the 1 cup). Mix all this in a saucepan and stir over low heat until it boils and thickens; allow to cool. Fold whipped cream into pudding mixture and spread over the 'set' jello. If desired, sprinkle Cheddar cheese on top.

Ann Liguori
Owner, Host and Executive Producer of Sports Innerview with
Ann Liguori WFAN-NY Radio Sports Talk Show Host

Soups & Salads

Orange Fluff

1 (16 oz.) ctn. small-curd cottage cheese
1 (3 oz.) pkg. orange jello
1 (8 oz.) can crushed pineapple, drained
3 (11 oz.) cans mandarin oranges, drained
1 (8 oz.) ctn. Cool Whip

Mix cottage cheese and dry jello together. Add drained fruit and mix thoroughly. Add Cool Whip and mix once more. Chill in refrigerator for at least one hour.

Janet Young
Boise-Treasure Valley, ID Chapter
Nancy Oliver Founder's Award Winner

Cherry Salad

1 (20 oz.) can crushed pineapple, drained
1 (21 oz.) can cherry pie filling
1 can sweetened condensed milk
12 oz. Cool Whip
2 c. miniature marshmallows

Mix all ingredients together and refrigerate for 2 hours before serving.

Kathy Thomas
Kansas City Metro and Tucson-Old Pueblo, AZ Chapters
Nancy Oliver Founder's Award Winner and
Former Association Board Member

Frozen Tropical Salad

1 (14 oz.) can whole berry cranberry sauce
1 (20 oz.) can crushed pineapple, drained
2 (11 oz.) cans mandarin orange segments, drained
1 (12 oz.) container Cool Whip

Mix everything together in a bowl and freeze overnight. Take out 2 hours before meal to soften, but not completely thaw. Optional add-ins include 1 to 1½ cups shredded coconut or ½ cup chopped pecans. Super quick and easy and can be made days before! Very refreshing for hot days and heavy meals.

Kim Cook
Washington, DC Metro Chapter

Mimi's Cranberry Apple Salad

1 (3 oz.) pkg. Jello strawberry gelatin
1/8 tsp. salt
1 1/4 c. boiling water
1 can jellied cranberry sauce
2 c. finely chopped apples

Dissolve gelatin and salt in boiling water. Break up cranberry sauce with fork. Add to gelatin mixture. Chill until very thick. Fold in apples. Chill until firm. Makes 6 to 8 servings. Great with chicken and turkey.

Diane Dushenski
Fox Cities/Green Bay, WI Chapter

Waldorf Salad

5 large apples, diced (Fuji, Gala, or Courtland)
2 Tbsp. lemon juice
2 1/2 c. chopped celery (5 full stalks)
1/4 tsp. nutmeg
1 c. yogurt (plain or vanilla, Greek style is most nutritious)
1/3 c. walnuts, chopped
1 Tbsp. sugar (optional)
1 to 3 drops vanilla extract

Chop celery and grind walnuts. Toss diced apples in lemon juice (unpeeled provides festive color). Combine apples with celery, walnuts, yogurt, nutmeg, sugar, and vanilla. Stir gently to blend. Chill before serving. Makes 6 to 8 servings.

Jan Bel Jan, ASGCA
Palm Beach County, FL Chapter
Golf Course Architect

Angel Hair Pasta Salad

1 lb. angel hair pasta (broken in small pieces)
1/2 c. olive oil
3 Tbsp. Cavender's Greek seasoning
1 (4 oz.) can chopped olives
7 oz. chopped pimentos
1/2 to 1 cup mayonnaise
3 to 4 green onions, chopped

Cook pasta per package. Combine pasta, olive oil, and seasoning. Combine olives, pimentos, mayonnaise, and green onions. Mix all ingredients together. The longer the dish cools the better, best if made the day before.

Karen Furtado
Southern New Hampshire Chapter
Former Association and Foundation Board President

Tuna Macaroni Salad

1½ c. elbow macaroni, uncooked
¼ c. French dressing
2 (6 oz.) cans chunk style tuna, drained
½ c. diced cucumber
¼ c. sliced radishes
¼ c. sliced carrots
1 tsp. onion salt
⅛ tsp. pepper
2 Tbsp. lemon juice
¼ c. sour cream

Cook macaroni as directed, drain well and run cold water over pasta to cool. In large bowl, toss macaroni with French dressing. Refrigerate covered 2 to 3 hours. At least 1 hour before serving time, add remaining ingredients and refrigerate until serving time. Serve garnished with salad greens and tomato wedges. Add additional French dressing to taste.

Ellen Brothers
Genesee County, MI Chapter

Company Tuna Salad

¼ tsp. curry powder
1 tsp. Worcestershire sauce
1 Tbsp. lemon juice
3 oz. cocktail onions
¾ c. mayonnaise
2 cans tuna
1 box frozen peas, uncooked
Chow mein noodles

Combine ingredients. Serve over chow mein noodles.

Becky Macaluso
Palm Beach County, FL Chapter
EWGA Managing Director, Chapter & Member Services

Tortellini Salad

¼ to ⅓ c. olive oil
2 Tbsp. red wine vinegar
1 tsp. Dijon mustard
½ tsp. honey
½ large (or 1 small) zucchini, quartered lengthwise and sliced crosswise into ¼ inch thick slices
9 oz. fresh cheese tortellini
1 red or orange bell pepper, cut into ½ inch square pieces
2 Tbsp. (or more) Parmesan cheese
2 Tbsp. chopped parsley
Salt and pepper to taste

Whisk together oil, vinegar, mustard, and honey and set aside. Drop zucchini slices into boiling water and blanch no more than 30 seconds, do not overcook. Immediately drop zucchini into a bowl of ice water to stop the cooking. Drain well on paper towels. Meanwhile, cook tortellini according to package instructions; rinse under cold water and drain well. Combine tortellini with zucchini, red pepper, Parmesan cheese, parsley, and dressing. Add salt and pepper to taste. Toss well and store in the refrigerator. Set salad out about 20 to 30 minutes before serving.

Molly Taylor
EWGA Foundation Intern

Black Bean Salad

Salad:

3 cans black beans, rinsed and drained
2 cans corn, drained
½ c. red onion, diced
1 red pepper, diced
Cilantro and/or parsley to taste

Combine all ingredients in a serving bowl.

Dressing:

½ c. lime juice
⅓ to ½ c. olive oil
2 garlic cloves, crushed
1 tsp. red pepper flakes or to taste

Mix dressing and pour over salad. Better to make it a day ahead and stir occasionally.

Lisa Van Divender
Cincinnati, OH Chapter

Soups & Salads

Broccoli Blue Cheese Salad

Vinaigrette Dressing:

2 Tbsp. red wine vinegar
10 Tbsp. (equals ½ cup plus 2 Tbsp.) extra virgin olive oil
1 garlic clove, minced
½ tsp. salt
¼ tsp. freshly ground pepper
2 tsp. Dijon mustard

Combine all ingredients in a container with a tight-fitting lid and shake well. Chill.

Salad:

4 c. broccoli florets
6 scallions, thinly sliced
5 oz. sliced water chestnuts
4 oz. Blue cheese crumbles
8 lettuce leaves
¼ c. lightly toasted pine nuts

Place broccoli in large saucepan. Pour boiling water over and let stand 2 minutes. Drain and immediately refresh with cold water. Drain again. Chill. Toss broccoli with scallions, water chestnuts, Blue cheese, and dressing. Serve on lettuce leaf, garnished with pine nuts. Serves 8. Recipe was adapted from One Magnificent Cookbook, The Junior League of Chicago and 10-Minute Cuisine, Henrietta Green and Marie-Pierre Moine.

Rosalyn Franta Kulik
Tampa Bay, FL Chapter

Bacon And Raisin Broccoli Salad

1½ c. fresh broccoli florets
4 strips bacon, cooked and crumbled
1 or 2 small boxes raisins to taste (prefer golden raisins if available)
2 to 3 Tbsp. mayonnaise and/or ranch dressing

Chop up broccoli florets. In a bowl combine broccoli, raisins, and bacon. Add mayonnaise and/or ranch dressing to desired taste. Mix together and refrigerate until ready to serve. Preparation time is less than 10 minutes.

Carolyn Clinkscales
Brevard County/Space Coast, FL Chapter

Corn, Black Bean, And Avocado Salad

2 c. canned black beans, drained and rinsed
½ c. corn kernels (canned, fresh, or frozen)
2 avocados, peeled, pitted, and diced
½ c. chopped purple onion
1 sweet red bell pepper, finely chopped
½ c. extra virgin olive oil
½ c. fresh cilantro, finely chopped
Juice of 2 fresh limes
1½ tsp. sea salt
½ tsp. ground cumin
½ tsp. turmeric
1 tsp. ground black pepper

In a medium bowl, combine beans, corn, avocados, onion, bell pepper, and cilantro. Mix gently to distribute ingredients evenly. In a small bowl, mix together salt, pepper, lime juice, spices, and oil. Pour over beans and vegetables. Toss to distribute. Serve immediately or cover and chill.

Lori Argall
Northern Nevada Chapter

Crunchy Romaine Toss

½ c. sugar
½ c. vegetable oil
¼ c. cider vinegar
2 tsp. soy sauce
Salt and pepper to taste
1 (3 oz.) pkg. Ramen noodles, broken
2 Tbsp. butter or margarine
1½ c. chopped broccoli
1 small bunch romaine, torn
4 green onions, chopped
½ c. chopped walnuts

In a jar with a tight fitting lid, combine the sugar, oil, vinegar, soy sauce, salt, and pepper; shake well. In a skillet, saute noodles in butter until golden. In a large bowl, combine noodles, broccoli, romaine, and onions. Toss with dressing and walnuts just before serving. Makes 6 to 8 servings.

Paula Dean
Quad-Cities, IA Chapter
Nancy Oliver Founder's Award Winner and
Former Association Board President

Broccoli Slaw

1 (10 oz.) pkg. broccoli slaw (in produce section)
1 bunch green onions, chopped
1 c. sliced almonds, toasted at 350° for 6 to 10 minutes (or use Sunkist Almond Accents)
5 Tbsp. sesame seeds, toasted in 3/4 teaspoon sesame oil until lightly browned
1 pkg. chicken Ramen noodles (crushed slightly in plastic bag with rolling pin)
1 seasoning packet from chicken Ramen noodles
1/4 c. canola oil
1/4 c. sugar
3 Tbsp. cider vinegar
1/2 tsp. salt
Crushed black pepper to taste

Combine seasoning packet with oil, sugar, vinegar, salt, and pepper. Chill. Prepare and combine almonds, sesame seeds, and Ramen noodles. Store in an airtight container until ready to use. Chop green onions and chill. A few hours before serving, combine all ingredients and chill. Salad will stay fresh for up to 12 hours. This is a family favorite and party pleaser! Serves 8.

Sharon Reich
Orlando, FL Chapter
EWGA Businesswoman Award Winner

Coleslaw

1 head cabbage, thinly sliced
Chopped scallions to taste
Dill weed to taste
Garlic salt to taste
Salt and pepper to taste
Mayonnaise to taste

Place sliced cabbage in mixing bowl. Add chopped scallions, dill weed, garlic salt, salt and pepper. Mix with mayonnaise. Cover and let set for at least an hour in the refrigerator.

Jean Shivers
Corpus Christi, TX Chapter

Cabbage Salad For 8

6 pieces thick cut peppered bacon
8 c. shredded red and white cabbage
Salt and caraway seeds to taste
½ bag Trader Joe's spicy pecans
Red wine vinegar (see instructions for quantity)
Crumbled Gorgonzola cheese to taste

Cut bacon into pieces and fry in a wok or frying pan; remove when crisp. Add cabbage to wok and sprinkle with salt and caraway seeds. Add pecans (you may want to add less depending on your group, these are spicy hot). Add red wine vinegar to the cabbage mixture (rule of thumb is if there are 3 tablespoons of bacon fat left, mix in 1 to 2 tablespoons of vinegar). Remove from the heat, add the bacon back in, top with Gorgonzola cheese, and toss lightly.

Kathie Coil
Tucson-Old Pueblo, AZ Chapter

Asian Slaw

½ c. sugar
¾ c. oil
⅓ c. white vinegar
2 pkg. beef flavored Ramen noodles
1 lb. shredded cabbage (broccoli slaw mix is a favorite)
1 c. sunflower seeds
6 or so green onions, finely chopped
1 c. sliced almonds

Crush noodles into bowl. Add slaw mix, sprinkle almonds, sunflower seeds, and green onion. Whisk together beef flavor seasoning packages, sugar, oil, and vinegar. Pour over ingredients. Stir well and chill 24 hours.

Ellen Brothers
Genesee County, MI Chapter

Soups & Salads

Oriental Salad

1 Bok Choy or Napa cabbage
4 to 8 green onions, sliced
¼ c. butter
2 pkg. Ramen noodles
½ c. sliced almonds

½ c. sesame or sunflower seeds
2 Tbsp. sugar
½ c. oil
½ c. red wine vinegar
2 Tbsp. soy sauce

First melt butter, add broken Ramen noodles and brown slightly. Add sesame seeds and almonds and brown, watch that it does not burn. Take off heat, sprinkle sugar over top and stir. Set aside and let cool. Slice Bok Choy or Napa cabbage and mix with onions. Mix oil, red wine vinegar and soy sauce to make dressing. When ready to serve, toss Ramen mix with cabbage and then add dressing. Serves 8.

Betty Abrams
Lehigh Valley, PA Chapter

Southern Cornbread Salad

1 (8x8 inch) dish cornbread cut into 1 inch cubes
1 (14.5 oz.) can red kidney beans, drained and rinsed
1 (15 oz.) can corn, drained
1 medium Vidalia onion, finely chopped

1 large green bell pepper, finely chopped
3 large tomatoes, chopped
2 c. grated sharp Cheddar cheese
1 (8 oz.) bottle ranch dressing

In bottom of large glass bowl, place cornbread cubes. Layer beans, corn, onion, bell pepper, tomatoes and cheese on top of cornbread. Spread ranch dressing evenly over cheese. Cover and refrigerate for 2 or more hours. Serves 8.

Karen McIntosh
Genesee County, MI Chapter

Grandma Vivi's Potato Salad

2 lb. new red potatoes
½ c. celery, finely chopped or sliced
2 Tbsp. fresh parsley, finely chopped
2 hard cooked eggs
1 c. mayonnaise
¼ c. Miracle Whip
½ c. sour cream
1 Tbsp. dill pickle juice
1 tsp. mustard
1 tsp. salt
Freshly ground pepper to taste
1 medium sweet onion, very finely chopped
Sweet paprika
Cherry or grape tomatoes, halved

Scrub potatoes. Place in pot in cold water to cover. Bring to a boil, cover and cook 15 to 20 minutes, or until tender. Drain and cool completely. Peel potatoes and cut into ½ inch cubes. Combine potatoes, celery and chopped parsley. Place eggs in small pot in cold water to cover. Bring to a boil. Remove from heat, cover and let stand 15 minutes. Drain. Place in ice water to immediately stop cooking. Combine mayonnaise, miracle whip, sour cream, pickle juice, mustard, salt, pepper and onions. Add mayonnaise mixture to potato mixture. Toss gently to coat. Cover and chill. Before serving, peel eggs and slice crosswise, or use egg slicer. Place on top of salad. Sprinkle with paprika. Add tomatoes and sprigs of fresh parsley to garnish. Makes 8 servings.

Connie Eldridge
Orange County, CA Chapter

Salad Olivia (Persian Potato Salad)

6 average size potatoes
4 chicken breasts, cooked
6 eggs, hard boiled
1 (10 oz.) pkg. frozen green peas, thawed
1¼ c. dill pickle relish
2 Tbsp. olive oil
¼ c. fresh lemon juice
½ c. mayonnaise, or enough to make moist
Salt and pepper to taste

Peel potatoes and cut into small cubes. Boil until fork tender, but do not overcook. Shred chicken into small pieces. Finely chop hard boiled eggs. Mix all ingredients, adding just enough mayonnaise to make the salad moist. Add salt and pepper to taste and chill thoroughly.

Susan Tajalli
Palm Beach County, FL Chapter

Tomato Caprese Salad With An "Extra Slice" And A "Hook"

3 large vine-ripened tomatoes (heirloom tomatoes optional)
1 large Vidalia (sweet) onion
2 ripe avocados
1 bunch fresh basil (at least 12 leaves), leaves removed, washed, and patted dry with a paper towel
1 lb. fresh Mozzarella cheese
3 to 4 Tbsp. extra virgin, best quality olive oil
Freshly ground sea salt to taste
Freshly ground black pepper to taste

Slice tomatoes about ¼ inch thick, into 12 slices. Slice avocados into 12 slices. Slice Mozzarella cheese about ¼ inch thick, into 12 slices. Slice onion into 12 slices. Keep fresh basil as full leaf. On a large serving platter arrange tomato, Mozzarella cheese slice, basil leaf, onion, and avocado, alternating and overlapping them. Drizzle with olive oil. Season with freshly ground sea salt and black pepper. Finish the salad by garnishing with a few small basil leaves. A variation on the classic tomato caprese salad (tomato, mozzarella, and basil) with two additional ingredients make this quickly prepared salad a hit. The "extra slice" is the Vidalia onion and "the hook" is the avocado. Because this salad is so simple (and gives you more time on the golf course!), top-quality, fresh ingredients are a must. Great "go to" dish year-round, but extra special in summer when locally grown heirloom tomatoes are available.

Kim Thomas
Washington, DC Metro Chapter
EWGA Women Who Lead Award Winner

Sliced Tomato With Balsamic Vinaigrette

1 Tbsp. balsamic vinegar
2 tsp. chopped fresh basil
1 tsp. olive oil
½ tsp. Dijon mustard
1 small garlic clove, crushed
1 large tomato, sliced
2 red leaf lettuce leaves
1 (¾ inch thick) slice Vidalia or sweet onion, separated into rings

Combine vinegar, basil, oil, mustard, and garlic in a small bowl. Stir with a whisk until well blended. Divide tomato slices evenly between 2 lettuce-lined plates. Arrange onion rings evenly over tomato. Drizzle vinaigrette mixture evenly over salads. Makes 2 servings.

Paula Dean
Quad-Cities, IA Chapter
Nancy Oliver Founder's Award Winner and
Former Association Board President

Kale Salad

1 bunch kale
Olive oil
Lemon
Salt to taste
Toasted pine nuts

Wash kale and remove large ribs; chop VERY fine. Squeeze juice from lemon and add with olive oil to kale to taste. Salt lightly. Add toasted pine nuts and toss before serving. For variation: toasted walnuts may be substituted for pine nuts, walnut oil may be substituted for olive oil, and a fruit flavored vinegar, like orange or raspberry for the lemon juice. Very simple, very nutritious and surprisingly delicious! The secret is finely chopping the kale.

Hollis Kerler
Milwaukee, WI Chapter
EWGA Director of Chapter Development

Fiesta Lime Salad

½ each - red, green, and yellow peppers, chopped
2 ribs celery, chopped
Corn from 2 to 3 ears
2 to 4 jalapenos, chopped fine
2 green onions, chopped
1 can black beans, rinsed
Zest of one lime
½ bunch cilantro
½ pkg. or more grape tomatoes, halved
Juice of 2 limes
2 Tbsp. white vinegar
1 tsp. chili powder
¼ c. oil (extra virgin olive oil is the best)
Salt, pepper, and hot pepper sauce to taste
6 to 8 c. lettuce of choice
Crushed tortilla chips, for garnish

To make dressing, mix lime juice, vinegar, chili powder, oil, salt, pepper, and pepper sauce. Set aside. Combine all remaining ingredients except lettuce and tortilla chips. Mix dressing with salad. Chop lettuce and mix just before serving for large group OR place lettuce leaves on plate and fill with dressed salad mix. Garnish with crushed tortilla chips.

Jan Schutte-Reed
Akron, OH Chapter

Height Of Summer Salad

2 c. watermelon chunks
2 c. fresh tomato, cut into chunks
1 c. crumbled Feta cheese
½ c. fresh black or green olives, chopped (not canned)
2 Tbsp. fresh thyme leaves, chopped finely
Olive oil
Balsamic vinegar
Salt
Pepper

Carefully mix together watermelon, tomato, Feta cheese, and olives, being careful not to mash ingredients. Sprinkle salad with thyme. Drizzle oil, vinegar, salt, and pepper to taste. Dressing is light. Mix gently. Serve at room temperature. Ingredient amounts are for proportion only. Easily increases for a crowd. Salad can sit for an hour to blend flavors, but does not keep well. Use fresh heirloom tomatoes if possible for maximum flavor. Can substitute other fresh ripe melon. Try cilantro, fresh basil, or marjoram in place of thyme for new experiences. A snap to make after a round of golf, usually refreshing, and always a surprise and conversation starter.

Valoree Dowell
Salt Lake City, UT Chapter

Mixed Citrus Green Salad

1 c. red seedless grapes, halved
1 (11 oz.) can mandarin oranges, drained
1 (8 oz.) can pineapple chunks, drained
2 (5 oz.) bags mixed salad greens
7 Tbsp. creamy poppyseed dressing
21 walnut halves

Combine grapes, mandarin oranges, pineapple and salad greens in a large bowl. Arrange 2 cups of salad on each of 7 plates and drizzle each with 1 tablespoon of dressing. Top each salad with 3 walnut halves. Makes 7 servings.

Kathy Burns
Jacksonville, FL Chapter

Strawberry & Spinach Salad

Salad:

1 pkg. baby spinach (may use lettuce if you prefer)
1 pt. strawberries, cleaned and thinly sliced
1½ c. crumbled Feta cheese
½ lb. bacon, cooked crisp and crumbled
½ medium red onion, thinly sliced in rings

Mix all ingredients together and set aside.

Dressing:

¼ c. sugar
1 tsp. grated onion
1 tsp. dry mustard
1½ tsp. poppy seeds
1 tsp. sesame seeds
⅓ c. cider vinegar
1 c. olive or vegetable oil

Mix dressing and toss dressing into spinach and strawberry mixture just before serving. Dressing may be cut in half. To make the salad look fancy, after slicing strawberries and onions, set a few aside to garnish the top after mixing in the salad dressing.

Patti Barr
Metro Detroit, MI Chapter

Soups & Salads

Orzo Salad

8 Tbsp. olive oil
8 Tbsp. lemon juice
8 oz. Feta cheese
25 Kalamata olives
1 c. fresh dill
4 Tbsp. red wine vinegar
5 c. cooked orzo
6 scallions, cut up
Tomatoes to taste (grape or cherry)
2½ lb. extra large shrimp, cooked and peeled

One day in advance, mix all ingredients except tomatoes and shrimp. Add just before serving, and toss well. Garnish with additional fresh dill. This makes a delicious main dish, enough for at least 6 or a side dish for 10 to 12. This makes it easy to enjoy company without last minute preparation in the kitchen. The dish can marinate for hours, then remove from fridge about 30 to 45 minutes before serving. Toss and enjoy!

Linda Landman
Long Island, NY Chapter

Taco Salad

1½ lb. ground beef
1 pkg. taco seasoning mix
1 pkg. cheese Doritos
2 large tomatoes, cubed
1 medium onion, diced
1 head lettuce
1 (8 oz.) pkg. grated Cheddar cheese (I prefer the Mexican blend.)
1 (16 oz.) bottle Russian dressing

Brown the ground beef sprinkling the taco seasoning mix over it as you cook, making sure to drain any excess fat. Set aside to cool. Cube the tomatoes. Dice the onion. Crush the Doritos while they are still in the bag. (a great tension reliever). Tear or shred the head of lettuce into the bowl (tearing makes the lettuce last longer without browning). Add all ingredients except the dressing a little at a time tossing along the way so that it is well mixed. Add the dressing, mix and enjoy.

Nancy Foran-Pinzon
Long Island, NY Chapter

Chicken Almond-Pear Salad

2 c. cooked chicken, cut into ½ inch cubes
½ c. green pepper, sliced lengthwise
½ c. chopped celery
3 Bartlett pears, cored and cut into ½ inch cubes
½ c. mayonnaise
½ tsp. prepared mustard
¼ tsp. ground ginger
½ tsp. seasoned salt
Lettuce
¼ c. toasted slivered almonds

Combine mayonnaise, mustard, ginger and salt and mix well. Set dressing aside. Toss together chicken, green pepper, and celery. Add pears and creamy mustard dressing. Mix gently. Serve on individual lettuce-lined plates (chilled). Garnish with almonds. Makes 4 servings.

Pat Ayres and Jan Bel Jan, ASGCA
Port St. Lucie-Treasure Coast, FL Chapter and Palm Beach County FL Chapter

Asian Vinaigrette Dressing

3 Tbsp. balsamic vinegar
3 Tbsp. soy sauce
1 tsp. sesame oil
½ c. olive oil
½ tsp. minced ginger
1 garlic clove, minced

Combine balsamic vinegar, soy sauce, and sesame oil in a medium size bowl. Add ginger and garlic. Drizzle olive oil into the bowl, whisking constantly. Makes ¾ cup.

Cindy McGeever
Greater Philadelphia, PA Chapter
Nancy Oliver Founder's Award Winner and
Former Association Board President

Caesar Salad Dressing

2 c. mayonnaise
3 whole eggs
½ pkg. onion soup mix (dry)
¼ tsp. curry powder
¼ tsp. garlic powder
⅔ c. Parmesan cheese
1 tsp. anchovy paste

Mix all ingredients thoroughly in a blender. Refrigerate.

Judith R. Shepp
Orlando, FL Chapter

Soups & Salads

Spinach Salad Dressing

¾ c. apple cider vinegar
1½ c. vegetable oil
¾ c. sugar

2 tsp. paprika
1 tsp. salt
1 tsp. dry mustard

Combine all ingredients in a sealed container. Shake well. Makes 1 quart.

Cindy McGeever
Greater Philadelphia, PA Chapter
Nancy Oliver Founder's Award Winner and
Former Association Board President

"All golfers, men and women, professional and amateur, are united by one thing — their desire to improve."

-Judy Rankin

Notes

Greens in Regulation

Vegetables

Vegetable Cooking Timetable

Vegetable	Preparation	Cooking	Time
Celery	Scrub thoroughly; cut off leaves and trim roots; slice to desired lengths.	Cook covered in small amount of boiling salted water or consommé.	10-15 minutes
Corn	Remove husks and silks from fresh corn. Rinse and cook whole.	Cook covered in small amount of boiling salted water.	6-8 minutes
Eggplant	Wash; if skin is tough, pare. Cut in ½ inch slices.	Dip in beaten egg, then in breadcrumbs. Brown in butter or oil.	Approx. 4 minutes
Mushrooms	Wash; cut off tips of stems. Leave whole or slice.	Add to melted butter in skillet; sprinkle with flour and mix. Cover and cook slowly, turning occasionally.	8-10 minutes
Okra	Wash pods; cut off stems; slice or leave whole.	Cook covered in small amount of boiling salted water.	8-15 minutes
Parsnips	Wash thoroughly; pare or scrape; slice lengthwise or crosswise.	Cook covered in small amount of boiling water.	15-20 minutes
Peas	Shell and wash	Cook covered in small amount of boiling salted water.	8-15 minutes
Spinach	Cut off roots and wash several times in lukewarm water, lifting out of water as you wash.	Cook covered without adding water. Reduce heat when steam forms; turn often while cooking.	3-5 minutes
Tomatoes	Wash ripened tomatoes.	Cook slowly, covered without adding water.	10-15 minutes
Zucchini	Wash, do not pare; slice thin.	Season and cook uncovered in butter in skillet for 5 minutes. Uncover and cook till tender, turning slices.	10 minutes total

Vegetables

Grilled Asparagus

1½ lb. (24) medium size
   asparagus, trimmed
2 Tbsp. extra virgin olive oil

Kosher salt
2 tsp. balsamic vinegar

Preheat grill. Toss the asparagus in olive oil; season with salt and sprinkle with the balsamic vinegar. Grill in a grill basket (or on pierced aluminum foil) about 5 to 6 inches from heat for 6 to 10 minutes. This is about 4 servings. Oven Option: Roast in 350° oven for 15 to 20 minutes. Even your pickiest eaters will love asparagus after trying it this way!

Ava (A.J.) Bessette
Albuquerque, NM and Brevard County/Space Coast, FL Chapters

"Golf is a game of coordination, rhythm and grace; women have these to a high degree."

-Babe Didrikson Zaharias

Vegetables

Best In The West Baked Beans

1 lb. ground sirloin or beef
10 slices bacon, cooked and crumbled (optional)
1½ c. chopped onion
¼ c. brown sugar
¼ c. white sugar
¼ c. ketchup
¼ c. barbeque sauce
2 Tbsp. yellow mustard
2 Tbsp. molasses
½ tsp. salt
½ tsp. chili powder
½ tsp. pepper
1 (16 oz.) can kidney beans
1 (16 oz.) can pork and beans
1 (16 oz.) can butter beans or lima beans

Brown meat and drain. Brown onion and add to cooked meat. Add combined sugars, sauces, and seasonings. Mix well and add beans. Pour into a 3 quart casserole and bake at 350° for 1 hour. Can also be heated or cooked in a crock pot. A great dish to carry to parties and cookouts in the crock pot. Makes 10 to 12 servings.

Margaret Downey
Jacksonville, FL Chapter
Foundation Board President and Association Board Member

Broccoli Puff

1 (10 oz.) pkg. chopped frozen broccoli
1 can cream of mushroom soup
½ c. shredded Cheddar cheese
¼ c. milk
¼ c. mayonnaise
1 egg, beaten
½ c. bread crumbs
2 Tbsp. butter, melted

Cook broccoli, drain well. Put in greased baking dish. Stir soup and cheese together; add milk, mayonnaise, and egg; blend well. Pour over broccoli. Combine bread and butter; sprinkle over top. Bake at 350° for 45 minutes.

Becky Macaluso
Palm Beach County, FL Chapter
EWGA Managing Director, Chapter & Member Services

Roasted Brussels Sprouts

1 lb. fresh Brussels sprouts
2 Tbsp. extra virgin olive oil
1 Tbsp. balsamic vinegar
1½ Tbsp. fresh grated Parmesan cheese
1 Tbsp. pignoli nuts (pine nuts)

Preheat oven to 450°. Trim Brussels sprouts, remove any discolored leaves and cut into quarters (or halves if small). Put sprouts in mixing bowl and toss with olive oil and balsamic vinegar. Cover roasting pan with foil if desired and spray with non-stick spray if needed. Arrange sprouts in a single layer on roasting pan, and roast 20 minutes, turning occasionally or until sprouts are slightly crisp and golden brown on edges. When sprouts are nearly done, toast pine nuts in a dry pan about 2 to 3 minutes, until barely starting to brown. (Be careful, they can go from lightly brown to overdone quite quickly.) Put cooked sprouts back into mixing bowl and toss with Parmesan cheese. Arrange on serving plate and sprinkle with pine nuts. Serve hot.

Jo-Ann Dixon
Northern New Jersey Chapter
Association and Foundation Board Member

Carrot Pudding

¾ c. margarine or butter
½ c. brown sugar
1 egg, beaten
1¼ c. self-rising cake flour, sifted
1 tsp. lemon juice
1 c. carrots, cooked and mashed (fresh or frozen)

Cream butter and sugar together; add egg, flour, lemon juice, and mashed carrots. Bake in greased pan for 1 hour at 350°. This is my daughter Dr. Marlene Wolf's favorite recipe!

Marlene Wolf, M.D. and Esther Rabinowitz
Fort Lauderdale Area, FL Chapter

Carrot Souffle

2 c. mashed cooked carrots
   (about 1¼ to 1½ lbs. carrots)
1 stick (½ c.) margarine, melted
¾ c. sugar
3 Tbsp. flour
1 tsp. baking powder
3 eggs, well beaten
¼ tsp. cinnamon

Preheat oven to 400°. Combine all ingredients. Pour into margarine-greased 9 inch pie pan. Bake at 400° for 15 minutes. Reduce to 350° and bake for 45 minutes, or until knife inserted into center comes out clean. May be made and baked ahead and served at room temperature. Also freezes beautifully.

Kathy Burns
Jacksonville, FL Chapter

Cheese-Frosted Cauliflower

1 medium head cauliflower
½ c. mayonnaise
1½ tsp. prepared mustard
¾ c. shredded American cheese

Cook cauliflower in small amount of salted boiling water just until tender about 10 to 15 minutes. Drain well. Place cauliflower in a 8x8x2 inch baking pan. Stir together mayonnaise and mustard; spread over cauliflower. Top with shredded cheese. Bake in a 375° oven 5 minutes or until cheese melts.

Sheri Harvey
Genesee County, MI Chapter

Corn With Bruschetta

4 ears sweet corn
Garlic powder to taste
Petite cut diced tomatoes (or fresh)
Minced garlic
Balsamic vinegar, small amount
Fresh or dried chopped basil
Salt and pepper to taste

Spray non-stick pan with cooking spray, sprinkle corn with garlic power, and set in prepared pan. Cook through just to heat, or grill, and remove kernels. Meanwhile, mix tomatoes, minced garlic, balsamic, basil, salt, and pepper. Add the bruschetta topping to the corn and enjoy!

Tiss Dahan
Senior Director of Global Apparel, TaylorMade-adidas Golf

Corn Pudding

1 (10 oz.) box frozen corn
½ c. sugar
3 Tbsp. flour
3 Tbsp. butter
3 eggs
2 c. milk

Preheat oven to 350°. Put corn in bowl to thaw. Add sugar and flour and stir until mushy. Melt butter in a 9x13 inch pan. Pour melted butter into corn mixture and stir. Add milk and stir. In a separate bowl mix eggs until foamy, then add to corn mixture. Bake 45 to 50 minutes.

Becky Macaluso
Palm Beach County, FL Chapter
EWGA Managing Director, Chapter & Member Services

Corn Pudding

1 box Jiffy corn muffin mix
1 (15 oz.) can corn, not drained
1 (15 oz.) can creamed corn
1 stick butter, melted
1 egg, beaten
1 (8 oz.) container sour cream

Mix all ingredients together and pour into greased 8x13 inch pan. Bake at 350° for 35 to 40 minutes.

Hollie West
Westchester, NY Chapter

"You have to play by the rules of golf just as you have to live by the rules of life. There is no other way."

-Babe Didrikson Zaharias

Eggplant Parmesan

1 eggplant
Sea salt
1 c. bread crumbs with Italian seasoning
1 c. Parmesan cheese, freshly grated

1 egg
1 jar tomato basil pasta sauce
1 c. Mozzarella cheese

Peel eggplant and slice in ½ inch pieces, crosswise. To remove excess moisture from eggplant, place slices in colander and sprinkle with sea salt. After a few minutes, wipe off moisture beads and salt with paper towels. Mix together bread crumbs and ½ cup of the Parmesan cheese. Whip the egg. Dip the eggplant in the egg and coat with bread crumb mixture on both sides. Place the eggplant slices on a baking tray. Turn oven on high broil and place tray 6 inches from broiler. Brown eggplant on both sides until tender. Preheat oven to 350°. In casserole dish, spoon pasta sauce to cover bottom. Layer with eggplant, Mozzarella cheese, Parmesan cheese, and sauce. Continue, ending with Parmesan on top. Cover and bake 30 minutes until hot and bubbly. Uncover and bake 5 minutes for more browning. Serve immediately, or at room temperature.

Connie Eldridge
Orange County, CA Chapter

The Best Eggplant Parmesan

Eggplant, sliced 1/8 inch thick
Eggs, beaten (enough to dip eggplant slices in)
Italian breadcrumbs (enough to coat eggplant slices)
Olive oil as needed for frying eggplant
Favorite store-bought or homemade marinara sauce
Mozzarella cheese
Parmesan cheese (optional)
Ricotta cheese (optional)

My kids hate eggplant but love this, go figure. The key is not to care about calories for this dish. The hardest thing to do is getting the eggplant ready to bake, it tastes so good you want to eat the eggplant as it is prepared. In fact, with marinara sauce as a dip it is an awesome appetizer (if you do this, cut eggplant 1/4 inch thick, 2 inches wide, and 3 to 4 inches long). For this recipe, take large ripe eggplants, peel gently, and slice. Dip slices in beaten eggs, then coat with breadcrumbs. Fry in olive oil until lightly brown, and lay on paper towels to remove excess grease and keep them crisp. To assemble, start with a thin layer of marinara sauce in the bottom of a pan. Add a layer of eggplant, a layer of Mozzarella and Parmesan cheese, and repeat. I like to alternate cheese layers with Mozzarella and Parmesan, but it's your call. If you are really feeling decadent, add Ricotta cheese as well. Depending on pan depth, you can get about 3 or 4 layers. Finish off the top with Parmesan and bake at 350° for 1 hour, or until the top layer of cheese is melted and slightly browned. Remove, cool 20 to 30 minutes, and enjoy!

MG Orender
President, Hampton Golf Clubs and Past President, PGA of America
EWGA Leadership Award Winner

Haricots Verts With Mustard Seeds And Toasted Coconut

½ lb. haricots verts, trimmed
1 Tbsp. olive oil
2 Tbsp. unsweetened coconut flakes (large)
½ tsp. mustard seeds
Salt to taste

Cook beans in a 3 quart saucepan of boiling salted water until tender-crisp, about 3 minutes, then drain. Rinse under cold running water to stop cooking and drain well. Heat ½ tablespoon oil in 10 inch heavy skillet over moderately high heat until hot, but not smoking. Cook coconut, stirring, until golden, about 2 minutes. Transfer with a slotted spoon to paper towels to drain. Cook mustard seed in remaining ½ tablespoon oil over medium-high heat, covered, shaking skillet until popping subsides, about 1 minute. Add beans to skillet with salt to taste, stirring occasionally, until heated through. Sprinkle with coconut and serve.

Luanne Jones
Houston, TX Chapter

Green Bean Casserole

3 cans sliced green beans, drained
2 cans stewed or diced tomatoes
1 onion, diced and sauteed in butter (or 3 Tbsp. dehydrated onion flakes)
1 to 2 Tbsp. flour (to thicken)
2 to 3 Tbsp. sugar
Salt and pepper to taste

Mix all ingredients well in a 3 quart casserole. Bake uncovered at 350° for 25 to 30 minutes.

Marlene Wolf, M.D. and Esther Rabinowitz
Fort Lauderdale Area, FL Chapter

Spinach Casserole

2 pkg. frozen spinach
1 pkg. Lipton onion soup mix (or any other brand)
1 c. sour cream
1 can dried onion rings

Cook frozen spinach per directions. Drain well. Mix together onion soup mix and sour cream. Add spinach. Put in greased casserole dish. Bake at 350° for 30 minutes. Garnish with onion rings.

Marlene Wolf, M.D.
Fort Lauderdale Area, FL Chapter

Spinach Squares

1 (10 oz.) pkg. frozen, chopped spinach
2 eggs
8 oz. sour cream
1 Tbsp. grated onion
½ c. Parmesan cheese
1 Tbsp. flour
2 Tbsp. butter
1 tsp. salt
⅛ tsp. pepper

Cook spinach and drain well. Beat eggs, add to spinach. Blend other ingredients. Place in a greased 9x9 inch square dish (don't use a larger dish unless you double the recipe or it will turn out too thin). Bake, uncovered, at 350° for 25 to 30 minutes. Cool slightly and cut into squares.

Becky Macaluso
Palm Beach County, FL Chapter
EWGA Managing Director, Chapter & Member Services

Eggs Florentine

Eggs Florentine:

- 4 c. spinach leaves
- 2 Tbsp. unsalted butter
- 2 Tbsp. finely chopped shallots
- 2 Tbsp. finely chopped fresh parsley
- Pinch of nutmeg
- Salt and pepper to taste
- 2 English muffins
- 4 large eggs

Saute the spinach, making two cups by cooking it gradually in the butter. Add shallots, salt, pepper, and nutmeg. Toss in until crispy. Poach the eggs in a microwave poacher for about 1 minute.

Hollandaise Sauce:

- 3 egg yolks
- 2 Tbsp. lemon juice
- 1/4 Tbsp. salt
- 1/2 tsp. sugar
- Pinch of cayenne pepper
- 1/2 c. butter, melted

In a blender, combine egg yolks, lemon juice, salt, sugar, and cayenne pepper. Blend at a low speed until it is thickened and smooth, gradually adding the hot melted butter.

Place half a toasted English muffin on each of four plates and top with 1/2 cup of sauteed spinach. Place the poached eggs on the spinach and spoon Hollandaise sauce over the open sandwich. Garnish with parsley and pepper.

Vita Anne Burdi
Long Island, NY Chapter

Squash Casserole

7 medium yellow squash
1 medium onion, thinly sliced
1 pt. sour cream
1 can cream of chicken soup
1 pkg. Pepperidge Farm stuffing mix
1 stick butter
Salt and pepper to taste

Steam squash and onion, season with salt and pepper. Mix together sour cream and soup and add to squash and onion. In 9x10 inch baking dish, melt butter. Stir in Pepperidge Farm mix. Remove 1/3 of mix for topping. Spread remaining over bottom of dish. Pour in squash mix, sprinkle remaining dressing over top. Bake at 400° for 25 minutes or until bubbly.

Maggi Braun
Charlotte, NC Chapter
Former Association and Foundation Board Member

Squash Casserole Supreme

2 summer squash
2 zucchini
2 c. mushrooms, diced
3 garlic cloves, minced
1/2 large yellow onion, diced
2 eggs
2 Tbsp. light sour cream
1 c. fat free Ricotta cheese
1 c. 2% shredded Colby Jack cheese
Cooking spray
Salt, pepper and cumin to taste

Cut zucchini and squash into thin slices. Add to pot with 1 teaspoon water and cook for 5 minutes. Remove from stove. Coat saute pan with cooking spray. Add diced mushrooms, garlic cloves and onion. Saute until tender. Add onion and mushroom mixture to squash. In separate container mix 2 eggs with 2 tablespoon sour cream. Coat baking dish with cooking spray. Distribute half of squash mixture in bottom of dish. Add half of ricotta cheese, half of egg mixture, and half of shredded cheese. Layer the other half of squash mixture over the top and use rest of Ricotta and egg mixture. Cover with foil and bake at 375° for 35 minutes. Remove foil and add the rest of the shredded cheese. Cook for additional 10 minutes. Then turn oven to broil for 2 to 3 minutes so cheese topping becomes crusty. Cool for 10 to 15 minutes before serving. Serves 9.

Karen McIntosh
Genesee County, MI Chapter

Greek Tomatoes

6 small plum tomatoes, cut in half
1 Tbsp. dry breadcrumbs
2 Tbsp. crumbled Feta cheese with basil and tomato

1/4 tsp. dried oregano
1/8 tsp. pepper

Preheat oven to 350°. Place tomato halves (cut side up) on baking sheet coated with cooking spray. Sprinkle breadcrumbs over each half and top with cheese. Sprinkle with oregano and pepper. Bake for 25 minutes. Serve warm.

Luanne Jones
Houston, TX Chapter

Root Vegetable Apple Gratin

6 slices bacon
2 Tbsp. vegetable oil
4 c. sliced leeks
4 c. sweet potatoes, peeled and cubed
2 c. parsnips, peeled and cubed

4 c. apples, peeled and cubed
1 c. chicken stock
6 oz. Goat cheese (or Blue cheese)
1/2 c. chopped almonds, pecans, or walnuts

Cook bacon, remove and drain fat. Add oil to same pan and wilt leeks. Add sweet potatoes and cook until almost done. Add parsnips, apples, and stock. Cook until tender and stock has reduced. Place into 2 quart casserole dish. Sprinkle cheese, nuts, and bacon on top. Bake at 375°, uncovered, 10 to 15 minutes to finish.

Marlene Goddu
Myrtle Beach, SC Chapter

Mixed Vegetable Casserole

2 large pkgs. mixed vegetables
1/4 c. water
1 tsp. salt
1/4 tsp. garlic salt
2 Tbsp. butter
1/4 c. butter
1/3 c. flour
2 c. milk
1/4 c. Parmesan cheese
1/8 tsp. garlic salt
2 Tbsp. dry vermouth
2 c. bread crumbs (stuffing mix)
3 Tbsp. butter, melted

Steam mixed vegetables in water for 5 minutes. Drain. Add salt, garlic salt and 2 tablespoon butter. Make cream sauce with 1/4 cup butter, flour and milk. When thickened, add Parmesan cheese, 1/8 teaspoon garlic salt, and dry vermouth. Top with bread crumbs. Drizzle with melted butter. Bake 30 to 40 minutes at 350°.

Danita Bounds
Kansas City Metro Chapter
Women Who Lead Award Winner

Vegetable Medley

3 Tbsp. olive oil
5 yellow squash, sliced
5 zucchini, sliced
2 1/2 onions, chopped
2 1/2 green peppers, chopped
5 garlic cloves, crushed
2 (16 oz.) cans diced tomatoes, undrained
1 1/4 tsp. dried basil
Salt and pepper to taste
1/2 c. grated Parmesan cheese

Preheat oven to 350°. In a large saute pan, heat olive oil over medium heat. Add squash, zucchini, onion, green pepper, and garlic. Saute until all vegetables are soft. Add tomatoes with juice. Season with basil, salt, and pepper. Transfer ingredients to a baking dish. Bake for 20 minutes in the preheated oven. Sprinkle with Parmesan cheese and bake another 10 minutes until hot and bubbly.

Cathy Morzella
Palm Beach County, FL Chapter
EWGA Accounting Assistant

Grilled Zucchini Sandwich

2 medium zucchini
8 each crimini or brown mushrooms
4 slices sweet onion
8 slices Gruyere or Swiss cheese
4 English muffins
1 jar traditional basil pesto
Olive oil
Salt and pepper

Slice zucchini lengthwise for grilling approximately 1/4 inch thick. Slice onion into discs for grilling approximately 1/4 inch thick. Slice mushrooms in half to make buttons for grilling. Place all veggies on a plate and lightly drizzle with olive oil, salt and pepper to taste. Slice English muffins and set aside. Heat grill on high. Place veggies on grill and slightly char the outside and grill until the center of the veggies are al dente. Remove, place on a plate and cut zucchini slices in half. Place English muffins face down on a low to medium heat grill. Lightly toast. Remove from grill and spread pesto on both halves of the muffin. Place a piece of cheese on one half; add the zucchini, onion and mushroom. Place another piece of cheese on the veggies and top with the other half of the muffin. Lightly brush the English muffin with olive oil and place back on the grill. Grill both sides of the English muffin sandwich until the cheese is melted and the muffin is lightly toasted. Cut in half and serve immediately. Enjoy!!

Elizabeth Rinehold
Santa Barbara, CA Chapter

Zucchini Quiche

3 c. zucchini, sliced thin and diced (no seeds)
1 small onion, chopped
1 c. biscuit mix
4 large eggs
1/2 c. vegetable oil
1/2 c. Parmesan cheese
1/2 tsp. marjoram
1 tsp. parsley flakes
1/4 tsp. salt
1/8 tsp. pepper

Mix together zucchini, onion, biscuit mix, eggs, oil, cheese, parsley, salt, and pepper until zucchini is evenly coated. Pour into buttered pie plate (10 to 12 inch) or an oblong dish (16 x 6 x 1 3/4 inch). Bake at 350° for 30 minutes or until golden. Serve warm.

Patricia Voll
Long Island, NY Chapter

Side Hill Lies

Pasta, Rice & Potatoes

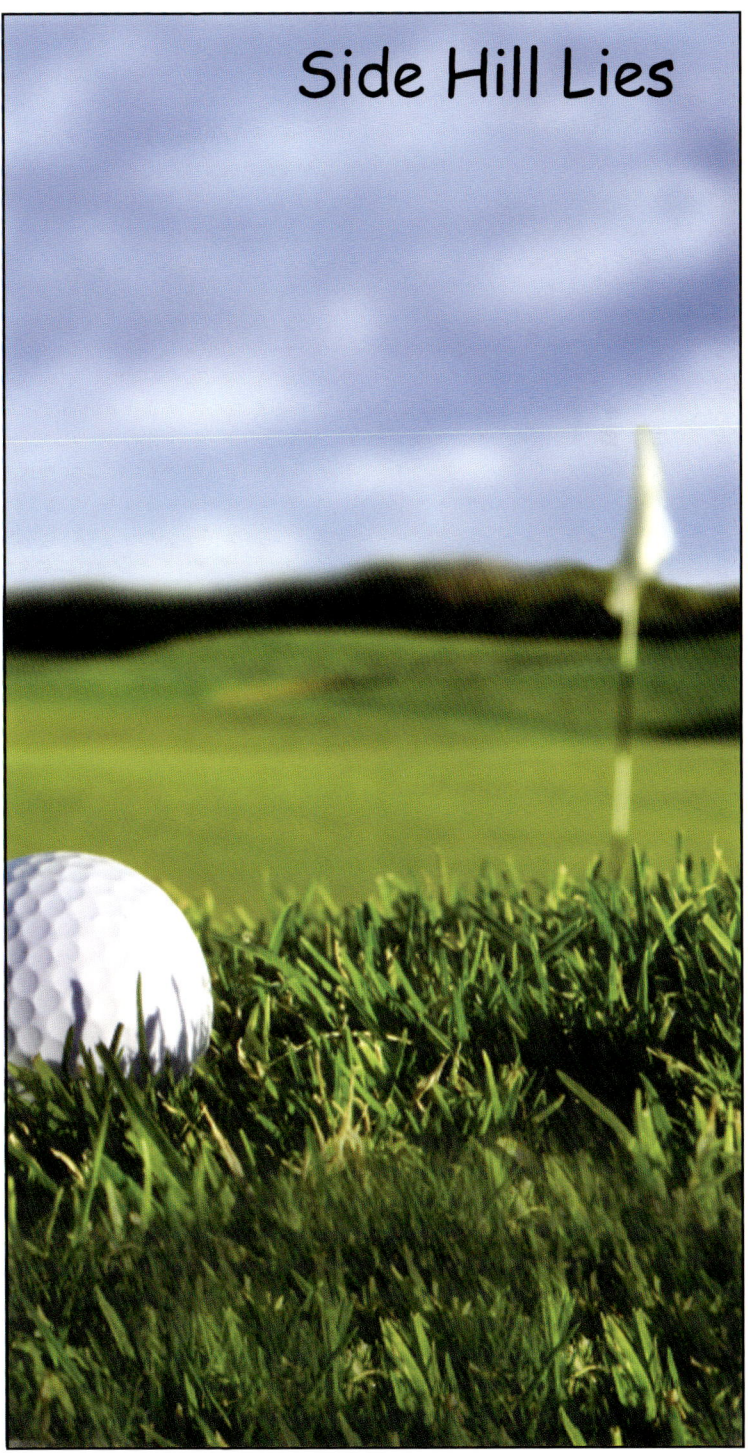

Cooking Guide for Egg, Milk, Meat and Cheese Dishes

Item	Oven Temperature	Approx. Baking Time
Soufflés	350-375°	30-60 minutes
Macaroni and Cheese	350-375°	25-45 minutes
Lasagna	350-375°	30-45 minutes
Meatloaf	350°	60-90 minutes
Meat Pie	400°	25-30 minutes
Casseroles	350-375°	25-40 minutes
Scalloped Potatoes	375-400°	50-60 minutes
Quiche	375-400°	35-45 minutes
Pizza	400-425°	20-30 minutes

Pasta, Rice & Potatoes

Marinara Sauce

Vegetable cooking spray
1½ Tbsp. olive oil
½ c. onion, chopped
4 garlic cloves, minced
2 Tbsp. fresh parsley, minced
1 tsp. dried whole oregano
1 tsp. dried whole basil
½ tsp. dried whole thyme

1 tsp. salt
¼ tsp. ground pepper
2 bay leaves
1 (28 oz.) can whole tomatoes, undrained and chopped
2 (6 oz.) cans tomato paste
¾ c. dry red wine
¾ c. water

Coat a Dutch oven with cooking spray; add oil. Place over medium heat until hot. Add onion and garlic; saute until tender. Add parsley and next five ingredients, stir one minute. Add remaining ingredients; reduce heat, and simmer, uncovered, 30 to 45 minutes, stirring often. Remove bay leaves. Serve over your favorite pasta.

Danita Bounds
Kansas City Metro Chapter
EWGA Women Who Lead Award Winner

Thursday Sauce

8 garlic cloves, whole
¼ c. canola oil or olive oil
1 (12 oz.) can tomato paste
1 tsp. salt
1 tsp. pepper

10 to 12 fresh basil leaves, whole (or ¼ tsp. chopped basil)
1 lb. of your favorite pasta

Brown garlic in oil over medium heat until golden brown. Empty contents of tomato paste can into oil and garlic. Fill empty can with water 2½ times. Add water to oil, garlic, and paste on stovetop. Stir until paste is broken up. Add salt, pepper, and fresh basil and stir until fully mixed. Bring to a boil over medium to high heat, then lower to a steady boil. Cook uncovered for 25 minutes, stirring occasionally (make sure steady but not too low boil). When timer goes off, continue to cook sauce, but now it is time to put the pot of water on high to make the pasta. Once boiling, add pasta and salt and cook according to directions. Strain pasta and add sauce. If you are only making the sauce, cook uncovered at a steady low boil for 45 minutes. Total preparation and cook time under 1 hour. Buon appetito!

Jackie Meli-Rizzo
Long Island, NY Chapter

Pasta, Rice & Potatoes

Annika's Bolognese Pasta

1 lb. ground beef
Pinch of pepper
1 yellow onion, chopped
1 carrot, chopped into small pieces
3 Tbsp. milk
1 c. beef stock
1 tsp. soy sauce
1 (28 oz.) can tomatoes, stewed or crushed
1 tsp. oregano
1 tsp. basil
¼ c. half and half
Fettucine pasta (or your favorite)
Parmesan cheese to taste

Start by browning the ground beef. Add a pinch of pepper to flavor the meat. When finished browning, put on paper towels to absorb the grease. Slowly saute the chopped onions until golden brown. Add the chopped carrots and blend together. Add the browned beef and the milk to thicken. Add the beef stock and soy sauce. Pour the canned tomatoes into the mix and let simmer for an hour. If using dried oregano and basil, add them before simmering. If using fresh herbs, add them at the end. When you are ready to serve, stir in the half and half to make it a little creamy and tasty! Serve hot over your favorite pasta - mine is fettucine - with some good Parmesan cheese. Enjoy!!

Annika Sorenstam, LPGA
World Golf Hall of Fame Member
EWGA Leadership Award Winner

Pasta Carbonara

2 Tbsp. butter
Generous ½ c. diced pancetta
1 garlic clove
12 oz. spaghetti
2 eggs, beaten
½ c. Parmesan cheese, freshly grated
½ c. Romano cheese, freshly grated
Salt and pepper to taste

Melt the butter in a pan, add the pancetta and garlic, and cook until the garlic turns brown. Remove and discard the garlic. Meanwhile, cook the spaghetti in a large pan of salted, boiling water until al dente, then drain and add the pancetta. Remove the pan from the heat, pour in the eggs, add half the Parmesan and half the Romano, and season with salt and pepper. Mix well so the egg coats the pasta. Add the remaining cheese, mix again, and serve.

Ty M. Votaw
Executive Vice President - Communications and International Affairs,
PGA TOUR

Garlic White Lasagna

1½ lb. Italian sausage
4 large garlic cloves, chopped
1 medium onion, chopped
1 (12 oz.) jar roasted red peppers
½ c. white wine
1 (10 oz.) pkg. frozen chopped spinach
1 (15 oz.) container Ricotta cheese
1 large egg
2 jars Alfredo sauce
1 pkg. non-cook lasagna noodles
2 (6 oz.) pkgs. Mozzarella cheese
1 c. shredded Parmesan cheese
½ tsp. salt
½ tsp. pepper

Preheat oven to 350°. Remove and discard sausage casing. Brown sausage in large skillet over medium heat; crumble sausage as it cooks. Drain sausage, reserving 1 tablespoon drippings in skillet. Cook garlic and onion in drippings until onion is tender. Stir in sausage, chopped red pepper, and wine. Bring to a boil then reduce heat and simmer uncovered until most of the liquid has evaporated, approximately 5 to 7 minutes. Microwave frozen spinach until hot and squeeze out excess liquid (be careful of steamed package). Combine spinach, Ricotta cheese, salt, pepper, and lightly beaten egg. Stir well. Spread 1 cup Alfredo sauce in a greased 13x9x2 inch baking dish. Layer with lasagna noodles. Top with half of spinach mixture and half of sausage mixture. Place 6 ounces Mozzarella cheese over sausage. Repeat layers, ending with noodles and Mozzarella cheese. Spread remaining Alfredo sauce over Mozzarella cheese. Sprinkle with Parmesan cheese. Let stand at room temperature for 30 minutes before baking (can refrigerate overnight). Cover with foil and bake for 1 hour, uncovering the last 15 minutes of baking. Let stand 15 minutes before serving.

Susan Tajalli
Palm Beach County, FL Chapter

Mexican Lasagna

1½ lb. ground beef, browned
1½ tsp. dried oregano
12 lasagna noodles, uncooked
1 (16 oz.) can refried beans
2 garlic cloves, minced
1 Tbsp. oil
2 tsp. ground cumin
2 c. water
2½ c. salsa
2 c. sour cream
¾ c. green onions, sliced
1 (2.25 oz.) can black olives, sliced
½ c. grated cheese (your favorite)

Preheat oven to 350°. Lightly spray a 13x9 inch baking dish with cooking oil. Saute garlic in oil, add beef and brown, add beans, oregano and cumin. Place 4 uncooked lasagna noodles in the bottom of baking dish. Spread ⅓ of the mixture over the noodles, makes three layers. Combine water and salsa, pour over noodles. Cover with foil. Bake 1½ hours or until noodles are tender. Combine sour cream, onions and olives and spoon over casserole; top with grated cheese. Bake uncovered until cheese melts. Remove from oven and let stand. You may be creative by adding avocado or fresh tomatoes to this delicious recipe.

Alice Miller
Northeast Bay, CA Chapter

Pesto Pasta

⅔ c. packed basil leaves, coarsely chopped (or 2 Tbsp. dried crushed basil leaves)
⅓ c. Parmesan cheese, grated
⅓ c. olive or vegetable oil
2 Tbsp. pine nuts or walnuts
½ tsp. salt
⅛ tsp. pepper
3 garlic cloves (or more for garlic lovers)
10 oz. uncooked spaghetti or other noodles
2 Tbsp. margarine or butter

Place all ingredients except spaghetti and margarine in a blender. Cover and blend on high speed until mixture is uniform consistency. Cook spaghetti as directed on package; drain. Toss spaghetti with basil mixture and margarine. Serve with additional Parmesan cheese if desired.

Joanne Cortese
Greater Philadelphia, PA Chapter

Chicken Pasta Primavera

Chicken:

1 pkg. boneless, skinless chicken breasts (3 to 4 breasts)
¼ c. olive oil, plus extra for roasting garlic
1 to 2 fresh garlic cloves, minced
1 tsp. Italian seasoning
1 head fresh garlic

Clean chicken breasts and pound to even thickness. Mix olive oil, 1 to 2 minced garlic cloves, and Italian seasoning in a large Ziploc bag. Place cleaned and pounded chicken in the bag to marinate for approximately 1 hour (longer is okay). Meanwhile, roast a head of garlic in the oven. Cut off the top, exposing the cloves. Place the garlic head in a small dish. Pour a small amount of olive oil on the garlic, cover, and roast in the oven for about 30 minutes at 375°. Fresh garlic will work fine in this recipe, but if you have time to roast the garlic, it adds a nice flavor.

Sauce:

2 c. chicken stock
½ c. olive oil
3 Tbsp. parsley, finely chopped
1 Tbsp. fresh basil, finely chopped or dried, or Italian seasoning (just rosemary would work as well)
3 fresh garlic cloves, minced (or 6 cloves of roasted garlic from above)

Mix all ingredients together and bring to a boil. Reduce heat and simmer for 30 minutes.

Veggies:

Assorted fresh vegetables **6 servings pasta (your favorite)**

Stir fry an assortment of your favorite vegetables - mushrooms, snow peas, broccoli, zucchini, asparagus, onion, and red pepper all work well. If you roasted garlic, add the remaining cloves, chopped, to the veggies. Do not overcook.

Grill the chicken and cut into bite-size pieces. Mix the chicken into the cooked vegetables. Cook your favorite pasta and drain. Toss the chicken and vegetables into the pasta and pour the sauce over the top. Serve and garnish with Parmesan cheese if desired.

Patty Evans
Northern Nevada Chapter

Bow Ties With Sausage, Tomatoes, And Cream

2 Tbsp. olive oil
1 lb. sausage
½ tsp. crushed red pepper
½ c. onion, diced
3 garlic cloves, minced
1 (28 oz.) can plum tomatoes, drained and coarsely chopped
1½ c. whipping cream
½ tsp. salt
12 oz. bow tie pasta, cooked and drained
3 Tbsp. fresh parsley, minced
Parmesan cheese to taste

Heat oil in a skillet. Add sausage and pepper flakes. Cook sausage about 7 minutes. Add onion and garlic, and cook until tender, about 7 minutes. Add tomatoes, cream, and salt. Simmer until mixture thickens, about 5 minutes. Add drained pasta to simmering sauce and heat until sauce thickens while stirring. Sprinkle with parsley and Parmesan cheese.

Vivian Zaffuto
Long Island, NY Chapter

Orzo Mushroom Casserole

1 (16 oz.) pkg. orzo
1 stick margarine
1 pkg. dried onion soup mix
1 (4 oz.) can mushrooms, drained

Cook orzo per directions. Drain. Add the rest of the ingredients and mix well. Bake in covered casserole dish at 350° for 1 hour on bottom shelf. Serve and enjoy!

Marlene Wolf, M.D. and Esther Rabinowitz
Fort Lauderdale Area, FL Chapter

Fabulous And Easy Wild Mushroom Ravioli

Ravioli:

2 lb. wild mushrooms (crimini, shiitake, or porcini)
2 garlic cloves, finely minced
4 shallots, finely minced
3 Tbsp. chopped parsley
½ stick butter
1 Tbsp. good olive oil
1 c. grated Parmesan
1 pkg. wonton wrappers
1 beaten egg (with 1 tsp. water)
Salt and pepper to taste

Wipe mushrooms clean and coarsely chop. Finely chop garlic, shallots, and parsley; set aside. Preheat saute pan and add butter and olive oil. When bubbling, add mushrooms, garlic, and shallots; reduce down until all liquid is absorbed. Take off of the heat and cool slightly. Add Parmesan to the mixture and roughly chop in a food processor. Open wontons and place a damp paper towel over skins so they do not dry out. Take one skin and place 1 teaspoon of the filling mixture in the middle. Dab some of the egg and water mixture along the edges of the skin. Place another skin on top, pressing all air and crimping the edges. Bring salted water to a boil and place ravioli in; remove when they come to the surface, about 1 to 2 minutes. Drain and add a little oil so they do not stick.

Sauce:

1 stick butter
2 shallots, minced
12 sage leaves
½ c. grated Parmesan

Heat saute pan with butter; add shallots and saute until brown. Saute ravioli until they get a little color. Add sage leaves. Remove, plate, and sprinkle with Parmesan and sage leaves. Serves 6.

Michelle Florea
Ft. Lauderdale Area, FL Chapter

Rotini With Spinach And Asiago Cheese

1 lb. rotini pasta
¼ c. olive oil
1 garlic clove, minced
1 bag fresh baby spinach
½ pt. cherry tomatoes, halved
1 c. Asiago cheese, grated
Salt to taste
¾ tsp. freshly ground black pepper

Cooking time: 15 minutes. Bring a large pot of salted water to a boil over high heat. Add the pasta and cook until tender but still firm to the bite, stirring occasionally, about 8 to 10 minutes. Drain pasta, reserving ½ cup of the cooking liquid. Meanwhile, warm olive oil in a large, heavy skillet over medium-high heat. Add the garlic and cook until fragrant, about 2 minutes. Add the spinach and tomatoes and cook until the spinach wilts, about 2 more minutes. Add the cooked pasta and toss. Add the cheese, salt, pepper, and the pasta cooking liquid and stir to combine. Transfer the pasta to a serving plate and serve.

Chin Oh
Kalamazoo/Battle Creek, MI Chapter

"Golf is not a game of great shots. It's a game of the most accurate misses. The people who win make the smallest mistakes."
-Gene Littler

Spicy Bacon Mac And Cheese

- 2 c. bacon, regular thick cut low salt, chopped into bite-size pieces
- 2 garlic cloves, diced
- 1 serrano pepper, minced
- 3 Tbsp. unsalted butter
- 1/3 c. flour
- 3 c. whole milk
- 1 c. crumbled Gorgonzola or Blue cheese
- 1 c. shredded Jack cheese
- 2 c. shredded sharp Cheddar cheese
- 2 tsp. hot sauce (the hotter the better)
- 2 Tbsp. Sauce Goddess BBQ Sweet Heat seasoning (or red pepper flakes)
- 1/2 tsp. salt
- 1/8 tsp. black pepper (6 turns or so on the pepper mill)
- 1 lb. dry pasta, any shape is fine
- 1/2 c. breadcrumbs
- 1 Tbsp. butter, melted

Start salted water boiling for your pasta. Preheat oven to 350°. Cook bacon on medium in fry pan with spatter screen until tender, about 10 minutes. Add garlic and pepper and cook for 2 minutes. Remove from pan. Leave 1 tablespoon or so of the bacon drippings. The more drippings the stronger the bacon flavor will be in the sauce. Add the first 3 tablespoons of butter to the pan. Slowly add flour and stir to create a roux (or medium thick flour/butter paste). Slowly add milk to create the white sauce, whisking constantly to prevent lumps. Add in hot sauce, Sauce Goddess BBQ Sweet Heat seasoning (or red pepper flakes), salt and pepper. Set aside 1/4 cup of the Gorgonzola and Jack cheeses and 1/2 cup of the Cheddar cheese for the topping. Add remaining cheeses in small batches slowly, adding more after the first amount has melted. Add the bacon and garlic back in. Stir to combine. Remove from heat. Cook pasta until almost done (still a bit firm when you eat it). You do not want overdone pasta for this because you cook it in the oven for 45 minutes. Drain pasta and add to the sauce. Give it a final taste and add salt and pepper if needed. Pour into a 9x13 inch baking dish. In a bowl, mix the remaining cheeses with 1/2 cup of breadcrumbs and 1 tablespoon of butter. Sprinkle this over the pasta and sauce. Bake covered for 15 minutes. Remove cover and continue baking for 30 minutes in a 350° oven until the top is golden brown and the cheese is melted. Enjoy!

Jennifer Reynolds
San Diego, CA Chapter

Baked Noodles And Vegetables

1½ pkg. medium noodles (I use a 1 lb. bag.), cooked and drained
1 (10.5 oz.) can cream of mushroom soup
1 large onion, sliced
1 green pepper, cut in strips
2 c. canned tomatoes
½ lb. medium sharp cheese, shredded
1 small bottle green olives, cut in halves
½ c. cream (I use half and half.)
1 (14.5 oz.) can shoestring green beans
Salt and pepper to taste
4 Tbsp. butter, melted

Mix all ingredients except noodles and butter. Stir cooked noodles into the mixture. Pour into an oblong glass baking dish and pour melted butter on top of mixture. Bake at 375° for 1 hour. Great for big family events, tastes even better warmed up. Freezes well.

Linda Moseley
Canton, OH Chapter

Beans And Rice Southwestern

1 (14 oz.) can premium black beans, rinsed
1 (14 oz.) can chopped tomatoes with chili peppers
1 (14 oz.) can corn (yellow or shoe peg), rinsed
2 Tbsp. barbeque sauce (your choice)
1 (4 oz.) can green chili peppers, chopped

Mix all ingredients on medium heat. Stir, cover, and simmer. Serve with Basmati rice. Makes 4 servings. Sour cream and shredded cheeses optional. Kids love the mix above rolled in soft flour tortillas. Protein, carbs, and veggies all in one dish!

Kathy Fraser
Charlotte, NC Chapter

Caribbean Rice

1 Tbsp. butter
1 garlic clove, minced
½ tsp. ground cumin
¼ tsp. salt
¼ tsp. cayenne pepper
1¼ c. water
¾ c. uncooked rice

1 (15 oz.) can black beans, drained and rinsed
1½ c. frozen corn kernels
2 scallions, chopped
2 Tbsp. fresh cilantro, chopped
2 tsp. lime zest, grated

In a pot, melt butter over medium heat. Add garlic, cumin, salt, and cayenne. Cook 1 minute. Add water; bring to a boil. Stir in rice and cover. Reduce heat to low and cook 15 minutes. Stir in beans and corn and simmer 5 minutes or until water is absorbed. Stir in scallions, cilantro, and lime zest. Transfer to bowl and serve.

Luanne Jones
Houston, TX Chapter

Luau Rice

¾ c. salad oil
1½ c. chopped onion
3 garlic cloves, crushed
2 Tbsp. curry
3 c. long grain white rice
6 c. water

4 tsp. salt
¼ tsp. white pepper
3 large tomatoes, seeded and diced
1 c. scallions, finely chopped

In a large heavy pot, heat oil over medium heat. Saute onions and garlic until onions are translucent. Add curry and cook 2 minutes. Add rice and cook 2 minutes, stirring constantly. Add water, salt, and pepper. Bring to a boil. Cover, reduce to low heat, and cook 30 minutes. Remove from heat. Uncover and let stand 5 minutes without stirring. Transfer to a large bowl and toss with fork. Cool (can be made ahead to this point). Cover and refrigerate for up to 24 hours. Just before serving, add diced tomatoes and scallions and toss.

Carla Washinko
Tampa Bay, FL Chapter
Nancy Oliver Founder's Award Winner and
Former Association Board President

Holiday Wild Rice

1 c. wild rice
½ c. butter
½ c. chopped slivered almonds
1 c. mushrooms, sliced
¾ c. chopped green onions
(including green tops)
3 c. chicken broth

Preheat oven to 350°. In a large pan, melt butter and saute wild rice, almonds, mushrooms and onions for 5 minutes. Turn into covered casserole dish or 9x13 inch glass pan. add chicken broth and cover tightly. Bake until liquid is absorbed and rice is opened, 1½ to 2 hours. Can be made ahead of time and reheated at 325° for 20 minutes.

Hollis Kerler
Milwaukee, WI Chapter
EWGA Director of Chapter Development

Grilled Fingerling Potatoes With Tarragon Vinaigrette

12 fingerling potatoes, halved
¼ c. white wine vinegar
1 Tbsp. chopped shallot
1 Tbsp. Dijon mustard
1 Tbsp. mayonnaise
2 Tbsp. chopped fresh tarragon leaves
¼ c. canola oil
Salt and pepper to taste

Preheat grill to medium temperature. Brush cut potatoes with canola oil and season with salt and pepper. Grill until lightly golden, turning until cooked through. Transfer to bowl. Combine vinegar, shallots, mustard, mayonnaise, and tarragon in food processor and blend until smooth. With motor running, slowly add ¼ cup of canola oil and blend until vinaigrette has emulsified. Add salt and pepper to taste. Drizzle vinaigrette over warm potatoes (they will absorb the vinaigrette better than cooled potatoes). Garnish with additional chopped tarragon. Recipe attributed to Bobby Flay.

Catherine Schiaffo
San Diego, CA Chapter

Scalloped Potatoes

3 medium potatoes (or about 1½ lb.)
½ c. onion, chopped
2 Tbsp. butter
1 c. whipping cream

4 slices bacon, cooked and crumbled
½ Tbsp. salt
1½ c. grated cheese (Velveeta or Cheddar)

Boil potatoes until fork tender but not falling apart. Cool, peel, and slice. Saute onion in butter. Place sliced potatoes in a 1½ quart casserole dish. Mix cream, onion, bacon, and salt together. Pour mixture over potatoes and top with grated cheese. Bake at 350° for 20 to 25 minutes until bubbling. Serves 4 to 5.

Patty Evans
Northern Nevada Chapter

Easy Potatoes

2 lb. frozen hash browns
¼ c. butter
¼ c. chopped onions
1½ tsp. salt
¼ tsp. pepper
8 oz. Cheddar cheese, shredded

8 oz. sour cream
1 (10.75 oz.) can condensed cream of chicken soup
2 Tbsp. butter, melted
½ c. corn flake crumbs

Preheat oven to 350°. Prepare the topping by mixing together 2 tablespoons melted butter and corn flake crumbs in a bowl, then set aside. Take the remaining ingredients and mix together in a bowl; place into a 9x13 inch baking dish. Crumble and sprinkle topping over top of potato mixture and bake uncovered 40 to 50 minutes at 350°. Serves 6 to 8.

Susan Naugle
Palm Beach County, FL Chapter
EWGA Director of Marketing

Hash Brown Party Potatoes

2 lb. frozen hash browns, thawed
1 stick margarine, melted
1 tsp. salt
½ tsp. pepper
1 (10.5 oz.) can cream of celery soup
16 oz. sour cream
½ c. chopped green onions
1½ c. shredded mild Cheddar cheese
2 c. crushed corn flakes
¼ c. margarine, melted

Preheat oven to 350°. Mix hash browns, margarine (1 stick), salt, pepper, celery soup, sour cream, green onions, and Cheddar cheese. Pour into a 9x13 inch pan or 2½ quart baking dish. Mix corn flakes and melted margarine (¼ cup) and spread over potato mixture. Bake about 1 hour and 15 minutes.

Kathy Thomas
Kansas City Metro and Tucson-Old Pueblo, AZ Chapters
Nancy Oliver Founder's Award Winner and
Former Association Board Member

Party Potatoes

2 (32 oz.) bags frozen hash brown potatoes
1 (10.5 oz.) can cheese soup
1 lb. sour cream
2 c. shredded sharp Cheddar cheese
1 stick butter or margarine
1 c. diced ham (optional)

Mix potatoes, soup, sour cream and cheese together in a 6x9 inch baking dish, saving out enough cheese to sprinkle on top. Cut butter into pats and place around on the mixture. Sprinkle remaining cheese on top and bake at 350° for 1 hour.

Sheri Harvey
Genesee County, MI Chapter

Sweet Potato Casserole

Potatoes:

- 2 lb. canned sweet potatoes, drained
- 3 eggs
- 1 stick butter or margarine, softened
- 1 (5 oz.) can skim milk
- 1 Tbsp. vanilla
- 1 c. sugar
- Dash cinnamon
- Dash nutmeg

Preheat oven to 325°. Combine all ingredients and beat well. Pour into casserole sprayed with PAM cooking oil.

Topping:

- 1 c. brown sugar
- 3 Tbsp. flour
- 1 stick butter or margarine, softened
- 1 c. nuts, chopped (prefer walnuts)

Blend all ingredients well and spread over top of sweet potatoes. Bake at 325 ° for about 30 to 40 minutes.

Patti Barr
Metro Detroit, MI Chapter

Down the Middle

Meat & Poultry

MEAT ROASTING GUIDE

Cut	Weight Pounds	Approx. Time (Hours) (325° oven)	Internal Temperature
BEEF			
Standing rib roast (10 inch) ribs (If using shorter cut (8-inch) ribs, allow 30 min. longer)	4	1¾	140° (rare)
		2	160° (medium)
		2½	170° (well done)
	8	2½	140° (rare)
		3	160° (medium)
		4½	170° (well done)
Rolled ribs	4	2	140° (rare)
		2½	160° (medium)
		3	170° (well done)
	6	3	140° (rare)
		3¼	160° (medium)
		4	170° (well done)
Rolled rump (Roast only if high quality. Otherwise, braise.)	5	2¼	140° (rare)
		3	160° (medium)
		3¼	170° (well done)
Sirloin tip (Roast only if high quality. Otherwise, braise.)	3	1½	140° (rare)
		2	160° (medium)
		2¼	170° (well done)
LAMB			
Leg	6	3	175° (medium)
		3½	180° (well done)
	8	4	175° (medium)
		4½	180° (well done)
VEAL			
Leg (piece)	5	2½ to 3	170° (well done)
Shoulder	6	3½	170° (well done)
Rolled shoulder	3 to 5	3 to 3½	170° (well done)

POULTRY ROASTING GUIDE

Type of Poultry	Ready-To-Cook Weight	Oven Temperature	Approx. Total Roasting Time
TURKEY	6 to 8 lb.	325°	2½ to 3 hr.
	8 to 12 lb.	325°	3 to 3½ hr.
	12 to 16 lb.	325°	3½ to 4 hr.
	16 to 20 lb.	325°	4 to 4½ hr.
	20 to 24 lb.	300°	5 to 6 hr.
CHICKEN (Unstuffed)	2 to 2½ lb.	400°	1 to 1½ hr.
	2½ to 4 lb.	400°	1½ to 2½ hr.
	4 to 8 lb.	325°	3 to 5 hr.
DUCK (Unstuffed)	3 to 5 lb.	325°	2½ to 3 hr.

NOTE: Small chickens are roasted at 400° so that they brown well in the short cooking time. They may also be done at 325° but will take longer and will not be as brown. Increase cooking time 15 to 20 minutes for stuffed chicken and duck.

Copyright © 2011 by Cookbook Publishers, Inc.

Meat & Poultry

Dad's Barbeque Sauce

1 small onion, chopped
Margarine or butter
1 to 2 c. ketchup
Blob of mustard
Small scoop of brown sugar
Smidgen of pepper
Dash of garlic salt
Dribble of Worcestershire sauce

In frying pan, saute onion in butter. Add remaining ingredients. Stir and simmer for 10 to 15 minutes. Serve on ribs, chicken, hamburgers or hotdogs. Enjoy!

Nancy Oliver
EWGA Founder

Texas Steak Rub

½ c. brown sugar
¼ c. granulated sugar
2 Tbsp. red chili powder (or any dark chili powder)
2 Tbsp. paprika
1 Tbsp. dry Mexican oregano
1 Tbsp. dry thyme
1 Tbsp. dry sweet basil
1 tsp. cayenne pepper
2 Tbsp. granulated garlic

Mix all ingredients together thoroughly. Generously rub on steak and grill to your desired temperature. I keep a jar of the rub on hand at all times to use on steaks, chicken and even mix into hamburger patties. This recipe is loosely based on a recipe from the Texas Beef Association.

Ava (A.J.) Bessette
Albuquerque, NM and Brevard/Space Coast, FL Chapters

Barbecue Sloppy Joe

1½ lb. lean ground beef
1 large onion, chopped fine
2 (8 oz.) cans tomato sauce
1½ tsp. chili powder
1½ tsp. paprika
¾ tsp. dry mustard
¾ tsp. Worcestershire sauce
3 Tbsp. white sugar
3 Tbsp. barbecue sauce
5 Tbsp. brown sugar

Saute onion. Brown ground beef; drain. Add rest of ingredients. Simmer, stirring frequently, about 30 to 60 minutes. Serve on hamburger buns. Good with coleslaw and chips. Can double recipe; freezes well. This recipe is from my mom, Helen Smith of Woodsfield, OH. Thanks, mom!

Marlene Wolf, M.D. and Gordon Smith
Fort Lauderdale Area, FL Chapter

Basil Burger With Bacon Chutney

Sweet Heat Basil Burger:

1¼ lb. ground turkey
3 Tbsp. fresh basil, diced
1 serrano pepper, minced
1 Tbsp. brown sugar
1 Tbsp. minced garlic
1 tsp. sea salt
1 tsp. black pepper

In a bowl, combine all ingredients. With wet hands, form the meat mixture into 4 burgers. Place burgers on wax or parchment paper and place in freezer for 15 minutes prior to cooking. AFTER you make the burger topping below, cook the burgers and spread it on top.

Bacon Chutney:

4 strips bacon, diced small
1 medium sweet onion, sliced thin
¾ c. Sauce Goddess Grill Glaze or your favorite BBQ sauce
1 c. water

In a saute pan, cook the bacon until close to crunchy. Remove and drain excess fat. Add onions, ¼ cup BBQ sauce, and ¼ cup water. Cook on low. Add water as needed until the onions are soft. Add more sauce and continue cooking until the mixture turns thick. Cook your burgers. Top your burger with this yummy bacon onion topping and maybe some Blue cheese. This "Bacon Chutney" stays good in the fridge for almost a week and is really good on sandwiches too.

Jennifer Reynolds
San Diego, CA Chapter

Michaela's Authentic Swedish Meatballs

2½ lb. minced lean beef (my mom uses 50% beef and 50% pork!)
1½ c. (or to taste) minced yellow onion
1 c. pre-soaked breadcrumbs (soak in milk)
2 eggs
Salt, pepper, and white pepper to taste

Start by soaking the breadcrumbs in milk until you get a texture similar to grits. Mix the meat, soaked breadcrumbs, onion, eggs, salt, pepper, and white pepper well in a bowl. Roll into medium sized meatballs (makes 30 to 35). Pan-fry for color and finish them in the oven in an oven safe dish with foil on top. Serve with brown sauce (heavy cream plus meat bouillon to taste plus food coloring), mashed or boiled potatoes and lingonberries! This is a very simple and authentic recipe for real Swedish meatballs. Yes, I'm Swedish-born and raised!!!

Michaela Wilson
Solheim Cup and Tournament Operations, PING

Swedish Meatballs

1 lb. ground beef
1 egg
1 small yellow onion, shredded
1 c. plain bread crumbs
3 Tbsp. water
2 tsp. salt
1 tsp. black pepper

Shred the onion and mix it with the egg, bread crumbs, water, salt, and pepper in a bowl. Let the mix sit for 10 minutes to harden a little, then add the ground beef. Mix everything thoroughly (preferably using clean hands), then roll into 1 inch diameter balls. Fry in a pan on medium heat for 15 to 20 minutes (keep moving the pan every few minutes to brown the meatballs evenly on all sides). Serve with boiled or mashed potatoes, beef gravy and lingonberry sauce (which can be found at IKEA or substitute with cranberry sauce).

Stina Sternberg
Senior Editor, Golf Digest

Mom's Meatballs

1 lb. ground beef
4 slices bread
½ c. water
2 eggs
1 tsp. salt
1 tsp. oregano
¼ c. grated Parmesan

Preheat oven to 375°. Soak bread slices in water, then stir and set aside. Beat eggs, add salt and oregano, then add to bread mixture. Add hamburger and Parmesan, mix and then roll mixture to form meatballs. Place in baking dish and bake 40 minutes at 375°. Serve with pasta and spaghetti sauce or on their own as an appetizer. Makes 12 to 16 meatballs. Preparation tip: wet hands prior to forming meatballs so mixture will not stick.

Susan Naugle
Palm Beach County, FL Chapter
EWGA Director of Marketing

Southwestern Tamale Pie

1 lb. ground beef
½ c. chopped onion
2 garlic cloves, finely chopped
1 Tbsp. chili powder
½ tsp. ground cumin
½ tsp. salt
1 (16 oz.) can whole tomatoes
1 (12 oz.) can whole kernel corn, drained
3 c. water
1 c. yellow corn meal
1 c. shredded Monterey Jack cheese

Saute ground beef, onion, and garlic in large skillet over medium heat, until beef is no longer pink. Drain off fat; stir in chili powder, cumin, salt, tomatoes (break up with fork) with juice of corn and tomatoes. Simmer uncovered for about 15 minutes or until thickened. Pour in casserole dish. In large saucepan, bring water to boil and slowly pour corn meal in pan. Stir constantly, until thickened. Spread corn meal mixture over meat mixture in baking dish. Bake uncovered for 35 minutes more. Sprinkle cheese on top and bake 5 to 10 minutes more until cheese is melted and bubbly.

Dawn Jeffers
Phoenix, AZ Chapter

Enchiladas

1½ lb. ground beef
1 packet McCormick's or
   Schilling enchilada sauce mix
1½ c. water
2 (8 oz.) cans tomato sauce
1 (16 oz.) can sliced black olives
12 large soft tortilla shells
2 c. shredded Mozzarella cheese
2 c. shredded mild Cheddar
   cheese

Brown ground beef and drain. In a saucepan, combine tomato sauce, water, olives, and sauce mix. Let simmer 5 minutes. Stir half of the sauce mixture in with the meat. Roll 2½ tablespoons of the meat and sauce mixture into each tortilla. Add a small amount of Mozzarella and Cheddar cheeses. Place shell seam down in a 9x13 inch greased pan. Spread remaining sauce evenly over enchiladas and top with remaining cheeses. Cook for 15 minutes in a 350° oven. Serves 12.

Linda Butkus
Omaha, NE Chapter

Taco Pizza

1 lb. ground beef
1 pkg. taco meat seasoning
⅔ c. taco sauce
⅔ c. pizza sauce
¼ c. refried beans
Pizza crust of your choice
1½ c. Mozzarella cheese
1 c. shredded Cheddar cheese
Shredded lettuce
Chopped tomato
Sliced black olives
Salsa

Brown beef, drain, and mix in seasoning according to packet instructions. Mix together taco sauce, pizza sauce, and beans. Spread evenly on pizza crust. Top with half the Mozzarella, the beef, and the other half of the Mozzarella. Bake 8 to 10 minutes at 450°. Mix Cheddar cheese, lettuce, tomatoes, and olives. Top pizza with mixture when it comes out of the oven. Drizzle with salsa of your choice. If you like taco pizza, you'll love this recipe. And....for all you Iowa golfers who love Happy Joe's Pizza...Enjoy!

Darlene 'Babe' Lamb
Kansas City Metro Chapter

Dinner-In-A-Dish Casserole

1 lb. ground beef (can be replaced with ground turkey)
¼ c. chopped onion
½ c. chopped green pepper
2 Tbsp. oil
1½ tsp. salt
¼ tsp. pepper
2 eggs
1 (12 oz.) can whole kernel corn, drained
4 medium tomatoes, sliced
½ c. dry bread crumbs
2 Tbsp. oil or margarine

Brown ground beef, onion, and green pepper in 2 tablespoons oil. Sprinkle with salt and pepper; continue to cook until meat is well browned. Remove from heat. Beat eggs slightly; add to meat mixture and blend. Place layers of corn, meat mixture, and tomatoes in a greased 2 quart casserole; repeat layers. Combine bread crumbs and oil. Sprinkle over top of mixture in casserole. Bake uncovered in oven at 400° for 30 minutes. Makes 4 servings.

Linda Moseley
Canton, OH Chapter

Barbequed Beef

3 to 4 lb. beef roast
½ c. brown sugar
1 tsp. horseradish
1 Tbsp. chili powder
1 tsp. Worcestershire sauce
1 small onion, chopped
½ c. catsup
⅓ c. vinegar
3 Tbsp. prepared mustard
1 to 2 Tbsp. lemon juice

Cover roast with water and boil until it falls apart. Shred or chop the beef. Reserve beef broth. Mix remaining ingredients and combine with beef. If too dry add a little of the beef broth. Simmer until onion is tender. Serve on buns with cole slaw. Makes approximately 16 medium size sandwiches.

Angie Niehoff
Palm Beach County, FL Chapter
Former Foundation Board President and Association Board Member

No Peek Mushroom Brisket

2 to 3 lb. beef brisket (boneless)
1 (10.25 oz.) can cream of mushroom soup (can use low-sodium, Healthy Request soup)
1 (15 oz.) can sliced mushrooms with liquid
1 (1 oz.) envelope dry onion soup mix
2/3 c. red wine
1/4 c. water

Preheat oven to 325°. Place meat in bottom of glass roasting dish or covered roasting dish. Mix all ingredients except for water. Pour on top of meat, adding water last. Stir a bit. Cover and bake in center of oven for 3 hours. No peeking, please. Meat is tender with rich gravy. Can cool, slice, and serve reheated the next day. Sauce is great over stroganoff noodles.

Marlene Wolf, M.D.
Fort Lauderdale Area, FL Chapter

"Golf is a game of inches. The most important are those between the ears."

-Arnold Palmer

Nancy's Mom Mim Bennett's Brisket

1 (5 lb.) brisket of beef
1 c. chopped celery
2 medium onions, chopped
1 c. Heinz chili sauce
¼ c. Worcestershire sauce
¼ c. red wine vinegar
Thickening agent: cornstarch and water or flour and butter roux
Kosher salt and fresh ground pepper (be generous with pepper)
¼ c. brown sugar
1 c. good quality cabernet or merlot

Mix brown sugar, chili sauce, vinegar, Worcestershire, and salt and pepper. Pour over meat and marinate in covered glass dish, very large Ziplock bag, or plastic container over night. Place brisket fat side up in large heavy duty foil-lined roasting pan. Include enough foil to cover and seal the meat. Mound with chopped celery and onion and pour marinade over. Grind on more pepper. Seal and roast in 300° oven, approximately 50 minutes per pound, or until tender. Slow cooking is the key. Remove from foil, let stand 25 minutes before slicing across the grain; arrange slices in decorative oven proof serving dish. Place all drippings and veggies from foil in sauce pot. Add wine, season to taste, and bring to a boil. Lower heat and cook until sauce is reduced by ⅓; skim fat. Thicken with cornstarch slurry or flour and butter roux. Heat until sauce is glossy. Pour over sliced brisket. Cover with foil and refrigerate or return to 350° oven and cook until bubbling hot. Remove foil and bake 10 minutes more or cool and refrigerate if serving later. Bring to room temperature, place in 325° oven until bubbly; remove foil and cook another 10 minutes. This recipe has been in our family for many, many years. It can easily be adapted to your palate by varying the seasonings and veggies. The secret is patience. Reheating makes it even better. Great for sandwiches. Remember that cooks and dogs (cats too) get the best scraps. Serve with horseradish mashed potatoes, garlic beans, and homemade applesauce. We serve with latkes (potato pancakes), sour cream, and applesauce for Hanukah.

Nancy Bennett Evans
Seattle, WA Chapter

San Antonio Brisket - Slow Cooker

5 to 7 lb. beef brisket
1 Tbsp. crushed garlic
6 Tbsp. Tony Chachere's original seasoning
2 tsp. red pepper
1 onion, chopped
2 (10.75 oz.) cans cream of mushroom soup
½ c. water

The slow cooker cannot be beat when it comes to tenderizing a brisket. And the best part of this meal is that it's ready when you've completed your 18 holes of golf! Use a 5 to 6 quart cooker. Trim brisket of fat. Press garlic into meat and generously sprinkle Tony Chachere's seasoning and red pepper over meat. Add onions, soup, and water (you can use reduced-fat mushroom soup if desired). Cook on low for 8 to 10 hours. Remove brisket. Add Kitchen Bouquet for color, if desired, mix, and your gravy is ready. Slice brisket and serve.

Brenda Peterson
San Antonio, TX Chapter

Corned Beef And Cabbage

2½ to 2 lb. corned beef brisket
1 tsp. whole black peppercorns
2 bay leaves
3 medium carrots, quartered
2 medium parsnips, cubed or cut into chunks
2 medium red onions, cut into wedges
1 small to medium head of cabbage

Trim meat. Put into large pot; add spices. Add enough water to cover the meat. Bring to boil, reduce heat, and simmer covered for 2 hours. Cut cabbage and add to the pot along with carrots, onions, and parsnips. Return to boiling; simmer covered until vegetables are tender. Serves 6 to 8 on a nice cool day.

Renee Powell, PGA, LPGA
Ohio Golf Hall of Fame Member
EWGA Leadership Award Winner

Vermouth Flank Steak

3 to 4 lb. flank steak
½ c. soy sauce
6 Tbsp. honey
4 Tbsp. vermouth, sweet or dry
3 tsp. garlic powder
1½ c. vegetable oil

Pat steak dry with paper towel and score both sides in a diamond pattern approximately ¼ inch deep. Place in a shallow non-metal dish or quality sealable plastic bag. In small bowl mix the remaining ingredients and pour over the steak. Refrigerate for 12 to 24 hours, turning several times. To grill, pour off marinade. Grill 5 to 6 minutes on the first side and 6 to 7 minutes on the second side, depending on personal taste. Slice thinly across grain and serve immediately. Makes 10 to 12 servings.

Christy Bartlett
Portland, OR Chapter
EWGA Recruiter of the Year Award Winner

Marinated Flank Steak

1 c. soy sauce
2 inch long piece of ginger root, cut into pieces
2 to 3 Tbsp. sugar
½ c. chopped onion
1½ to 3 lb. flank steak

Combine all ingredients except steak in a jar and shake. Make the marinade the evening before and do not refrigerate. Marinate the meat 2 hours on each side, in the refrigerator. Grill 4 to 6 minutes per side for a 2 pound steak. Halfway through grilling on each side, turn the steak 90 degrees to get more grill marks.

Dana Rader, LPGA
National President, LPGA Teaching and Club Professional

Rita's Rump Roast

1 rump roast (approx. 4 lb.)
1 pkg. onion soup mix
1 beef bouillon square
2½ c. water

Flour
Seasoning salt
Olive oil (to grease skillet)

Preheat oven to 350°. Take rump roast and cut the fat off. On a dinner plate, cover surface with flour and sprinkle with seasoning salt. Then roll the rump roast around on the plate to coat it with flour. Use olive oil to grease skillet. Place rump roast in skillet on low heat setting to brown the rump roast for a few minutes until sides are brown (this helps to seal in the flavor). Place rump roast into pan suitable for oven. Add onion soup mix to 1½ cups boiling water and mix. Set aside. Take 1 cup boiling water and drop 1 beef bouillon square into it, mix, then pour both the onion soup mix and the beef bouillon over rump roast and cover before placing in oven. Bake rump roast for 2½ hours. For best results and easy slicing, cook the night before you plan to serve and place rump roast, together with liquid drippings (in separate container) in refrigerator overnight. Prior to serving, skim the fat off top layer of drippings to use liquid as consomme. Cut rump roast into slices, then reheat rump roast and consomme to serving temperature. Pour consomme over top of rump roast slices and serve with your favorite vegetables!

Susan Naugle
Palm Beach County, FL Chapter
EWGA Director of Marketing

Walt's Roast & Gravy

3 lb. chuck or round roast (flat cut, 2 to 3 inches thick)
A-1 steak sauce
1 pkg. dry onion soup mix

2 cans cream of mushroom soup
1 can cream of celery soup

Place roast in large foil bag and set in shallow cooking dish. Pour a generous coating of A-1 steak sauce over roast. Sprinkle onion soup mix over top and then add soups. Close foil bag securely being careful to not push bag down on top of roast. Bake at 350° for 3 hours. Carrots can be added if desired. Be careful when opening bag. Place roast on a platter and pour gravy into serving dish. Serve with mashed potatoes.

Ellen Brothers
Genesee County, MI Chapter

Grilled Tri Tip With Citrus Garlic Marinade

1 tri tip, approx. 2 lbs.
½ c. soy sauce (low sodium okay)
1 orange
1 lemon
1 lime
2 garlic cloves, smashed
2 Tbsp. olive oil

Combine soy sauce, juice from all citrus fruits, garlic, and oil in a bowl. Place marinade in a Ziploc bag with meat. Marinate 2 to 3 hours, turning occasionally (in refrigerator). Heat grill to medium temperature. Remove tri tip and reserve marinade. Let meat come to room temperature before grilling. Bring the reserved marinade to a boil to use as basting liquid. Sear all sides of tri tip over direct heat then move to indirect heat until internal temperature is 140° (for medium rare). Baste with marinade while grilling. Allow meat to rest 5 to 10 minutes before slicing on a bias to serve.

Catherine Schiaffo
San Diego, CA Chapter

Crock Pot Italian Beef

1 pkg. Good Seasons Italian dressing
1 pkg. Good Seasons Zesty Italian dressing
1 can beer
1 roast

Place all ingredients in crock pot. Cook until meat is tender and comes off the bone. Shred meat and return to crock pot juice. Heats up easily in microwave.

Darlene 'Babe' Lamb
Kansas City Metro Chapter

Easy Oven Barbecued Ribs

1 slab pork ribs
1 bottle Famous Dave's Sweet & Sassy barbecue sauce
2 dashes Worcestershire sauce
1 c. ketchup
2 Tbsp. mustard
½ box brown sugar

Season the ribs with a little salt and pepper. Top broil the ribs until they are slightly brown. Mix together the barbecue sauce and all remaining ingredients in a bowl. Cover the ribs with the barbecue sauce mixture. Bake in a covered roaster or pan covered with heavy foil for 5 to 7 hours at 250°. If you are only baking one slab, the baking time might be less.

Linda Eader
Metro Detroit, MI Chapter

Babyback Ribs

Babyback ribs
Texjoy, paprika, garlic powder, lemon pepper (in equal parts)
Brown sugar (twice as much as other spices)

Pull the membrane off the back of the babyback ribs. Make a rub with the spices and brown sugar. Rub generously over the front and back of ribs. Double wrap in foil and refrigerate overnight. Bake for 1½ hours at 350°, then finish on grill for 20 minutes. If you do not want to grill, bake for an additional 30 minutes.

Zona Trahan
Houston, TX Chapter
Nancy Oliver Founder's Award Winner

Slow Cooker Pork Ribs

1 lb. pork ribs
¾ c. brown sugar
½ c. tamari (soy sauce)
½ c. ketchup
1 Tbsp. vinegar
3 to 4 garlic cloves, minced
Salt and pepper to taste
1 medium onion, sliced

Combine all ingredients except the ribs and onion in a bowl. In a skillet (or slow cooker insert) brown the ribs on all sides. Add the ribs to the sauce and turn to coat them. Place the sliced onion in the slow cooker. Add the ribs and sauce. Cover and cook on low for 4 to 5 hours or on high for 2 to 3 hours.

Shelia Sampolesi
Seattle, WA Chapter
Former Association Board Member

Tasty Pork Tenderloin

3 to 4 lb. pork tenderloin
2 Tbsp. sugar
1 tsp. salt
1 tsp. ground sage
1 tsp. marjoram
¼ tsp. celery seed
¼ tsp. Dijon mustard
3 to 4 fennel seeds (optional)

Preheat oven to 350°. Take the sugar, salt, sage, marjoram, celery seed and Dijon mustard and mix in a bowl. Cover pork tenderloin with the mixture. Pierce tenderloin with fork to make holes in which to insert the fennel seed (optional). Place tenderloin in baking dish and bake (approximately 20 minutes per pound) at 350°.

Susan Naugle
Palm Beach County, FL Chapter
EWGA Director of Marketing

Pork Medallions With Mustard Cream Sauce

1 (1 lb.) pork tenderloin
⅓ c. all-purpose flour
½ tsp. salt
¼ tsp. pepper
3 Tbsp. butter
3 green onions, sliced (white and green parts separated)
⅓ c. dry white wine
1 c. whipping cream
¼ c. country style Dijon mustard

Cut tenderloin crosswise into ½ inch thick pieces. Pound between sheets of waxed paper to thickness of ¼ inch. Combine flour, salt, and pepper into a shallow dish. Melt 1 tablespoon of butter in a heavy large skillet over medium-high heat. Dredge pork in seasoned flour, shaking off excess. Add ⅓ of pork to skillet and saute until brown and cooked through, about 2 minutes per side. Transfer to platter and keep warm. Repeat with remaining pork in two more batches, adding 1 tablespoon of butter to the skillet for each batch. Add white parts of green onions to skillet and saute until just tender, about 1 minute. Stir in white wine and boil until liquid is reduced to 2 tablespoons, about 3 minutes. Add whipping cream and simmer until thickened to sauce, about 5 minutes. Whisk in mustard. Season sauce to taste with salt and pepper. Spoon sauce over pork. Garnish tenderloin with remaining green onions and serve.

Catherine Schiaffo
San Diego, CA Chapter

"The real way to enjoy playing golf is to take pleasure not in the score, but in the execution of the strokes."

-Bobby Jones

Pork Chops Al Tamarindo With Cannellini Beans And Tomatoes

Pork Chops:

4 small thin sliced pork chops (can be boneless)	Garlic salt to taste
	Pepper to taste
1 can Goya tamarind juice	

Sprinkle pork chops liberally on both sides with garlic salt and pepper. Brown on both sides in a non-stick frying pan coated with olive oil on medium-high heat for 4 minutes per side. Pour juice in pan and reduce heat to medium-low. Allow juice to reduce to a (thick) sauce consistency, about 10 minutes. Serve sauce on top of pork chops with beans and tomatoes on the side (recipes follow).

Cannellini Beans:

1 can cannellini beans	Salt to taste
Extra virgin olive oil	Pepper to taste
¼ c. chopped sweet onion	

Rinse beans in a colander with cold water and place in a microwave-safe dish. Add onion, olive oil, salt, and pepper. Heat in microwave for 2 minutes and serve warm.

Tomatoes:

1 heirloom tomato	4 Tbsp. extra virgin olive oil
Fresh basil leaves	Salt to taste
2 Tbsp. sherry vinegar	Pepper to taste

Slice tomato and top with fresh basil leaves, salt, and pepper. Dress with oil and vinegar.

Clarise Snyder
Boston, MA Chapter

Pork Chop Stew

4 center cut boneless pork chops
2 Tbsp. cooking oil
1 (10.75 oz.) can cream of mushroom soup
1 c. water
4 celery stalks
1 (16 oz.) bag small peeled carrots
4 to 6 red potatoes
1 onion
Salt, pepper, and garlic to taste

Brown pork chops in oil. Mix cream of mushroom soup with 1 can of water. Add soup to pork chops. Cut up celery, onion, carrots, and potatoes. Add to pork chops and soup. Bring to a boil. Put lid on pan and slowly cook on low for around 2 to 3 hours.

Linda Vollstedt
Former Arizona State Women's Golf Coach
EWGA Leadership Award Winner

Pulled Pork Sandwiches

4½ lb. pork shoulder roast
14 oz. KC Masterpiece barbecue sauce
1 Tbsp. fresh lemon juice
1 tsp. brown sugar
1 medium onion, chopped
3 pkg. hamburger rolls

Place pork in Crock Pot slow cooker. Cover and cook on low for 7 to 8 hours or on high for 5 hours. Remove pork, shred meat with 2 forks. Discard bones and any liquid in slow cooker. Return shredded pork to slow cooker, add barbecue sauce, lemon juice, brown sugar and onion mix. Cover; cook on low for 1½ to 2 hours or on high for 1 hour. Serve on hamburger buns or hard rolls with cole slaw and perhaps some vinegar splash for a North Carolina style pulled pork.

Jo-Ann Dixon
Northern New Jersey Chapter
Association and Foundation Board Member

Goat Cheese, Artichoke, And Smoked Ham Strata

2 c. whole milk
¼ c. olive oil
8 c. (1 inch cubes) sourdough bread, crusts trimmed
1½ c. whipping cream
5 large eggs
1 Tbsp. chopped garlic
1½ tsp. salt
¾ tsp. black pepper
½ tsp. ground nutmeg
12 oz. soft Goat cheese (such as Montrachet), crumbled
2 Tbsp. chopped fresh sage
1 Tbsp. chopped fresh thyme
1½ tsp. herbes de Provence
12 oz. smoked ham, chopped
3 (6.5 oz.) jars marinated artichoke hearts, drained, halved lengthwise
1 c. packed grated Fontina cheese
1½ c. packed grated Parmesan cheese

Preheat oven to 350°. Butter 13x9x2 inch glass baking dish. Whisk milk and oil in large bowl. Stir in bread. Let stand until liquid is absorbed, about 10 minutes. Whisk cream and next 5 ingredients in another bowl to blend. Add Goat cheese. Mix herbs in small bowl to blend. Place half of bread mixture in prepared dish. Top with half of ham, artichoke hearts, herbs, and cheeses. Pour half of cream mixture over. Repeat layering with remaining bread, ham, artichoke hearts, herbs, cheeses, and cream mixture. (Can be made 1 day ahead. Cover and chill.) Bake uncovered until firm in center and brown around edges, about 1 hour. Serves 8 to 10.

Kristen Skivington
Genesee County, MI Chapter

Meat & Poultry

Sausage & Fruit Stuffed Acorn Squash

2 large cooked acorn squash
16 oz. Roll of Country sausage, hot or maple flavored
1 onion, finely chopped
1 garlic clove, minced
1 tart apple, cored, but unpeeled, and chopped
½ c. raisins
1 Tbsp. dry sherry or apple cider vinegar
1 Tbsp. butter
2 tsp. brown sugar

Cook squash whole in the microwave for 12 to 14 minutes or until soft. Brown and crumble sausage in large skillet, reserve small amount of drippings. Set aside and keep warm. Saute onion and garlic in reserved sausage drippings until translucent. Add chopped apple, raisins, browned sausage and sherry, bring to boil, lower heat and cover. Simmer for about 4 minutes. Split the two cooked squash in half lengthwise and clean out the seeds. Place them in a covered oven-proof pan or microwave dish, cut side up. Sprinkle with brown sugar and dot with butter. Fill the squash with the sausage mixture. Any extra can be placed around the squash. Cover and bake in 350° oven until hot. Serves 4.

Ava (A.J.) Bessette
Albuquerque, NM and Brevard/Space Coast, FL Chapters

Sausage Strata

6 slices bread
1 lb. bulk pork sausage
1 tsp. mustard
1 c. shredded Swiss cheese
3 eggs, slightly beaten
2 c. milk
½ tsp. salt
Dash pepper
Dash nutmeg

Trim bread crusts and line bottom of greased 9x13 inch (or 6x10 inch) pan. Brown sausage and drain. Spoon sausage over bread. Sprinkle with cheese. Combine other ingredients and pour over cheese. Bake at 350° for 35 minutes or until set. Easy to prepare ahead of time and serve for overnight guests!

Le Ann Finger, PGA, LPGA
Palm Beach County, FL Chapter
National Promotions Specialist, PGA of America

Sausage & Squash Casserole

½ lb. sweet Italian sausage
½ c. chopped onion
2 Tbsp. butter
2 Tbsp. flour
½ tsp. Italian seasoning
⅛ tsp. each salt and pepper
1 c. milk

1½ c. shredded Mozzarella cheese
2 c. cooked egg noodles, drained
½ c. each halved zucchini and/or summer squash
½ c. chopped tomatoes

Preheat oven to 350°. Cook sausage and onion in skillet until sausage is brown and crumbly. Drain and set aside. Melt butter, stir in flour and seasonings until smooth, remove from heat and add milk. Bring to boil over medium heat, stir constantly for one minute, reduce to low. Stir in half the cheese; stir in cooked sausage mixture, noodles, squash and tomatoes. Put in buttered 1 quart casserole. Bake 25 to 30 minutes or until hot and bubbly. Sprinkle with other half of cheese. Cook until cheese melts. Enjoy!

Joan Choiniere
Greater Springfield, MA Chapter

"I have always had a drive that pushed me to try for perfection, and golf is a game in which perfection stays just out of reach."
-Betsy Rawls

Lamb Curry With Condiments

Lamb Curry:

- 2 Tbsp. olive oil
- 3 lb. lamb shoulder, cut into 2 inch chunks (we use leg of lamb)
- ½ c. chopped onion
- 2 garlic cloves, minced
- 1 Tbsp. minced fresh ginger
- 2 tsp. best quality curry powder
- ½ tsp. freshly grated nutmeg
- ½ tsp. ground cumin
- ½ tsp. ground cardamom
- ¼ tsp. ground cloves
- ¼ tsp. cayenne pepper
- 2 c. homemade beef stock or canned broth
- 1 c. new basic tomato sauce (recipe below)
- ¼ c. orange marmalade
- ¼ c. mango chutney (recipe below)
- ¼ c. cream of coconut
- 2 Tbsp. fresh lemon juice
- 1 tsp. salt
- ½ c. golden raisins
- Toasted unsweetened coconut
- 3 to 4 c. cooked white rice

Heat 1 tablespoon of the oil in a flameproof casserole or Dutch oven. Brown the lamb, in batches, over medium high heat, and set aside. Add the remaining oil and saute the onion, garlic, and ginger over medium heat, 5 minutes. Then stir in all the spices. Stir in the stock, tomato sauce, marmalade, chutney, cream of coconut, lemon juice, and salt. Return the lamb to the casserole. Sprinkle the mixture with the raisins, and bring to a boil. Lower the heat, cover, and simmer for 1½ hours. Sprinkle the curry with toasted coconut and serve over rice. Instead of coconut for garnish, we use selections of unsalted peanuts, onion rings and mango chutney.

New Basic Tomato Sauce:

- 2 (35 oz.) cans plum tomatoes
- ¼ c. olive oil
- ¼ c. chopped onions
- ½ c. finely chopped carrot
- 4 garlic cloves, finely chopped
- ¼ c. dry red wine
- 2 Tbsp. tomato paste
- ½ c. chopped fresh Italian (flat leaf) parsley
- 1 Tbsp. dried oregano
- 1 Tbsp. dried basil
- ½ tsp. ground nutmeg
- ½ tsp. freshly ground black pepper
- Salt to taste
- Pinch of dried red pepper flakes (optional)

Continued

Drain the tomatoes, reserving 1 cup of the juice. Crush the tomatoes with the back of a spoon, and set aside. Heat the oil in a saucepan over medium low heat. Add the onions, carrot, and garlic. Cook, stirring until the onions and garlic have wilted, about 10 minutes. Add the tomatoes, reserved juice, wine, tomato paste, and remaining ingredients. Cover and cook over medium heat for 15 minutes, stirring once. Remove the cover and simmer another 45 minutes, stirring occasionally. Makes 6 cups (sauce freezes well).

Mango Chutney:

4 c. under ripe mangoes, diced
1 c. raisins
1 c. dates, chopped
4 oz. green ginger, chopped
1 tsp. mustard seed

4 c. sugar
2 garlic cloves, minced
2 hot peppers, chopped
4 c. red wine vinegar
½ lb. onions, chopped

Add fruit and peppers to vinegar and allow to steep until the next day. To mangoes add sugar, ginger, garlic, onions and other seasonings. Boil all ingredients together gently until chutney is thick and brown. This works well with pears, peaches or apples too. Serve on roasted meats or baked potatoes OR mix 1½ cups mayonnaise, ¼ cup of the chutney and ½ teaspoon curry powder for a delicious dressing for salads or hot vegetables.

Deborah Gross
Dayton, OH Chapter
EWGA Businesswoman of the Year Award Winner

Rack Of Lamb For Two

1 8-rib rack of lamb
4 Tbsp. olive oil
2 Tbsp. Dijon mustard
2 Tbsp. soy sauce

1 Tbsp. chopped fresh parsley
2 grinds black pepper
1 garlic clove, finely chopped

Cut excess fat from the rack of lamb. Whisk all ingredients together until it forms a fairly thick consistency. Coat both sides of rack. Broil each side for 5 minutes (medium rare); turn oven to 400° and bake for 10 minutes. Remove from oven, let stand for 5 minutes, and carve. Serve with a Rhone or syrah wine; a full bodied cabernet would also do well.

Jane Blalock, LPGA
CEO, Jane Blalock Company
New England Sports Hall of Fame Member

Turkey Meatloaf Apricot

Meatloaf:

1¼ lb. ground turkey
1 medium onion, diced
2 garlic cloves, minced
15 black olives, rinsed and minced
½ c. dried apricots, minced
1 serrano pepper, minced

½ c. oatmeal
1 whole egg plus 2 egg whites (extra large)
2 tsp. sea salt
1 Tbsp. black pepper
¼ c. fresh thyme leaves

Preheat oven to 350°. Separate eggs and whisk to combine. Add onions, olives, apricots, peppers, garlic, and herbs to saute pan. Add salt and pepper. Cook until onions are barley translucent. Transfer to a large bowl. Add oatmeal. Stir to combine. Add meat and eggs. Mix completely. Spray a loaf pan with a oil spray very lightly. Place meatloaf mixture into loaf pan and bake at 350° for 60 minutes (your oven may vary). It should be 140° on your meat thermometer. Remove from oven and pour ½ of the glaze (recipe below) on top of loaf, spread if needed. Return to oven until internal temperature reaches 165° (approximately 15 minutes more). Carry over will take the meatloaf to 170° to 180°. Let meatloaf cool for 10 minutes. Place a platter on top of the loaf pan and carefully flip over. Pour remaining glaze over loaf as evenly as possible. Slice and enjoy.

Apricot Glaze:

½ c. apricot preserves
1 Tbsp. plus 1 tsp. rice wine vinegar
3 sprigs fresh thyme leaves

2 Tbsp. water
1 Tbsp. red pepper flakes (optional)

Combine all ingredients to create a glaze for the meatloaf.

Jennifer Reynolds
San Diego, CA Chapter

Chicken Cassoulet

8 skinned and boned chicken thighs
2 cans mushroom soup
1 can pitted black olives
1 green pepper, diced
¾ c. vermouth or white wine
3 cans navy beans
1 medium onion, diced
1 c. shredded Parmesan cheese
1 Tbsp. small capers
1 Tbsp. chopped garlic
3 tsp. dried rosemary
2 Tbsp. butter
3 Tbsp. olive oil
1 c. bread crumbs
½ c. flour
1 tsp. salt
½ tsp. black pepper
Fresh loaf of French bread

Preheat oven to 350°. Lightly dust chicken with flour and brown in hot oil over medium-high heat. Remove chicken and set aside. In same pan, saute onions and green peppers until onions are transparent. Add garlic, rosemary, and mushroom soup with two cans water (or chicken broth). Stir and cook for 3 minutes. Stir in capers and vermouth (or wine) and cook 5 additional minutes. Lightly coat 2½ quart pan with cooking spray and spoon in enough of the gravy to coat the pan. Place chicken, drained and rinsed beans, and black olives in the pan. Top with the rest of the mushroom gravy mixture. Add salt and pepper, then sprinkle with cheese and bread crumbs and dot with butter. Bake at 350° for 35 to 40 minutes and let sit for 10 minutes. Serve with warmed French bread.

Susan Tajalli
Palm Beach County, FL Chapter

"The important thing is to be prepared for both bad shots and the bad breaks the course can dish out even on good shots."

-Bob Rotella

Chicken And Wild Rice Casserole

Casserole:

- 1 medium onion, peeled and diced
- 2 Tbsp. butter or vegetable oil
- 1 (10.75 oz.) can condensed cream of celery soup (cream of chicken, cream of mushroom, and Cheddar cheese soups also work well)
- 1 (4 oz.) jar pimentos
- 2 (14.5 oz.) cans French style green beans, drained and rinsed
- 3 c. chicken, cooked and diced (can add more)
- 1 c. mayonnaise
- 1 (6 oz.) box long-grain wild rice, cooked according to package directions
- 1 c. grated sharp Cheddar cheese (can add more)
- 1 pinch House Seasoning (recipe below)

Preheat oven to 350°. Heat butter or oil in a small skillet over medium heat. Add onion and saute until translucent, about 5 minutes. Remove from heat and transfer to a large bowl. Add all remaining ingredients to bowl and mix together until thoroughly combined. Pour into a greased 3 quart casserole dish. Bake for 25 to 35 minutes or until bubbly. Let stand for a few minutes before serving.

House Seasoning:

- 1 c. salt
- ¼ c. ground black pepper
- ¼ c. garlic powder

Combine all ingredients. Store in covered container.

Cyndi Blanchette
Charlotte, NC Chapter

Cajun Stew

1 sweet onion, diced
4 celery hearts, diced
2 small green peppers, diced
2 carrots, peeled and diced
3 garlic cloves, chopped
2 cans petite cut tomatoes, juice and all (no salt added, if possible)
Zatarain's Cajun seasoning to taste
1 pkg. smoked chicken Andouille sausage, cut into 1/4 inch slices and cut in half
12 oz. shrimp, cut into thirds
2 chicken breasts, cut into chunks
1/4 c. fresh squeezed orange juice
2 cans kidney beans, rinsed and drained
1 can kidney beans, rinsed, drained, and pureed with some chicken stock
Okra, cut up (as much you like)

Saute onion, celery, peppers, and carrots in a large pot until translucent. Add garlic and saute. Add tomatoes and seasoning, and let simmer. In the meantime, in a large saute pan, saute sausage. Add shrimp and cook through. Drain and add to vegetable base. Brown chicken and add to vegetable base. Let simmer and add orange juice. Add kidney beans as well as the pureed bean and stock mixture. Add okra, if desired. Let simmer.

Tiss Dahan
Senior Director of Global Apparel, TaylorMade-adidas Golf

King Ranch Casserole

1 (26 oz.) can cream of chicken soup
1 (14 oz.) can cream of mushroom soup
2 (10 oz.) cans diced tomatoes with green chilies
1 (14 oz.) can chicken broth
3 1/3 c. cooked, diced chicken
20 corn tortillas (broken to fit pan)
1 c. chopped onion
3 1/3 c. shredded Cheddar cheese

Preheat oven to 350°. Lightly mist 9x13 inch casserole dish with non-stick cooking spray. Blend soup, tomatoes, green chilies, and chicken broth until smooth. Layer half of the chicken, tortillas, onion, cheese, and soup mixture. Repeat layers ending with shredded Cheddar cheese. Bake 1 hour. Serves 8 to 10.

Kathy Whitworth, LPGA
World Golf Hall of Fame Member
EWGA Leadership Award Winner

Chicken Breast Hot Dish

6 boneless, skinless chicken breasts
1 jar dried beef
1 (8 oz.) pkg. cream cheese
1 (16 oz.) ctn. sour cream
1 large can cream of chicken soup (family size)

Grease 9x13 inch Pyrex pan and line the bottom with dried beef slices. Place chicken on top of dried beef. Mix cream cheese, sour cream, and soup into a gravy mixture and pour over chicken. Bake at 350° for 1 to 1¼ hours. Serve with rice, as soup mixture makes a great gravy. Optional: may wrap chicken breasts in bacon for additional flavoring; however, bacon makes gravy somewhat greasy (and not as tasty!). A great Midwest Hotdish!

Le Ann Finger, PGA, LPGA
Palm Beach County, FL Chapter
National Promotions Specialist, PGA of America

Chicken Golf Balls

6 whole chicken breasts
12 slices bacon, cook slightly and drain fat
1 pkg. dried beef (rinse the salt off)
1½ c. sour cream
2 cans cream of chicken soup
3 oz. cream cheese
Sharp cheese

Pepper, but do not salt chicken breasts. Cut each breast in half and roll into a ball. Wrap bacon around each ball. Place layer of dried beef in the bottom of a baking dish. Arrange the bacon-wrapped chicken balls on top of the beef. Cover with mixture of soup, sour cream, and cream cheese. Cover tightly with foil. Bake in a 325° oven for 2 hours. When done, remove foil and grate cheese on top. Serve with rice and enjoy!

Trina Fleming
Orange County, CA Chapter

Chicken Stew With Cornmeal Dumplings

Chicken Stew:

- 1 (9 oz.) pkg. frozen peas
- 2 c. cubed, cooked white chicken meat
- 2 c. diced, raw potatoes
- 1 (13 oz.) can V-8 juice
- ½ c. sliced celery
- ½ c. finely chopped onion
- ½ c. finely chopped carrots
- 1 Tbsp. chili powder
- ½ tsp. salt
- 6 drops bottled hot pepper sauce
- 4 to 5 cans chicken broth (I use low sodium or you can use the chicken broth from cooking the chicken.)

Put everything into a pot except the peas and cook until the potatoes are almost done, about 25 minutes, then add the peas.

Cornmeal Dumplings:

- 1¼ c. Bisquick
- ½ c. cornmeal
- 1 c. shredded sharp cheese
- ⅔ c. milk

Mix all of the ingredients together. As soon as the stew comes back to a boil after adding the peas, drop tablespoons of dumpling mixture on top of the boiling stew. Let simmer for 10 minutes, then cover and cook another 10 to 20 minutes. Dumplings should be done about that time. Sprinkle a little shredded cheese on top of the dumplings before serving. You can adjust the seasonings of the stew to your liking. I usually add pepper and a little bit more hot sauce.

Donna Cox
Greater Knoxville, TN Chapter

Meat & Poultry

Hot Chicken And Chips Retro

4 c. chopped roasted boneless, skinless chicken breast
¼ c. chopped green onions
¼ c. chopped red bell peppers
2 Tbsp. finely chopped fresh, flat leaf parsley
1 (8 oz.) can sliced water chestnuts, drained and chopped
½ c. low-fat mayonnaise
¼ c. reduced-fat sour cream
2 Tbsp. fresh lemon juice
2 tsp. Dijon mustard
½ tsp. salt
½ tsp. freshly ground black pepper
¾ (3 oz.) shredded Swiss cheese
¾ c. crushed baked potato chips

Preheat oven to 400°. Combine chicken, green onion, bell pepper, parsley, and water chestnuts in a large bowl and stir well. Combine mayonnaise, sour cream, lemon juice, mustard, salt, and pepper in a small bowl and stir with a whisk. Add mayonnaise mixture to chicken mixture, stirring well to combine. Spoon mixture into 9x11 inch baking dish coated with cooking spray and sprinkle with cheese. Top cheese evenly with chips. Bake 13 minutes or until filling is bubbly and chips are golden. Makes 6 servings. This recipe has a nostalgic appeal that dates back to the 1950s and 1960s, when I would make it for "pot lucks."

Del Murray
Omaha, NE Chapter

Chicken Casserole

4 boneless chicken breasts
1 pkg. frozen broccoli florets
1 can cream of chicken soup
¼ lb. grated Cheddar sharp cheese
½ c. mayonnaise
1 small onion, chopped
¼ small package stuffing mix (Pepperidge Farm cornbread)
½ c. melted butter

To make the sauce, combine cream of chicken soup, cheese, mayonnaise and onion in small bowl and set aside. Clean chicken breast and boil; cut up in small pieces. Place a layer of chicken in oblong glass baking dish. Spread the frozen broccoli florets on top of the chicken. Spread the sauce mixture on top of the broccoli. Melt the butter and pour on top of the sauce mixture and then sprinkle the stuffing on top. Bake at 350° for 45 minutes.

Shirley Vallee
Polk County, FL Chapter

Crockpot Chicken Enchilada Casserole

1 (19 oz.) can enchilada sauce
6 boneless chicken breast halves (or store bought roasted chicken)
2 cans cream of chicken soup
1 small can sliced black olives
½ c. chopped onion
1 (4 oz.) can chopped mild green chili peppers
16 to 20 corn tortillas
16 oz. shredded Cheddar cheese

Cook and shred chicken (or shred roasted chicken). Mix soup, olives, chili peppers and onions. Cut tortillas in wedges. Layer crockpot with sauce, tortillas, soup mix, chicken and cheese to the top, ending with cheese. Cover and cook on LOW for 5 to 7 hours. Tip: Disposable slow cooker liners make clean up a snap. Find them in the aisle by foil. Serves 8 to 10.

Karen Carlson
Northern Colorado Chapter
EWGA Chapter Development Representative

Chicken Empanada

1 chicken, cooked and deboned (rotisserie chicken works well)
1 large onion, chopped
1 green pepper, chopped
Olive oil
2 Tbsp. garlic, chopped
1 can diced tomatoes
1 small jar sliced Spanish olives
Salt and pepper to taste
1 small jar pimentos
1 c. Vino Seco (Spanish cooking wine)
2 small cans tomato sauce
1 c. raisins
1 c. frozen green peas
1 box Pillsbury refrigerated pie shells

Preheat oven to 375°. Remove skin from chicken and tear up into small chunks. In large skillet, saute onion, garlic, and green pepper in olive oil. Add chicken, tomatoes, drained olives, drained pimentos, raisins, peas, tomato sauce, and Vino Seco. Cook on medium-low heat until most liquid is absorbed, about 30 minutes. Prepare pie crust according to directions for a 2 crust pie. Add chicken mixture to bottom crust and top with second crust. Make slits in top crust for steam. Bake until crust is golden, approximately 30 minutes.

Susan Tajalli
Palm Beach County, FL Chapter

Chicken Pot Pie

Vegetables:

1 (12.5 oz.) can chicken breasts
2 cans mixed vegetables
2 cans cream of chicken soup
1 can cream of celery soup
½ onion, chopped

Mix chicken breasts, mixed vegetables, cream of chicken soup, cream of celery soup and chopped onion. Pour into casserole dish.

Crust:

1 c. flour
1 c. milk
¾ c. mayonnaise

Mix flour, milk and mayonnaise together and pour on top of vegetable mixture. Bake 45 to 60 minutes at 350° until golden brown.

Linda Keaton
Huntsville, AL Chapter

Chicken Pot Pie

1 lb. pre-cooked diced chicken breast
1 can cubed potatoes
2 cans mixed vegetables
3 cans cream of chicken soup
2 boxes Pillsbury pie shells (2 per box)
½ c. frozen diced onions

Easy as 1-2-3! Add 1 can of diced potatoes, 2 cans of mixed vegetables and 3 cans of cream of chicken soup into a large mixing bowl. Add the onions and pre-cooked, diced chicken breasts to the bowl and stir until all is well mixed. Salt, pepper and/or additional seasoning to your taste.

Take 2 pie pans and add a pie crust to the bottom of each. Drop in half of the mixture into each pie pan and spread around. Put the second pie crust on top of each. Roll and crimp edges. Poke holes in the top of each pie crust with a toothpick. Cook at 350° for about an hour or until pie crust is golden brown. Makes 2 pies, enough to feed 2 hungry foursomes.

Karen Alesch
Fox Cities/Green Bay, WI Chapter
EWGA Women Who Lead Award Winner

Quick Chicken Pot Pie

2 c. cooked chicken
1 can mixed vegetables, drained
2 cans cream of potato soup
½ c. milk

Parsley, seasoned or garlic salt to taste
1 box Pillsbury ready-to-bake pie crusts

Place the bottom pie crust in a pie pan. Set aside the top crust. Mix chicken, soup, mixed vegetables, milk and seasoning together in a bowl. Spread the mixture onto the pie crust that is in the pie pan. Top with the remaining pie crust. Make slits in the top crust to vent. Bake on bottom rack on a cookie sheet for 1 to 1¼ hours at 375°. The chicken can be cooked the day before for faster preparation. Canned chicken can also be used. I use stewed chicken breast.

Linda Eader
Metro Detroit, MI Chapter

Chicken Cacciatore

2½ to 3 lb. boneless, skinless chicken
1 Tbsp. olive oil
2 fresh garlic cloves
Oregano

2 Tbsp. basil
1 lb. mushrooms
1 (13 oz.) can crushed tomatoes
Salt and pepper to taste

Cube chicken and brown in oil and garlic about 10 minutes. Add a generous amount of oregano and the basil, as well as the mushrooms. Cook an additional 10 minutes (longer if using fresh mushrooms). Add the canned tomatoes and simmer an additional 20 to 25 minutes. Spoon over pasta and serve with garlic bread. Serves 4 to 6.

Sandra Donahue
Jacksonville, FL Chapter

Chicken Tetrazzini

- ¼ c. unsalted butter
- 1 (8 oz.) pkg. sliced mushrooms
- ⅓ c. all-purpose flour
- 1 (14 oz.) can low-sodium chicken broth
- 1⅓ c. half and half
- 3 Tbsp. dry sherry (optional)
- ½ tsp. kosher salt
- ¼ tsp. coarse ground black pepper
- ⅛ tsp. ground nutmeg
- 3 (1 lb.) cooked boneless, skinless chicken cut into strips or shredded
- ½ lb. spaghetti, broken in half and cooked according to pkg. directions
- ½ c. grated Parmesan cheese

Preheat oven to 425°. Melt butter in a large, non-stick skillet over medium-high heat. Add mushrooms, saute 4 minutes or until browned. Sprinkle with flour and toss to combine. Add broth and half and half: cook, stirring often, until mixture comes to a boil. Reduce heat and simmer 2 minutes, stirring constantly. Stir in sherry (if using), salt, pepper and nutmeg. Remove from heat and stir in chicken. Combine spaghetti and chicken mixture, toss gently and spoon into a 9x13 inch baking dish or shallow 3 quart baking dish; sprinkle with cheese. Bake 20 minutes or until golden brown and bubbly. Serves 8. (350 calories and 14g fat per serving)

Contributor Unknown

"Golf is a science, the study of a lifetime, in which you can exhaust yourself but never your subject."

-David Forgan

Fast Fettuccine Cacciatore

8 oz. fettuccine, uncooked
2 tsp. vegetable oil
1 lb. boneless, skinless chicken breasts, chopped
1 c. green bell pepper, chopped
1 c. mushrooms, sliced
1 (14.5 oz.) can diced tomatoes, undrained
1/4 c. zesty Italian or balsamic dressing
1 c. shredded Italian, Mozzarella and Parmesan cheese blend
1 c. fresh basil leaves, chopped

Cook pasta as directed on package. Simultaneously, heat oil in large skillet on medium-high heat. Add chicken and cook until no longer pink. Add peppers and mushrooms. Cook for 3 minutes stirring occasionally. Stir in tomatoes with their liquid and the dressing. Reduce heat to medium-low; simmer for 5 minutes or until chicken is cooked through. Toss pasta with chicken mixture. Sprinkle with cheese and basil. Makes four 2 cup servings.

Karen McIntosh
Genesee County, MI Chapter

Petto Di Pollo Farcito With Formaggio Di Capra E Peperoni Rossi Arrostiti

4 boneless, skinless chicken breasts
1 jar red roasted peppers
1 pkg. Goat cheese
1/4 c. Ken's lite Caesar salad dressing
1 Tbsp. dried basil
1 Tbsp. dried oregano
1/2 Tbsp. black pepper
1/4 tsp. sea salt (optional)

Chicken breast stuffed with Goat cheese and red roasted peppers.

Preheat oven to 350°. Split chicken breast leaving a pocket in each breast. Slice Goat cheese into 1/4 inch slices and place 2 inside each chicken breast. Add 2 to 3 slices of the red roasted peppers inside of chicken breast. Close each chicken breast with tooth picks. Season outside of each breast with Ken's dressing and all dried seasonings. Cook time approximately 35 to 45 minutes until chicken is cooked. Remove tooth picks before plating.

Paula Talese
Fort Lauderdale Area, FL Chapter

Sauteed Chicken Breast With Mustard Sage Sauce

4 boneless, skinless chicken breast halves
Flour
3 Tbsp. olive oil
½ c. white wine
6 whole, fresh sage leaves
1½ c. low-sodium chicken broth
1½ Tbsp. grain mustard
2 Tbsp. butter
Sea salt and pepper

Dredge the chicken in flour to coat. Add the oil to a pan and saute chicken over medium-high heat for 4 to 5 minutes on the first side. Turn chicken and cook for an additional 6 to 9 minutes, or until cooked through. Remove from pan. Add the wine to the pan and using a wooden spoon, scrape up the browned bits that have collected on the pan. Over high heat, cook wine about 4 minutes. Add sage leaves and chicken broth and continue cooking until reduced. Remove from heat and whisk in mustard and butter to thicken sauce. Add salt and pepper to taste, and serve over chicken.

Marlene Mattox
San Antonio, TX Chapter

Rosemary Chicken

2 tsp. olive oil
1½ tsp. fresh rosemary (or dried)
¼ tsp. salt
¼ tsp. peppercorn medley (black, pink, green, white peppercorns, all spice and coriander) or black pepper
1 lb. (approx. 8) boneless, skinless chicken thighs
1 (14.5 oz.) can stewed tomatoes, undrained
1 (15 oz.) can navy beans, drained
¼ c. chopped, pitted Kalamata olives

Heat oil in a large skillet over medium high heat. Combine rosemary, salt and pepper; sprinkle over one side of the chicken. Place chicken in pan, seasoned side down; cook 3 minutes. Reduce heat to medium; turn chicken. Add tomatoes and beans; cover and simmer 10 minutes or until chicken is done. Sir in olives. Makes 4 servings.

Ava (A.J.) Bessette
Albuquerque, NM and Brevard County/Space Coast, FL Chapters

Easy Low Fat Chicken Parm

2 to 3 boneless, skinless chicken breasts
1 Tbsp. panko or Italian style bread crumbs for each side of chicken
1 Tbsp. marinara sauce for each piece of chicken
1 Tbsp. Parmesan cheese for each piece of chicken

Preheat oven to 350°. Line a rectangle baking dish with aluminum foil. Rinse each chicken breast with water and place in pan. Spray each piece of chicken with cooking spray (both sides). Sprinkle bread crumbs on both sides. Bake for 45 minutes. Check to see if they are done (should be white inside). Add marinara sauce and cheese on top of each piece. Serve and enjoy!

Debbie Silverman
Fort Lauderdale Area, FL Chapter

Mozzarella Chicken

Chicken breasts, boneless and skinless
Onion powder, garlic powder, and seasoned salt to taste
Mozzarella cheese, sliced or shredded
Creamy French dressing

Pound chicken so it will cook evenly. Place in frying pan sprayed with non-stick spray. Season with onion powder, garlic powder, and seasoned salt to taste on both sides. Saute in fry pan until fully cooked and golden. Sprinkle or place slices of cheese on each chicken breast. Cover until cheese melts. Serve with French dressing on the side or drizzled on top.

Marylou Lenegan
Charlotte, NC Chapter

Chicken In Wine Sauce

4 large boneless, skinless chicken breasts
4 Tbsp. butter, melted, plus more for casserole
Kosher salt and freshly ground black pepper
6 oz. (about 8 slices) Swiss cheese
1 (10.75 oz.) can condensed cream of chicken soup
¼ c. white wine
1 c. herb flavored stuffing mix, crushed

Preheat oven to 350°. Add the chicken to a shallow buttered casserole and season with salt and pepper, to taste. Layer the cheese slices on top. In a medium bowl, add the soup and wine. Season with salt and pepper and pour over the cheese. Sprinkle stuffing mix on top and drizzle with melted butter (if desired, use more melted butter). Bake for 45 minutes. Remove from oven and serve.

Barbara McArthur
Long Island, NY Chapter

"I was fortunate enough to be on the winning team once, and I was fortunate, too, to be on the losing team once."
-Laura Diaz

Pine Nut And Feta Stuffed Chicken

2 bags Pepperidge Farm corn bread stuffing
1 lb. Feta cheese
½ lb. pine nuts

2 large roasters (kosher is the best if you can get them fresh)

Make a basting material that can also be used to flavor the stuffing. I like Pirates Gold (name brand in most grocery stores). I pour the bottle in a mixing bowl and add cilantro, sage, and Montreal Chicken seasoning. Season to taste. I pour a little of this into the corn bread stuffing, liquid and seasoning. I then go back to the basting and add more sage, and cilantro. This is to rub on the chicken; I go heavy with the herbs so it becomes a slurry rather than a liquid. I mix the corn bread stuffing that is now a bit damp from the basting material, add Feta cheese and pine nuts. If it needs more liquid, use chicken broth. Let it sit for 30 minutes to check the texture, mix the flavors, and make sure you don't need a little more chicken broth so it does not dry out while baking. Stuff the birds, liberally rub the basting slurry on the chickens and place them in the preheated oven. Temperature and cooking time will vary based on the size of the chickens and your oven. Enjoy! My wife especially likes this. The measurements are to taste and rarely if ever done by me, so make it to your personal preferences.

MG Orender
President, Hampton Golf Clubs and Past President, PGA of America
EWGA Leadership Award Winner

Chicken With Chocolate

1 (3 lb.) chicken, disjointed
Salt and pepper
All purpose flour
2 Tbsp. butter
2 Tbsp. olive oil
1½ c. basic chicken stock or
    canned chicken broth
1 oz. bitter chocolate, melted
½ tsp. cinnamon
½ c. blanched almonds
½ c. finely chopped onions
1 c. grated carrots
½ c. raisins
12 pitted prunes
Chopped parsley
Whole almonds

Season chicken with salt and pepper; dredge with flour. Melt butter and oil in large skillet. Add chicken; brown on both sides. Remove chicken to oven-proof dish. Add 2 tablespoons flour to pan drippings; cook until browned, stirring constantly. Add stock gradually; cool, stirring until thickened. Blend in chocolate and cinnamon; add salt and pepper, if needed. Stir in remaining ingredients (except parsley and whole almonds); pour over chicken. Bake, covered, in preheated 325° oven for 45 minutes. Garnish with chopped parsley and blanched whole almonds. Makes 4 servings.

Carol Malysz
Rhode Island Chapter
EWGA Businesswoman of the Year Award Winner

Grilled Chicken Ala Rosie

3 boneless, skinless chicken breasts
6 slices Muenster cheese, or your favorite type
Roasted red peppers (from jar), drained
BBQ sauce to taste
Jane's Crazy Salt to taste
Favorite marinating concoction of herbs, rubs, or dressings

Marinate chicken in your favorite concoction of herbs, rubs or dressings, the longer the better for up to 3 hours in fridge. Add a dash of Jane's Crazy Salt on one side of chicken just before grilling for good flavor. Spray grill with Pam so the chicken does not stick. Grill chicken as usual on your gas or charcoal grill. On final turn of chicken, drape drained roasted red pepper on chicken and top with cheese. Once cheese is melted, use tongs or spatula to carefully remove chicken into dish for serving. Drip favorite BBQ sauce on top of cheese before serving (we like Emeril's). Serve with grilled asparagus and salad.

Rosie Jones, LPGA
RosieJones Golf Getaways
2011 USA Solheim Cup Captain

Quick Coq Au Vin

- 4 slices bacon, coarsely chopped
- 4 boneless, skinless chicken breast halves
- 3 Tbsp. chopped fresh Italian parsley, divided
- 8 oz. large baby bella mushrooms, halved
- 8 large shallots, peeled and halved
- 2 garlic cloves, pressed
- 1½ c. dry red wine
- 1½ c. low salt chicken broth, divided
- 4 tsp. all purpose flour

Preheat oven to 300°. Saute bacon in large non-stick skillet over medium-high heat until crisp. Using slotted spoon, transfer to bowl. Sprinkle chicken with salt, pepper and 1 tablespoon parsley. Add to drippings in skillet. Saute until cooked through (6 minutes/side). Transfer to pie dish, place in oven to keep warm. Add mushrooms and shallots to skillet; sprinkle lightly with salt and pepper. Saute until brown, about 4 minutes. Add garlic; toss 10 seconds. Add wine, 1¼ cups broth, bacon, and 1 tablespoon parsley. Bring to boil; stirring for 10 minutes. Place flour in small cup. Add ¼ cup broth, stirring until smooth. Add flour mixture to sauce. Cook until sauce thickens; 3 to 4 minutes. Season with salt and pepper. Arrange chicken on platter; stir juices from pie dish into sauce and spoon over chicken.

Nona Footz
Fairfield County, CT Chapter
Foundation Board Vice President and Association Board Member

Mango BBQ Chicken With Mango Salsa

BBQ Sauce and Chicken:

6 boneless, skinless chicken breasts
1 c. canned crushed tomatoes
½ c. cubed peeled mango
2 Tbsp. distilled white vinegar
1 Tbsp. sugar
2 tsp. canned chopped chipotle chilies in adobo sauce
Salt to taste

Combine all ingredients (other than chicken) in processor and blend until smooth. Season with salt. (Can be prepared 1 day ahead; cover and chill.) To cook chicken, prepare BBQ grill at medium-high heat. Brush chicken with BBQ sauce and grill until cooked through, basting often with sauce, about 4 minutes per side. Serve with salsa (recipe to follow).

Salsa:

1 c. cubed peeled mango
1 c. cubed seeded tomato
½ c. finely chopped onion
¼ c. finely chopped green onion
2 Tbsp. chopped cilantro
2 Tbsp. olive oil
2 Tbsp. fresh lime juice
1 jalapeno pepper, seeded and minced

Combine all ingredients in a bowl and season to taste with salt and pepper.

Liz Tobin
Long Island, NY Chapter

Chicken And Cheese Enchiladas

2 c. bite-size pieces cooked chicken
2½ c. grated Monterey Jack cheese (about 8 oz.)
½ c. chopped red onion
1 (12 oz.) pkg. 7 inch flour tortilla shells (or 10 inch)
2 Tbsp. butter
2 Tbsp. flour
2 c. chicken broth
1½ c. sour cream
2 (4 oz.) cans diced green chilies, drained
½ c. sliced scallions

Preheat oven to 350°. In medium bowl, mix chicken, 1½ cups cheese, and chopped red onion. Place ⅓ cup mixture on bottom half of each tortilla and roll up. Arrange rolled tortillas seam side down, in 13x9x2 inch baking dish. Set aside. Melt butter in heavy 2 quart saucepan over low heat. Sprinkle in flour, stirring constantly 5 full minutes. Add broth, continuing to stir. Increase heat to medium, stirring about 3 minutes until mixture begins to bubble and thicken. Remove from heat; fold in sour cream and chilies. Pour sauce over rolled tortillas in baking dish, then bake, uncovered, 15 minutes. Sprinkle with remaining cheese and scallions. Bake 5 minutes longer, until cheese melts. Makes 6 servings.

Darla Huff
Charlotte, NC Chapter

Crock Pot Chicken Tortilla/Tacos

3 to 4 boneless, skinless chicken breasts, washed and fat removed
1 can black beans, drained and rinsed
1 (16 oz.) bag frozen corn
1 (24 oz.) jar salsa
1 pkg. taco seasoning mix

Place all ingredients in crock pot on low for 4 to 6 hours (put this on before you go play golf and it is ready to eat when you're finished playing). Remove crock pot lid and use a fork to shred chicken breasts. Stir with a spoon and serve on flour or whole grain tortilla or taco shells with shredded lettuce, tomato, cilantro, onion, red or green chilies, salsa, shredded cheese, sour cream, jalapenos, etc. or just serve with a side salad. Enjoy while you think about your great golf day!

Teresa Riggs
Greater Knoxville, TN Chapter

Mexican Albondigas

2 small tomatoes
5 garlic cloves
1 small yellow onion
1 lb. ground chicken
¼ c. white rice, cooked
2 cans chicken broth
1 handful cilantro, chopped
1 egg
3 mint leaves, chopped
5 small red potatoes, cut in half
3 carrots, cut into small pieces

In a blender, blend tomatoes, 5 garlic cloves, and half of the onion. In a bowl, add chicken, rice, half of the cilantro, egg, and the other half of the onion (finely chopped). In a large pot, add chicken broth (add water until pot is ¾ full), tomato mixture, remaining cilantro, and mint leaves. Cook over medium heat until it boils, and then add potatoes and carrots. Make small balls out of the chicken mixture, and drop into pot until done. Do not stir, just shake the pot gently. Serve with warm corn tortillas.

Lisa Landa
San Francisco Bay Area, CA Chapter

"Golf is 90% inspiration and 10% perspiration." -Johnny Miller

Green Chicken Enchiladas

2 (4 oz.) cans diced green chilie peppers
2 (7 oz.) cans Herdez sausa verde (Stick to the brand if you can. I am told it is important.)
1 (10 oz.) can cream of mushroom soup (your preferred brand)
4 skinless chicken breasts (or your preferred chicken parts)
20 flour tortillas
1 bag Mexican cheese (or similar cheese available in your location)

Cut the chicken into strips that can easily be shredded later. Boil chicken until it is cooked. While the chicken is cooking, open all of the canned ingredients and pour the contents into a pan. Let the mixture simmer until it is smooth and creamy (you can allow it to simmer until you are ready to use it). When the chicken is cooked, shred it using a couple of forks (one to hold it down as it will be HOT and one to do the actual shredding). Open the bag of shredded cheese and get the tortillas out of their bag as well. Place three or four tortillas at a time into the microwave for 10 to 15 seconds. This softens them up so you can roll them without tearing. One at a time, put some chicken and some cheese into a tortilla and roll the tortilla into an enchilada looking shape and place it in a casserole dish. Continue doing this until you run out of chicken and cheese or until your casserole dish is full. When you have finished filling the dish with enchiladas, pour the green sauce over the top until they are all covered and there is sauce between them, around them, and over them (if there is some sauce left over, it is excellent as a dip for chips). Sprinkle grated cheese all over the top of the enchiladas. Here is the cool part: if you are actually making this to eat right now, all you have to do is put it in an oven preheated to 350° for about 15 minutes to melt the cheese and reheat the chicken. The other cool thing is that you can make these days in advance and put them in the freezer; then thaw them out and stick them in the oven just to get everything hot and melted right before you serve it. Serves 4 to 10 people, depending on how hungry everyone is.

Robin K. Anderson
Houston, TX Chapter
EWGA Businesswoman of the Year Award Winner

Chicken Enchiladas With Mexican Rice

Chicken Enchiladas:

1 can cream of mushroom soup
8 oz. sour cream
1 can refried beans
10 soft flour tortillas

2 c. shredded Cheddar cheese
2 c. shredded Colby Jack cheese
3 to 4 chicken breast halves, cooked and shredded

In saucepan over low heat, blend soup and sour cream. Down the center of each tortilla, spread a line of beans, salsa, chicken and Cheddar cheese. Roll into tube and place in 9x13 inch pan. Repeat with remaining tortillas and same ingredients. All ten should fit in a row. Pour sauce over top, cover with Colby Jack cheese. Bake at 350° for 20 minutes.

Mexican Rice:

2 pkg. Lipton Mexican rice (or brand of choice)

2 cans stewed tomatoes, undrained

In saucepan, combine rice mix and stewed tomatoes (instead of water listed on package). Cook as directed. Add water as necessary to achieve desired tenderness.

Ellen Brothers
Genesee County, MI Chapter

Pastel De Montezuma

6 c. boned and skinned cooked chicken breast
1 (14 oz.) can tomatillos, drained
1 small white onion, diced
4 garlic cloves
1 (4 oz.) can diced green chilies
1 bunch fresh cilantro, de-stemmed
1 tsp. salt
½ tsp. sugar
1 pt. sour cream
1 doz. (6 inch) corn tortillas cut into 1½ inch strips
1½ lb. shredded Jack cheese

Preheat oven to 375°. Make a green sauce by combining tomatillos, onion, garlic, green chilies, cilantro, salt and sugar in a blender. Process until pureed. Arrange casserole by placing half the chicken pieces in a lightly greased 9x13 inch baking dish. Spread half the green sauce, then half the sour cream. Top with half the tortilla pieces and then half the cheese. Repeat layers with remaining ingredients, ending with the cheese. Cover dish with foil and bake in a 375° oven for 40 to 45 minutes. uncover and bake 8 minutes until cheese is bubbly and casserole is hot throughout.

Meg Thompson
Sonoma-Marin-Napa, CA Chapter

Chicken Enchiladas

4 chicken breasts
1 small onion, chopped
2 c. Mozzarella cheese, shredded
1 can diced green chilies or jalapenos
1 Tbsp. butter
1 can chicken broth
1 pt. sour cream
1 pkg. tortillas, burrito size

Cook chicken and slice into small pieces (can use food processor). Chop onion and add to chicken. Add 1 cup of Mozzarella cheese and mix well. Divide mixture among the tortillas and wrap. Place in 9x13 inch pan. Preheat oven to 350°. In saucepan, melt butter. Add chilies or jalapenos and heat through. Add chicken broth and bring to a boil. Add sour cream and stir until heated through. Pour sauce over tortillas and bake for 20 minutes. Sprinkle remaining cup of cheese over top and bake for 5 more minutes or until cheese is melted. Serves 8 to 10.

Christy Bartlett
Portland, OR Chapter
EWGA Recruiter of the Year Award Winner

Quiche With Hash Brown Crust

3 c. frozen shredded hash browns
2 Tbsp. butter, melted
4 eggs
1 c. half and half or milk
Seasoned salt and pepper to taste
1 c. diced ham
1 c. chopped broccoli
1 c. shredded cheese

Thaw hash browns; squeeze liquid out in colander and dry between paper towels. Press into the bottom and sides of a lightly greased 9 or 10 inch pie pan. Drizzle melted butter over hash browns. Bake 25 minutes at 425°.

Beat eggs, half and half or milk, seasoned salt and pepper. Layer ham, broccoli and cheese in cooked crust and pour egg mixture over the top. Bake at 350° for 30 to 35 minutes until golden brown and knife comes out mostly clean. Baking time can vary depending on the depth of the pie pan. Filling variations: 1 cup cooked, crumbled sausage and 1 cup Cheddar cheese or just veggies - broccoli, mushrooms, spinach and/or onions.

Karen Carlson
Northern Colorado Chapter
EWGA Chapter Development Representative

Breakfast Casserole

4 c. cubed, day-old bread (white or French)
2 c. shredded sharp Cheddar cheese
10 eggs, lightly beaten
4 c. milk
1 tsp. dry mustard
1 tsp. salt
1/4 tsp. onion powder
Dash ground black pepper
10 slices bacon, cooked and crumbled
1/2 c. sliced mushrooms
1/2 c. chopped tomatoes

Grease heavily with butter a 9x13 inch baking dish. Arrange bread cubes in dish and sprinkle with cheese. Beat together eggs, milk, mustard, salt, onion powder, and pepper to taste. Pour evenly over bread and cheese. Sprinkle with bacon, mushrooms, and tomato. Cover and chill up to 24 hours. Preheat oven to 325°. Bake uncovered until set (about 1 hour). Serves approximately 12 people.

Linda Reid
Sacramento, CA Chapter

Meat & Poultry

Chili Egg Puff

10 eggs
½ c. flour
½ tsp. baking powder
½ tsp. salt

1 pt. cottage cheese
½ lb. Jack cheese, grated
½ c. margarine, melted
1 can diced Ortega chilies

Beat eggs until light and lemon-colored. Add flour, baking powder, salt, cottage cheese, Jack cheese and melted butter. Stir in chilies. Pour in greased 9x13 inch dish. Bake at 350° for approximately 35 minutes. Make sure it is done in the middle. A delicious brunch favorite, especially around the holidays. Provides plenty of protein and fortitude for an 18-hole round of golf!

Karen Moraghan
Northern New Jersey Chapter
Association Board Member

"Good golf is easier to play — and far more pleasant — than bad golf."
-Babe Didrikson Zaharias

Notes

Casual Water

Seafood

MICROWAVE HINTS

1. Place an open box of hardened brown sugar in the microwave oven with 1 cup hot water. Microwave at high for 1½ to 2 minutes for ½ pound or 2 to 3 minutes for 1 pound.
2. Soften hard ice cream by microwaving at 30% power. One pint will take 15 to 30 seconds; one quart, 30 to 45 seconds; and one-half gallon, 45 seconds to one minute.
3. One stick of butter or margarine will soften in 1 minute when microwaved at 20% power.
4. Soften one 8-ounce package of cream cheese by microwaving at 30% power for 2 to 2½ minutes. One 3-ounce package of cream cheese will soften in 1½ to 2 minutes.
5. Thaw frozen orange juice right in the container. Remove the top metal lid. Place the opened container in the microwave and heat on high power 30 seconds for 6 ounces and 45 seconds for 12 ounces.
6. Thaw whipped topping...a 4½ ounce carton will thaw in 1 minute on the defrost setting. Whipped topping should be slightly firm in the center but it will blend well when stirred. Do not overthaw!
7. Soften jello that has set up too hard - perhaps you were to chill it until slightly thickened and forgot it. Heat on a low power setting for a very short time.
8. Dissolve gelatin in the microwave. Measure liquid in a measuring cup, add jello and heat. There will be less stirring to dissolve the gelatin.
9. Heat hot packs in a microwave oven. A wet fingertip towel will take about 25 seconds. It depends on the temperature of the water used to wet the towel.
10. To scald milk, cook 1 cup milk for 2-2½ minutes, stirring once each minute.
11. To make dry bread crumbs, cut 6 slices bread into ½-inch cubes. Microwave in 3-quart casserole 6-7 minutes, or until dry, stirring after 3 minutes. Crush in blender.
12. Refresh stale potato chips, crackers, or other snacks of such type by putting a plateful in the microwave oven for about 30-45 seconds. Let stand for 1 minute to crisp. Cereals can also be crisped.
13. Melt almond bark for candy or dipping pretzels. One pound will take about 2 minutes, stirring twice. If it hardens while dipping candy, microwave for a few seconds longer.
14. Nuts will be easier to shell if you place 2 cups of nuts in a 1-quart casserole with 1 cup of water. Cook for 4 to 5 minutes and the nut meats will slip out whole after cracking the shell.
15. When thawing hamburger meat, the outside will many times begin cooking before the meat is completely thawed. Defrost for 3 minutes, then remove the outside portions that have defrosted. Continue defrosting the hamburger, taking off the defrosted outside portions at short intervals.
16. To drain the fat from hamburger while it is cooking in the microwave oven (one pound cooks in 5 minutes on high), cook it in a plastic colander placed inside a casserole dish.
17. Cubed meat and chopped vegetables will cook more evenly if cut uniformly.
18. When baking large cakes, brownies, or moist bars, place a juice glass in the center of the baking dish to prevent a soggy middle and ensure uniform baking throughout.
19. Since cakes and quick breads rise higher in a microwave oven, fill pans just half full of batter.
20. For stamp collectors: Place a few drops of water on stamp to be removed from envelope. Heat in the microwave for 20 seconds and the stamp will come right off.
21. Using a round dish instead of a square one eliminates overcooked corners in baking cakes.
22. When preparing chicken in a dish, place meaty pieces around the edges and the bony pieces in the center of the dish.
23. Shaping meatloaf into a ring eliminates undercooked center. A glass set in the center of a dish can serve as the mold.
24. Treat fresh meat cuts for 15 to 20 seconds on high in the microwave oven. This cuts down on meat-spoiling types of bacteria.
25. A crusty coating of chopped walnuts surrounding many microwave-cooked cakes and quick breads enhances the looks and eating quality. Sprinkle a layer of medium finely chopped walnuts evenly onto the bottom and sides of a ring pan or Bundt cake pan. Pour in batter and microwave as recipe directs.
26. Do not salt foods on the surface as it causes dehydration (meats and vegetables) and toughens the food. Salt the meat after you remove it from the oven unless the recipe calls for using salt in the mixture.
27. Heat leftover custard and use it as frosting for a cake.
28. Melt marshmallow creme in the microwave oven. Half of a 7-ounce jar will melt in 35-40 seconds on high. Stir to blend.
29. Toast coconut in the microwave. Watch closely because it browns quickly once it begins to brown. Spread ½ cup coconut in a pie plate and cook for 3-4 minutes, stirring every 30 seconds after 2 minutes.
30. Place a cake dish up on another dish or on a roasting rack if you have difficulty getting the bottom of the cake done. This also works for potatoes and other foods that don't quite get done on the bottom.

Copyright © 2011 by Cookbook Publishers, Inc.

Seafood

Bouillabaisse

1 shallot, finely chopped
2 garlic cloves, finely chopped
1 carrot, finely chopped
1 3/4 oz. celery root, finely chopped
1/2 pepper, chopped (red, green or yellow)
1 squash, chopped
2 Tbsp. butter
Small pinch of saffron
2 bay leafs
1 tsp. dried thyme
27 oz. fish bouillon
1 (17.5 oz.) can crushed tomatoes
A little white wine
24 to 28 oz. salmon, halibut, shrimp, scallops, or any firm seafood available, cut in 1 inch cubes
Salt and white pepper to taste
Parsley for decoration

Finely chop shallots, garlic, carrots, and celery root. Chop peppers and squash. Melt the butter in a large pot. Fry the saffron, veggies, bay leaf and thyme. Then add the bouillon, tomatoes, and wine, and let it boil for 10 minutes. Add the fish, cut up in 1 inch cubes. Simmer for 4 to 5 minutes or until done. Salt and pepper to taste. Serve with rouille, great bread and cheese.

Pia Nilsson, LPGA and Lynn Marriott, PGA, LPGA
Co-founders and Coaches of VISION54
EWGA Leadership Award Winners

Steamers On The Grill

2 doz. littleneck clams, scrubbed
2 garlic cloves, chopped
2 pinches red pepper flakes
1½ Tbsp. extra virgin olive oil
1½ Tbsp. butter
Salt and pepper to taste
Chopped tomato to taste (optional)
1 lb. spaghetti, prepared according to directions
1 Tbsp. chopped Italian parsley
Grated Parmesan cheese to taste

With extra heavy duty aluminum foil, make a pouch and add clams, garlic, red pepper flakes, oil, butter, salt, pepper, and tomatoes. Seal pouch and place on cookie sheet or disposable foil pan and place on preheated grill over medium-high heat. Grill for 15 to 18 minutes or until clams open. Open pouch very carefully, be careful of steam. Pour clams and broth over cooked pasta and sprinkle with parsley and grated Parmesan cheese.

Virginia Campioni
Eastern Shore, MD Chapter

Crab Quesadillas

½ lb. jumbo lump crab meat
¼ c. chopped green onions
2 Tbsp. sour cream
1 jalapeno pepper, seeded and finely chopped
1 Tbsp. minced fresh cilantro
¾ tsp. minced garlic
½ c. shredded Monterrey Jack cheese
4 flour tortillas

Preheat broiler. Combine crab with green onions, sour cream, jalapeno, cilantro, and garlic. Stir well. Sprinkle 2 tablespoons of cheese on each tortilla. Divide crab mixture evenly among tortillas. Fold in half, pressing gently to seal. Place filled tortillas on a baking sheet. Broil for 1 minute or until tortilla is lightly browned.

Luanne Jones
Houston, TX Chapter

Easy But Delicious Crawfish Etouffee

1 yellow onion, chopped
2 Tbsp. butter
Batch of celery, chopped
½ garlic clove, minced
1 bell pepper, chopped
1 (10 oz.) can Ro-Tel tomatoes (original)
1 (10.75 oz.) can Campbell's golden mushroom soup
1 (10.75 oz.) can Campbell's cream of chicken soup
2 Tbsp. Worcestershire sauce
2 lb. crawfish tails (most groceries carry these in frozen seafood section)

In a deep cast iron skillet or medium saucepan brown onion in butter. Add celery, garlic and bell pepper and simmer for 5 minutes. Add the remaining ingredients (do not add water). Stir well, cover and let simmer over low heat for at least 30 minutes. Serve over white or brown rice. Great with warm French bread!

Zona Trahan
Houston, TX Chapter
Nancy Oliver Founder's Award Winner

Baked Fish Fillets

1 lb. mild fish fillets
1 Tbsp. lemon juice
½ tsp. paprika
2 Tbsp. butter
2 Tbsp. flour
Dash salt and pepper
½ c. milk
½ c. buttered bread crumbs
1 Tbsp. parsley

Cut fillets in serving pieces. Place in greased shallow baking dish. Sprinkle with lemon juice, paprika, salt and pepper. In saucepan, melt butter; blend in flour, dash salt and pepper. Add milk, cook and stir until thick and bubbly. Pour sauce over fillets. Sprinkle with crumbs. Bake at 350° for 35 minutes. Garnish with parsley.

Becky Macaluso
Palm Beach County, FL Chapter
EWGA Managing Director, Chapter & Member Services

Fried Fish Fillets With Nut Crust

¼ c. mayonnaise
1 Tbsp. Dijon mustard
1 Tbsp. lemon juice
½ c. finely chopped nuts, such as pecans, pistachios, or macadamia nuts
⅓ c. panko breadcrumbs
⅓ c. corn starch
½ tsp. ground black pepper
1 lb. fish fillets, such as tilapia, salmon, cod, or grouper
Flour for dredging
Vegetable oil for frying

Blend mayonnaise, mustard, and lemon juice in a small bowl. Combine nuts, panko bread crumbs, cornstarch, and pepper on a separate large plate. Lay fillets on sheet of wax paper. Dredge fillets in flour, shaking off excess. Spread mayonnaise mixture evenly over both sides of fillets. Press fillets into nut mixture. Heat a large non-stick skillet over medium-high heat. Add enough oil to make about ½ an inch in the skillet. Heat to 350°. Cook fish in 2 batches for 3 to 5 minutes per side, depending on the thickness. Fry until golden and crispy. Drain on a wire rack or paper towels. Serve with lemon wedges. Serves 4.

Marlene Mattox
San Antonio, TX Chapter

Fish Florentine

6 frozen breaded fish portions
1 (10 oz.) pkg. frozen chopped spinach
1 can cheese soup
1 (8 oz.) can water chestnuts, drained
3 Tbsp. bacon bits

Prepare fish following package directions. Cook spinach following package directions, drain well. In a saucepan stir soup, water chestnuts, and bacon bits into spinach; heat through. Turn into a 10x6x2 inch baking dish. Top with fish. Bake in a 350° oven for 10 minutes or until hot. Garnish with halved lemon slices.

Sheri Harvey
Genesee County, MI Chapter

Flounder Galliano

5 oz. slivered almonds
6 oz. butter
2 oz. Galliano liqueur
2 oz. lemon juice
1 Tbsp. dried dill
Salt and pepper to taste
4 flounder fillets

Saute almonds in butter until lightly toasted, browning butter (10 to 20 minutes at 340°). Add Galliano, lemon juice, and seasonings. Add fillets. Cook at 380° until fish flakes, turning once. Spoon Galliano, almonds and butter over fish as it cooks. Precede with several martinis and have a little white wine with dinner! Bon Appetit!

Gretchen Stelter
Genesee County, MI Chapter

Mahi Mahi Fish Tacos With Slaw

Slaw:

1/3 c. vegetable oil
2 Tbsp. sugar
2 Tbsp. rice vinegar
1/8 tsp. sesame oil (or more to taste)
3/4 head of cabbage
3 green onions
1/2 can diced green chilies
2 to 3 Tbsp. finely chopped cilantro

Whisk together vegetable oil, vinegar, sugar, and sesame oil. Meanwhile, chop cabbage and green onions and mix with green chilies and cilantro. Toss everything with the prepared dressing.

Mahi Mahi:

3/4 to 1 lb. fresh or frozen mahi mahi
Remaining 1/2 can diced green chilies
Juice of 1 lime
1 Tbsp. finely chopped cilantro
3 Tbsp. olive oil
Shredded cheese
Diced tomato

Mix together lime juice, green chilies, cilantro, and olive oil. Marinate fish for one hour. Grill mahi mahi on a hot grill, approximately 5 to 7 minutes on each side. Serve fish in warmed flour or corn tortillas. Top with prepared slaw, tomatoes, and cheese to taste, or serve over crunchy chips as a taco salad.

Patty Evans
Northern Nevada Chapter

Basil-Crusted Salmon

Cooking spray
1 tsp. olive oil
2 tsp. minced garlic
3 Tbsp. finely chopped fresh basil
1 Tbsp. lemon juice
1 to 1½ c. soft breadcrumbs, lightly toasted
¼ c. freshly grated Parmigiano Reggiano cheese
6 (4 oz.) salmon fillets

Coat large non-stick skillet with cooking spray. Add oil. Over medium-high heat, saute garlic 30 seconds. Add basil and lemon juice; saute 1 minute. Add breadcrumbs, cheese and pepper. Toss well. Preheat oven to 350°. Place fillets in a 9X13 inch baking dish coated with cooking spray. Spoon breadcrumb mixture evenly over fish. Cover and bake for 15 minutes. Remove cover and continue to bake for 10 minutes or until salmon flakes easily when tested with a fork.

Kathy Burns
Jacksonville, FL Chapter

Salmon With Basil And Champagne Sauce

Salmon fillet (approx. 2 lbs.)
1 c. pine nuts
1 c. basil leaves
2 Tbsp. olive oil
¼ stick butter
¼ c. chopped shallot
2 c. champagne
2 c. whipping cream

Put pine nuts, basil, and olive oil in food processor and blend until smooth (add more oil if necessary). Melt butter and saute shallots in saucepan. On high heat, add champagne and cook until reduced, about 10 minutes. Add cream and cook until thick, about 8 minutes. Season with salt and pepper to taste. Broil salmon brushed with olive oil and salt and pepper. Cook until almost done. Put pine nut mixture on fish and return to broiler until warm. Serve with cream sauce. Enjoy!

Penelope 'Penny' Rahman
Palm Beach County, FL Chapter

Grilled Salmon With East-West Spice Rub

Spice Rub Mixture:

1 Tbsp. sugar
1½ tsp. five-spice powder
1½ tsp. ground coriander
1½ tsp. black pepper
½ tsp. salt

Combine all ingredients in a small bowl. Set aside.

Glaze:

Zest of one orange
½ c. fresh orange juice
½ c. low-sodium soy sauce
⅓ c. honey
2 Tbsp. minced green onions
1 Tbsp. minced peeled fresh ginger
1½ tsp. dark sesame oil
4 garlic cloves, minced
1 (3 inch) cinnamon stick

Combine all ingredients in a saucepan. Bring to a boil. Reduce heat and simmer 10 minutes. Strain through a sieve. Set aside.

Remaining Ingredients:

8 (6 oz.) salmon fillets (about 2 inches thick)
Spinach leaves
Red, yellow, and orange bell pepper, cored and sliced
Slivered almonds
Dried cranberries
Mandarin orange slices, drained

Rub fillets with spice mixture. Cover, refrigerate 10 minutes or all day. Prepare grill. Place salmon skin side down on a grill rack coated with cooking spray. Grill 16 minutes, covered or until fish flakes easily when tested with a fork. Remove skin; discard. Lay spinach on a plate and add sliced peppers, almonds, cranberries, and Mandarin oranges. Top with grilled salmon fillet and serve with glaze as a dressing.

Jayne Black
Boise-Treasure Valley, ID Chapter

Seafood

Grilled Salmon With Spice Blends

1 sheet heavy aluminum foil
1 lb. salmon fillets
⅓ c. white wine
2 tsp. Worcestershire sauce
1 tsp. olive oil
2 tsp. dried herb-season blend (like McCormick Grill Mates Salmon Seasoning)
2 tsp. bottled minced garlic
Lemon slices (optional)

Preheat gas grill to medium-high (about 400°). Place on a cookie sheet a sheet of aluminum foil that is about 2 inches larger than the salmon on all sides. Fold up the edges, crimping to form a 1 inch high lip all the way around the fish. Mix wine and Worcestershire sauce in a 1 cup measure. Pour over fish. Drizzle with the oil, then sprinkle the seasoning and garlic evenly over the fish. Slide the fish in the foil from the cookie sheet onto the grill rack. Cook until the fish is opaque throughout, about 10 minutes, depending upon thickness, or to desired doneness. Remove from grill. Top with lemon slices, if desired.

Kathy Burns
Jacksonville, FL Chapter

"Success in this game depends less on strength of body than strength of mind and character."

-Arnold Palmer

Roasted Salmon Platter

Marinade:

2 lemons, zested and juiced
2 Tbsp. olive oil
1 Tbsp. Dijon mustard
1 Tbsp. whole grain mustard
2 garlic cloves, minced
1 Tbsp. kosher salt

Whisk together ingredients and set aside.

Main Ingredients:

1 whole salmon fillet (approx. 3 lbs.)
6 medium Yukon Gold potatoes
1 lb. fresh asparagus
4 small tomatoes, cut in wedges
8 hard cooked eggs, cut in halves
1 bunch arugula or spring mix greens
1 c. assorted fancy olives, black and green

Cover a sheet pan with aluminum foil, place salmon on sheet and drizzle with marinade. Let marinate for at least 15 minutes. Preheat oven to 500°. Place potatoes and 1 tablespoon of salt in a large pot of water. Bring to a boil, lower heat and simmer for 10 to 15 minutes, until potatoes are barely tender. Drain and then leave potatoes in pot covered with a clean dish towel for 15 to 20 minutes. When cool enough to handle, slice in thick slices and set aside. Roast salmon for 12 to 15 minutes. Remove to large platter, let rest for 15 minutes, break into serving size pieces. Blanch asparagus in boiling salted water, drain immediately, and immerse in ice water. Drain again and set aside.

Vinaigrette:

¼ c. white vinegar
1 tsp. Dijon vinegar
1 tsp. kosher salt
½ tsp. freshly ground black pepper
½ c. olive oil

Whisk together thoroughly all ingredients

Arrange salmon, potatoes, asparagus, tomatoes, eggs, arugula, and olives on a large flat platter. Drizzle some vinaigrette over the vegetables and serve the rest on the side. The dish may be served hot, cold or room temperature!! Prepare ahead, play a round of golf, and put on a dinner fit for a queen!

Maggi Braun
Charlotte, NC Chapter
Former Association and Foundation Board Member

Seafood

Honey-Mustard Glazed Salmon Steaks

2 (6 to 8 oz.) salmon steaks
2 tsp. honey
1 Tbsp. Dijon mustard
Pinch of thyme (optional)

Place salmon steaks in microwave-safe dish. In a separate bowl, combine remaining ingredients. Drizzle mustard glaze evenly over salmon steaks. Microwave on high 3 to 4 minutes (more or less depending on your microwave). Allow to stand 2 minutes before serving. Serves 2.

Denise Camens
New York City, NY Chapter

Layer Up Salmon Pizza

1 large wheat Bollo pizza crust
1 c. Goat cheese
8 oz. sun dried tomato slices to cover sauce
10 oz. tomato sauce or pasta sauce
½ tsp. cracked peppercorns
Sprinkle of fresh chives
2 (8 oz.) cans salmon, drained

Place toppings on crust and bake on baking sheet at 350° for 45 minutes. Serve with chilled sangria and friends after 18 holes. The tartness of the Goat cheese and sweetness of the sangria is wonderful to the tongue.

Gigi Edwards Bryant
Austin, TX Chapter

Salmon Loaf

1 (15½ oz.) can red salmon, undrained
2 eggs, beaten
½ c. plain breadcrumbs
2 Tbsp. chopped parsley
⅛ tsp. pepper
1 small onion, chopped (or onion flakes)
2 Tbsp. lemon juice

Preheat oven to 350°. Generously spray an 8½ x 2½ inch loaf pan with cooking spray. In large bowl, flake salmon (I remove skin). Add all remaining ingredients and mix well with salmon and its liquid (I use a separate bowl and then mix it together.). Press into loaf pan. Bake for 50 to 60 minutes, until toothpick comes out clean. Let stand 5 minutes. Loosen edges; lift out of pan. Cut into 4 slices.

Marlene Wolf, M.D. and Esther Rabinowitz
Fort Lauderdale Area, FL Chapter

Spicy Baked Shrimp

½ c. olive oil
2 Tbsp. Cajun seasoning (or to taste)
2 Tbsp. fresh lemon juice
2 Tbsp. chopped fresh parsley (or 1 Tbsp. dried parsley)
1 Tbsp. honey
1 Tbsp. soy sauce
1 lb. uncooked large shrimp, shelled and deveined

Combine oil, Cajun seasoning, lemon juice, parsley, honey, and soy sauce in a 9x13 inch baking dish. Add shrimp and toss to coat. Refrigerate covered 1 hour, stirring occasionally. Can be refrigerated 2 to 3 hours or more to prepare ahead of time. Preheat oven to 350° and bake until shrimp are cooked through, stirring occasionally, about 10 to 12 minutes. Serve with yellow rice and French bread. Easy, quick, and yummy! Courtesy of Bon Appetit.

Sherry Greene
LPGA Foundation Programs Director

Grilled Lemon Garlic Shrimp

4 garlic cloves, minced
2 shallots, minced
1 bay leaf
2 Tbsp. fresh thyme leaves
¼ c. fresh parsley, chopped
1 tsp. red pepper flakes
1 tsp. Dijon mustard
½ c. olive oil
Zest of 1 lemon
2 Tbsp. fresh lemon juice
Kosher salt
Black pepper
1 tsp. "Fire and Flavor" Everyday Rub
1 to 2 lemons, halved
16 giant shrimp, peeled and deveined

Whisk all ingredients except shrimp and halved lemons in a bowl. Reserve 2 to 3 tablespoons to drizzle over shrimp when cooked. Toss shrimp in marinade until coated. Cover and refrigerate 1 to 2 hours, tossing occasionally. Remove shrimp; season with salt and pepper. Place shrimp on skewers or butterfly and place on grill directly. Slice lemons and brush with oil. Grill lemons and shrimp until golden brown on each side (approximately 1½ minutes). Place grilled shrimp on serving platter. Drizzle with reserved marinade and squeeze grilled lemon over shrimp. Serves 4. Recipe attributed to Carissa Giacalone.

Catherine Schiaffo
San Diego, CA Chapter

Shrimp Quinoa

1 lb. shrimp
1 c. quinoa
2 Tbsp. olive oil
1 1/3 Tbsp. garlic, chopped
2 c. broccoli, chopped
1/2 c. sundried tomatoes, chopped
1/4 c. black olives, sliced
2/3 c. artichoke hearts, chopped
2 Tbsp. capers
1/2 tsp. garlic powder
Sea salt to taste
Cracked black pepper to taste

Cook quinoa according to package directions. Heat olive oil over medium heat. Saute shrimp, garlic, and broccoli, seasoned with garlic powder, salt, and pepper, about 5 minutes. Add sundried tomatoes, black olives, artichoke hearts, and capers, and cook another 5 minutes. Add olive oil if needed to prevent sticking. Add cooked quinoa, stirring to mix ingredients, and heat until hot, about 5 more minutes. If desired, may substitute chicken or sausage for shrimp, or omit for vegetarian; rice or pasta for quinoa; spinach, zucchini, and/or yellow squash for broccoli. Quinoa (pronounced keen-wa) is a complete protein grain and can be found in the health foods department of most grocery stores. It is grown in the Andes Mountains and was so important to the Inca culture that they referred to it as the Mother Grain. Eat, enjoy, and may you have the 'mother' of all rounds of golf!

Bonnie Ogden
Greater Knoxville, TN Chapter

Shrimp Santorini

1 small onion
2 garlic cloves
2 Tbsp. olive oil
1 c. tomato sauce, homemade or store bought
1/4 tsp. pepper
1 lb. shrimp, cleaned
1/4 lb. Feta cheese

Chop onion and garlic and saute in olive oil until golden brown. Add tomato sauce and pepper. Layer shrimp in a baking pan and top with tomato sauce mixture. Sprinkle crumbled Feta cheese over tomato sauce. Bake 350° for approximately 15 to 30 minutes (depending on size of shrimp) until cooked through. Serve over rice or pasta. Enjoy!

Jackie Orfanos, M.D.
New York City, NY Chapter

Shrimp Scampi

2 garlic cloves
½ tsp. salt
½ tsp. oregano
¼ tsp. basil
3 Tbsp. extra virgin olive oil
½ stick butter
1 lb. large shrimp, cleaned and deveined
½ c. coarsely chopped fresh parsley
Parmesan cheese, grated
Freshly ground pepper

Mince garlic; crush and blend with salt, oregano, and basil. Heat butter, olive oil, and garlic mixture in frying pan. When very hot, add shrimp and cook, stirring constantly, until shrimp are pink and firm. Add parsley and toss well. Sprinkle with Parmesan cheese and freshly ground pepper. Serve over rice.

Gretchen Stelter and George Kuehn Sr.
Genesee County, MI Chapter

Sesame Seed And Cracked Black Pepper Crusted Tuna Steaks

½ c. white sesame seeds
2 Tbsp. fresh coarsely cracked black peppercorns
2 (8 to 10 oz.) tuna steaks
3 Tbsp. peanut oil
Kosher salt to taste
Peanut oil for sauteing
Store-bought Asian spicy dipping sauce (optional)

Combine sesame seeds and cracked pepper in small dish and mix well. Rub tuna with 3 tablespoons peanut oil. Season with salt. Press sesame seed mixture onto both sides of steaks. Sear in hot oil in a saute pan 2 to 3 minutes on each side or until tuna is rare. Serve with a spicy Asian sauce if desired.

Luanne Jones
Houston, TX Chapter

Notes

Putt for Dough

Breads & Rolls

Common Baking Dishes and Pans

Spring Form Pan	 Layer Cake or Pie Pan	 Ring Mold	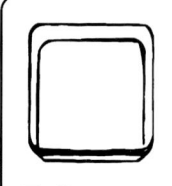 Baking or Square Pan

Loaf Pan	 Brioche Pan	 Angel Cake Pan	 Bundt Tube

Equivalent Dishes

4-CUP BAKING DISH
= 9" pie plate
= 8" x 1¼" layer cake pan
= 7⅜" x 3⅝" x 2¼" loaf pan

6-CUP BAKING DISH
= 8" or 9" x 1½" layer cake pan
= 10" pie pan
= 8½" x 3⅝" x 2⅝" loaf pan

8-CUP BAKING DISH
= 8" x 8" x 2" square pan
= 11" x 7" x 1½" baking pan
= 9" x 5" x 3" loaf pan

10-CUP BAKING DISH
= 9" x 9" x 2" square pan
= 11¾" x 7½" x 1¾" baking pan
= 15" x 10" x 1" flat jelly roll pan

12-CUP BAKING DISH OR MORE
= 13½" x 8½" x 2" glass baking dish
= 13" x 9" x 2" metal baking pan
= 14" x 10½" x 2½" roasting pan

Total Volume of Pans

TUBE PANS
7½" x 3" Bundt tube   6 cups
9" x 3½" fancy or Bundt tube   9 cups
9" x 3½" angel cake pan   12 cups
10" x 3¾" Bundt tube   12 cups
9" x 3½" fancy tube mold   12 cups
10" x 4" fancy tube mold   16 cups
10" x 4" angel cake pan   18 cups

SPRING FORM PANS
8" x 3" pan   12 cups
9" x 3" pan   16 cups

RING MOLDS
8½" x 2¼" mold   4½ cups
9¼" x 2¾" mold   8 cups

BRIOCHE PAN
9½" x 3¼" pan   8 cups

Copyright © 2011 by Cookbook Publishers, Inc.

Breads & Rolls

Brioche

Dough:

- ⅓ c. very warm water (110° to 115°)
- ¼ oz. package active dry yeast
- 10½ oz. cake flour
- 10 oz. all-purpose flour
- ⅓ c. sugar
- 2½ tsp. fine sea salt
- 6 eggs (at room temperature)
- 10 oz. unsalted butter (at room temperature), cut into 1 inch cubes
- 1 egg
- 1 egg yolk
- 1½ Tbsp. water

Combine water and yeast in small bowl. Let set for 10 minutes, then stir until yeast is dissolved. Set aside. Sift together the flours, sugar and salt into the bowl of a mixer fitted with the dough hook. Add the eggs and beat for 1 minute at low speed, scraping down the sides with a rubber spatula as needed. Slowly add the dissolved yeast and continue beating at low speed for 5 minutes. Stop the machine, scrape any dough off the dough hook, and beat for another 5 minutes. Add the butter cubes, about ¼ of them at a time, beating for about 1 minute after each addition. Once all the butter has been added, beat for 10 to 15 minutes more. Place the dough in a large floured mixing bowl and cover with plastic wrap. Set aside in a warm place until doubled in size, about 3 hours.

Continued

Turn the dough out onto a generously floured work surface and gently work the air bubbles out by folding the dough several times while lightly pressing down on it. Return the dough to the bowl, cover with plastic wrap, and refrigerate overnight. Generously butter two 8½ x 4½ x 3 inch loaf pans. Turn the dough out onto a floured work surface. With floured hands, divide the dough in half and shape it into two rectangles to fit the loaf pans. Place the dough in the pans and let the dough rise uncovered in a warm place until it is about ½ inch above the top of the pans, about 3 hours. Preheat the oven to 350°. Prepare Egg Wash by whisking together the egg, egg yolk and water. Using a pastry brush, brush the tops of the loaves with the egg wash. Bake the brioche until it is well-browned on top about 35 to 40 minutes. Remove from the oven and immediately turn the brioche out onto a wire rack.

Shelia Sampolesi
Seattle, WA Chapter
Former Association Board Member

Sally Lunn Bread

3½ to 4 c. all-purpose flour, divided
⅓ c. sugar
1 tsp. salt
1 pkg. dry yeast

½ c. milk
½ c. water
1 stick margarine
3 eggs (room temperature)

Mix 1¼ cup flour, sugar, salt, and yeast in a large bowl and set aside. Combine milk, water, and margarine in a saucepan. Heat over low until mixture is warm (margarine does not need to melt). Gradually add liquid to dry ingredients and beat 2 minutes at medium speed. Add eggs and 1 cup of flour (or enough flour to make a thick batter). Beat on high for 2 minutes. Stir in enough additional flour to make a stiff batter. Cover bowl. Let rise until doubled in size. Stir batter down and beat well, about 30 seconds. Turn out into a well-greased and floured tube pan. Cover and let rise until doubled in size. Bake at 325° for 40 to 45 minutes. Remove from pan and cool on wire rack.

Lisa Weistart
Marketing Manager, Adams Golf

Mashed Potato Rolls

1 c. milk
1 pkg. active dry yeast
½ c. lukewarm water
1 c. mashed potatoes
¾ c. vegetable oil
½ c. sugar
1 tsp. salt
2 beaten eggs
6 to 8 c. all purpose flour

Scald milk. Set aside to cool to lukewarm. Dissolve yeast in the warm water. With electric mixer, mix mashed potatoes, oil, sugar, salt and eggs; cream well. Mix lukewarm milk and dissolved yeast water together; add to creamed mixture. Mix all together a few minutes at medium speed of mixer. By hand, work in 6 to 8 cup of sifted flour until you can handle the dough. Toss on floured board and knead well. Place in a large bowl and let rise until double in bulk. Knead again lightly. Rub top with melted butter; place in covered dish and store in refrigerator until ready to use (preferably over night). 2 to 2½ hours before needed, roll out like biscuit dough, cut with biscuit cutter and place on lightly greased baking pan. You may also form into Parker house or cloverleaf rolls. Cover lightly with clean cloth and let rise in a warm place. Bake at 400° for 15 to 20 minutes or until light brown. This dough does not have to be used all at once. It can be stored in the refrigerator for several days.

Maggi Braun
Charlotte, NC Chapter
Former Association and Foundation Board Member

Banana Bread

1½ c. sugar
⅔ c. melted butter
1 c. mashed ripe bananas
2 eggs
1 c. chopped nuts (your choice, optional)
4 Tbsp. buttermilk
2 c. flour
1 tsp. baking soda

Cream sugar and butter; add eggs, bananas, buttermilk and nuts. Lastly, add flour and soda. Mix well. Bake in 2 greased bread pans at 350° for 45 to 50 minutes, or until done. Can make small holiday gifts by using 4 baby loaf pans and baking 40 to 45 minutes.

Kathy Thomas
Kansas City Metro and Tucson-Old Pueblo, AZ Chapters
Nancy Oliver Founder's Award Winner and
Former Association Board Member

Banana Bread/Cake

1¼ c. flour
1 c. sugar
½ tsp. salt
1 tsp. baking soda

½ c. butter or margarine
2 unbeaten eggs
1½ or 2 ripe bananas

Recipe calls to sift dry ingredients (I do not sift and it turns out great). Add bananas (mashed), eggs, and margarine, and beat at low speed until just blended. Grease and flour a 10½ x 3⅝ x 2⅝ inch pan. Pour batter into pan. Bake 45 minutes in a 350° oven. Test center with toothpick. I like to double the recipe and bake in a 9x13 inch pan. Variations: add a few blueberries and bake, sprinkle chopped walnuts on top, or serve it with just powdered sugar on top. To make it more dessert-like, I sometimes make a chocolate frosting or lemon frosting and frost the top of the cake. Either way it should be moist and delicious. Enjoy!

Barbie Adler
Chicago Metro, IL Chapter

Blueberry Pound Cake

1 c. sugar
½ lb. butter, softened
4 large eggs

2 c. flour
2 c. fresh blueberries
2 Tbsp. grated lemon rind

Preheat oven to 300°. Lightly grease one loaf pan. In large bowl, cream butter and sugar until light and fluffy. Beat in eggs, one at a time. Gently fold in all but 3 tablespoons of the flour, ½ cup at a time. Toss blueberries with lemon rind and remaining flour. Fold blueberry mixture into batter and pour into pan. Bake for 1 hour and 30 to 50 minutes, depending on size of pan (test center of cake with toothpick). Cool completely and unmold. Let stand overnight before serving. Recipe can be doubled, and frozen for later use. Delicious!

Linda C. Murphy
Pittsburgh, PA Chapter

Lemon Bread

½ c. butter
1 c. white sugar
2 eggs
Grated rind of 1 lemon
1½ c. all purpose flour

1 tsp. vanilla or almond extract
1 tsp. baking powder
¼ to ½ tsp. salt
½ c. milk

Cream butter and sugar; add eggs and lemon rind. Combine dry ingredients and add alternately with milk. Put in loaf pan and bake at 325° for 1 hour. While still hot and before removing from pan, glaze with mixture of ½ cup powdered sugar and juice of half a lemon. Let cool in pan. If desired, ½ cup of cherries and ½ cup of walnuts may be added to mixture.

Marlene Wolf, M.D. and Sue Jesse
Fort Lauderdale Area, FL Chapter

Monkey Bread

1 pkg. biscuits (6 pack)
1 c. sugar

2 Tbsp. cinnamon
1¼ sticks margarine

Cut biscuits into quarters. Combine sugar and cinnamon. Roll biscuit pieces in sugar/cinnamon mix and put into Bundt pan. Melt butter and add leftover sugar/cinnamon mix; bring to boil. Pour over biscuits. Bake at 350° for 25 minutes. Remove from pan while still hot by pouring upside down on a plate. Do not try to cut it, just pull off bites and enjoy.

Becky Macaluso
Palm Beach County, FL Chapter
EWGA Managing Director, Chapter & Member Services

Breads & Rolls

Pumpkin Bread

1½ c. plus 2 Tbsp. sifted flour
1½ c. sugar
¾ tsp. salt
1 tsp. baking soda
½ tsp. cinnamon
½ tsp. nutmeg
½ c. shortening, melted (Crisco)
2 eggs, slightly beaten
⅓ c. water
1 c. pumpkin (1 can is 2 c.)

Preheat oven to 350°. Sift together flour, sugar, salt, baking soda, and spices into a large mixing bowl. In another bowl, beat together shortening, eggs, water, and pumpkin. Make a well in the dry ingredients and add the pumpkin mixture. Mix by hand only until all dry ingredients are moist. Bake in greased and floured 9x5x3 inch loaf pan for 60 to 65 minutes.

Marlene Wolf, M.D.
Fort Lauderdale Area, FL Chapter

Zucchini Bread

3 eggs, beaten
1 c. oil
1 c. brown sugar
1 c. white sugar
3 c. flour
2 c. zucchini, peeled and grated
3 tsp. vanilla
3 tsp. cinnamon
1 tsp. salt
1 tsp. baking soda
¼ tsp. baking powder
1 c. chopped nuts

Preheat oven to 350°. Blend dry ingredients. Beat eggs until light and foamy. Add oil, sugar and vanilla to the eggs and continue beating. Stir in grated zucchini. Add nuts. Stir in dry ingredients just until blended. Pour into 2 greased and floured, 5x9 inch bread pans. Bake at 350° for 1 hour. Let cool in pans for 10 minutes.

Renee Pecuch
Lehigh Valley, PA Chapter

Zucchini Bread

3 eggs, slightly beaten
2 c. sugar
1 c. oil
2 tsp. vanilla
3 c. flour
1 tsp. salt

1 tsp. baking soda
1 tsp. cinnamon
¼ tsp. baking powder
2 c. grated zucchini squash
1 c. coarsely chopped walnuts

Combine eggs, sugar, oil, and vanilla. Add flour, salt, baking soda, cinnamon, and baking powder. Stir. Add zucchini and walnuts. Pour into 2 loaf pans. Bake 1 hour at 350°.

Everette Dupree
Palm Beach County, FL Chapter
EWGA Director of Finance

Basic Muffin Recipe

3 c. all purpose flour
2 c. sugar
2 tsp. baking soda
½ tsp. salt
2 eggs

2 sticks butter, melted and cooled
¾ c. milk
2 tsp. vanilla (or other flavoring)

Combine flour, sugar, baking powder, baking soda, and salt in a mixing bowl. In a separate bowl, combine eggs, butter, milk, and vanilla. Add wet ingredients to dry ingredients. Once mixed, store in refrigerator overnight. The next morning, choose any of the following items to mix in: 1 cup granola, 1 cup walnuts, 1 cup blueberries, 1 cup coconut, 1 cup dried cranberries, 1 cup crushed pineapple (drained), or 2 mashed bananas plus 1 chopped banana. Fold mix-ins into batter. Brush tops of muffin pans with oil so muffins won't stick. Use a large ice cream scoop for even size. Bake 25 to 30 minutes at 350°.

Barbara McLaughlin
Naples, FL, Chapter

Pumpkin Spice Muffins

1 box spice or carrot cake mix (2 layer)
1 (15 oz.) can pumpkin (not pie filling)
1 c. Hershey's cinnamon chips (or all of 10 oz. pkg.)
½ c. water or applesauce or caramel syrup
½ to 1 c. chopped pecans (optional)

Preheat oven to 400°. Combine all ingredients. Fill paper-lined muffin cups about ⅔ full. (Lightly coating the paper liners with cooking spray before adding the muffin mixture makes it easier to remove the muffins after baking.) Bake at 400° for 16 to 18 minutes. Makes about 48 medium-size muffins. Great for fall!

Kathy Burns
Jacksonville, FL Chapter

Walnut Muffins

2 c. dark brown sugar
4 eggs
1½ c. whole wheat flour
1½ c. chopped walnuts (6 oz. pkg.)
½ c. margarine, melted
¼ tsp. black walnut extract (good substitute is banana extract)

Mix ingredients in the order given. (I have no clue why. That's just the instruction I was given. Personally, I just dump everything in the bowl at the same time and hope for the best). Spoon the batter into greased and floured mini-muffin tins. Do NOT use large tins or cupcake papers and do not fill to the top. (Again, I don't know why, but in this case I follow the instructions as given). Bake at 350° for 10 to 15 minutes (Another clue is they have been in long enough is if the smoke detector starts screaming. This will deliver you some pretty crunchy muffins, and they will taste like charcoal. Your best bet is to use an actual timer.). Recipe makes about 6 dozen depending on how much of the batter you spoon into each mini-muffin slot.

Robin K. Anderson
Houston, TX Chapter
EWGA Businesswoman of the Year Award Winner

Easy Moist Cornbread

2 boxes Jiffy cornbread mix (see additional ingredients on box)
1 can creamed corn

Preheat oven to 400°. Make cornbread mix as directed on the box. Add the creamed corn. Pour mixture into 9x13 inch pan lightly coated with cooking spray. Bake at 400° about 20 minutes or until golden and bread has started to pull away from sides of pan.

Kathy Burns
Jacksonville, FL Chapter

Hutterite Corn Bread

2 c. flour
2 c. sugar
2 c. cornmeal
2 c. whipping cream
2 eggs
2 tsp. baking soda
2 tsp. vinegar (white or clear)
2 tsp. salt

Mix all ingredients and pour into an ungreased 9x13 inch pan. Bake at 350° for 35 minutes.

Ronna Jo Ricco
Spokane/Inland Northwest, WA Chapter
EWGA Women Who Lead Award Winner

Beer Bread

3 c. self-rising flour
1 can beer, room temperature
6 Tbsp. sugar

Grease a loaf pan. Mix ingredients, put in pan, and bake at 375° for 1 hour and 10 minutes. Cool and serve.

Becky Macaluso
Palm Beach County, FL Chapter
EWGA Managing Director, Chapter & Member Services

Beer-Cheese Triangles

2 c. packaged biscuit mix
½ c. shredded Cheddar cheese
½ c. beer

In mixing bowl stir together biscuit mix and shredded cheese. Make a well in the center, add beer all at once. Stir just until mixture clings together. Knead gently on a lightly floured surface for 5 strokes. Roll or pat dough into a 6 inch circle. Cut into 10 wedges. Place on a greased baking sheet. Bake in a 450° oven for 8 to 10 minutes.

Sheri Harvey
Genesee County, MI Chapter

Prosciutto Muffins

2 Tbsp. butter
1½ c. finely chopped onion
½ c. prosciutto (about 2 oz.), diced
2 c. whole wheat pastry flour
1 tsp. fresh rosemary, minced
1½ tsp. baking powder
½ tsp. baking soda
½ tsp. salt
⅛ tsp. freshly ground pepper
1 c. non-fat buttermilk
2 large eggs
2 Tbsp. extra virgin olive oil

Preheat oven to 400°. Coat 12 muffin cups with cooking spray. Melt butter in a large skillet over medium heat. Add onion and cook, stirring until golden, about 5 minutes. Stir in prosciutto and cook, stirring for 2 minutes. Remove from the heat. Whisk flour, rosemary, baking powder, baking soda, salt and pepper in a large bowl until combined. Whisk buttermilk, eggs and oil in a medium bowl until blended. Fold the onion mixture and buttermilk mixture into the dry ingredients with a rubber spatula until evenly moistened. Divide the batter among the prepared muffin cups. Bake the muffins until lightly browned and a toothpick inserted in the center comes out clean, 18 to 20 minutes. Serve warm.

Jo-Ann Dixon
Northern New Jersey Chapter
Association and Foundation Board Member

Kitty's French Bread Melt

1 loaf French bread
8 oz. Swiss cheese, diced
2 (4 oz.) cans mushrooms, drained
2 sticks margarine
2 Tbsp. poppy seeds
1 tsp. dry mustard
1 tsp. Lawry seasoning salt
1 tsp. lemon juice
2 Tbsp. minced onion

Cut French bread diagonally both ways, not completely through. Melt butter and add minced onion, poppy seeds, mustard, seasoning salt, and lemon juice. Drizzle this mixture inside the opening of the bread. Stuff with diced Swiss cheese and mushrooms. Bake at 350° until cheese melts.

Becky Macaluso
Palm Beach County, FL Chapter
EWGA Managing Director, Chapter & Member Services

Pineapple Stuffing

¼ lb. butter, softened
1 c. sugar
4 extra large eggs
Dash cinnamon
Dash nutmeg
8 slices bread, cubed
20 oz. crushed pineapple, drained

Cream butter and sugar together. Add eggs one at a time. Add spices. Fold in bread and crushed pineapple. Spread evenly in a 9x13 inch pan or baking dish. I usually double the recipe. Bake in a 350° oven, uncovered, for 1 hour.

Cindy McGeever
Greater Philadelphia, PA Chapter
Nancy Oliver Founder's Award Winner and
Former Association Board President

Green Tomato Breakfast Cake

1/3 c. butter, softened
1 c. sugar
2 eggs
1 tsp. vanilla extract
1 c. all-purpose flour
1 tsp. baking powder
1/8 tsp. salt
2 green tomatoes, cored and cut into eighths
2 tsp. granulated sugar
1/2 tsp. ground cinnamon

Preheat oven to 350°. Coat a 9 inch round cake pan or baking dish with cooking spray. Combine butter and sugar and beat with a mixer at medium speed until fluffy. Beat in eggs and vanilla. Combine flour, baking powder and salt. Stir into the butter mixture. Beat well. Spoon batter into prepared pan. Arrange green tomato pieces in concentric circles over batter. Sprinkle lightly with sugar and cinnamon. Bake 50 to 60 minutes until cake is firm and golden. Serves 8. (210 calories and 9g fat per serving) Just as good for dessert as it is for breakfast!

Contributor Unknown

Sour Cream Coffee Cake

1 c. butter (2 sticks)
2 eggs
2 c. sugar
1 c. sour cream
1/2 tsp. vanilla
2 c. cake flour
1 tsp. baking powder
1/4 tsp. salt
1/2 c. chopped pecans
1/4 c. packed brown sugar
2 tsp. cinnamon

Cream butter, eggs, and sugar until fluffy. Fold in sour cream and vanilla. Sift flour baking soda, and salt, and add to above mixture. Meanwhile, mix pecans, brown sugar, and cinnamon for topping. Into a greased Bundt pan, add half of the topping and half of the batter. Repeat. Bake at 350° for 55 to 60 minutes. Test center. Cool in pan about 15 minutes before turning out. Serve warm. Freezes beautifully. Rich, but worth it! A Christmas morning tradition at our house!

Karen Moraghan
Northern New Jersey Chapter
Association Board Member

Creme Brulee French Toast

½ c. unsalted butter (1 stick)
1 c. packed brown sugar
2 Tbsp. corn syrup
1 (8 to 9 inch) round loaf Challah bread

5 large eggs
1½ c. half and half
1 tsp. vanilla
1 tsp. Grand Marnier
¼ tsp. salt

In a small, heavy saucepan, melt butter with brown sugar and corn syrup over medium heat, stirring until smooth. Pour into 9x13 inch baking dish. Cut 6 (1 inch) thick slices from center portion of bread reserving ends for another use, and trim crusts. Arrange bread slices in one layer of baking dish, squeezing them slightly to fit. In a bowl, whisk together eggs, half and half, vanilla, Grand Marnier and salt until combined well. Pour evenly over bread. Chill bread mixture, covered at least 8 hours and up to 1 day. Preheat oven to 350°. Bring bread to room temperature before placing in the oven. Bake bread mixture, uncovered, in the middle of the oven until puffed, and edges are pale golden, 35 to 40 minutes.

Variations: I could not find a round loaf of Challah bread, so I used a braided loaf from my local bakery. I cut 8 (1 inch) slices from the middle out, reserving the ends. I am not sure what for, but seems like a nice enough bread!!! I did not trim the crusts. They are just too pretty. It all fit in my baking dish without too much squeezing. It might have been a little moister on the top with less bread, but we all thought it turned out just great. I did not add the salt. I might try a little cinnamon (maybe a ½ teaspoon or so) in the egg mixture next time to spice it up a bit.

Tyra Jarvis
Sacramento, CA Chapter
Nancy Oliver Founder's Award Winner and
Former Association Board President

Easy French Toast Strata

Strata:

1 loaf of French bread
8 oz. cream cheese, cubed in small pieces
8 eggs
2½ c. milk
6 tsp. melted butter
¼ c. maple syrup

Cut or tear French bread into small cubes (about 12 cups). Place ½ of the cubes in a greased 13x9x2 inch baking dish. Top with cream cheese cubes and then the rest of the bread cubes. With a blender or mixer, combine eggs, milk, and syrup. Add melted butter slowly so that it does not solidify. Pour evenly over bread and cream cheese. Use a spatula to press down and moisten all the bread. Cover and refrigerate 2 to 24 hours. Bring to room temperature and bake at 325° for 35 to 40 minutes (add 5 to 10 minutes if not at room temperature) or until center is set and edges are browned. Let stand 10 minutes before cutting and serve with apple cider syrup. This is a great make ahead breakfast!!

Apple Cider Syrup:

1 c. sugar
8 tsp. cornstarch
1 tsp. ground cinnamon
2 c. apple cider or apple juice
4 Tbsp. butter

In a small sauce pan combine all ingredients (except butter) and cook over medium heat until thick and bubbly. Cook for 2 minutes more. Stir in butter and serve with strata.

Renee Birklund
Canton, OH Chapter

Breads & Rolls

Night Before French Toast

1 to 2 loaves French bread, without seeds
8 eggs
3 c. milk
1 Tbsp. vanilla
¾ tsp. salt
4 Tbsp. sugar
2 Tbsp. butter
Cinnamon

Grease 13x9x2 inch baking pan. Cube bread into 1 inch pieces and arrange evenly in the pan. In a large bowl whisk together eggs, milk, sugar, salt, and vanilla. Pour over bread in pan. Cover with foil and refrigerate for 4 or more hours. When ready to cook, heat oven to 350°. Dot bread mixture with butter and sprinkle with cinnamon. Bake for 40 to 45 minutes, uncovered (or bake with the foil on for 20 minutes and remove for last 20 to 25 minutes). When toast is puffy and brown, remove from the oven and let stand for 5 minutes before serving. Serve with syrup, honey, yogurt, berries, or sour cream. Enjoy!

Patricia Voll
Long Island, NY, Chapter

Special Occasion French Toast

2 Tbsp. Karo syrup (white)
1 stick butter
1 c. brown sugar
½ c. pecans
10 to 12 slices of Texas toast (thick)
5 eggs
1½ c. milk
1 tsp. vanilla
Cinnamon to taste

Combine syrup, butter, and brown sugar in a small pan. Simmer until syrupy. Pour into a 9x13 inch non-stick pan. Sprinkle pecans in the bottom of pan on top of mixture. Place the bread 2 layers deep in the pan. Beat the eggs, milk and vanilla together then pour evenly over the bread. Sprinkle with cinnamon. Cover and let sit in refrigerator overnight. Bake at 350° for 45 minutes. Flip over onto serving dish to serve. Serve hot, immediately.

Zona Trahan
Houston, TX Chapter
Nancy Oliver Founder's Award Winner

Ski Team Buttermilk Pancakes

1 pt. buttermilk
3 eggs
1 stick butter, melted
2 c. flour

1 scant tsp. baking soda
1 level tsp. baking powder
1 tsp. salt

Mix in order: buttermilk, eggs, melted butter, flour, baking soda, baking powder, and salt in blender. Heat griddle to 400° to 420°. Bake without greasing skillet or griddle. If batter seems too thick to pour well, mix in a little more buttermilk to thin. One of the following items may be added to the mix: blueberries, diced apples, sliced bananas, chopped strawberries, or other fruit. For a little kick you may add a shot of Irish whiskey (good for cold weather!). This recipe may be multiplied, made, and refrigerated the day before if you are preparing for a crowd. Fruit should be folded in just before baking to reduce color bleeding.

Gretchen Stelter and Hugh Stelter
Genesee County, MI Chapter

Swedish Pancakes

¾ c. all purpose flour
1 Tbsp. sugar
1 tsp. salt

4 eggs
¾ c. milk

Combine ingredients in blender or bowl, and mix until smooth. Heat 10 inch non-stick skillet over medium heat. Add scant tablespoon butter to pan. When melted, pour in ¼ cup batter. Swirl to coat bottom of pan. When top loses shine, flip. Pancake should be lightly browned. Fold in half and then in half again. Serve with syrup, powdered sugar or lingonberries.

Carolyn Caplan
Miami, FL and Cleveland, OH Chapters

The Sweet Spot

Desserts

EQUIVALENT CHART

3 tsp.	1 Tbsp.
2 Tbsp.	⅛ c.
4 Tbsp.	¼ c.
8 Tbsp.	½ c.
16 Tbsp.	1 c.
5 Tbsp. + 1 tsp.	⅓ c.
12 Tbsp.	¾ c.
4 oz.	½ c.
8 oz.	1 c.
16 oz.	1 lb.
1 oz.	2 Tbsp. fat or liquid
2 c.	1 pt.
2 pt.	1 qt.
1 qt.	4 c.
⅝ c.	½ c. + 2 Tbsp.
⅞ c.	¾ c. + 2 Tbsp.
1 jigger	1½ fl. oz. (3 Tbsp.)
8 to 10 egg whites	1 c.
12 to 14 egg yolks	1 c.
1 c. unwhipped cream	2 c. whipped
1 lb. shredded American cheese	4 c.
¼ lb. crumbled Bleu cheese	1 c.
1 lemon	3 Tbsp. juice
1 orange	⅓ c. juice
1 lb. unshelled walnuts	1½ to 1¾ c. shelled
2 c. fat	1 lb.
1 lb. butter	2 c. or 4 sticks
2 c. granulated sugar	1 lb.
3½-4 c. unsifted powdered sugar	1 lb.
2¼ c. packed brown sugar	1 lb.
4 c. sifted flour	1 lb.
4½ c. cake flour	1 lb.
3½ c. unsifted whole wheat flour	1 lb.
4 oz. (1 to 1¼ c.) uncooked macaroni	2¼ c. cooked
7 oz. spaghetti	4 c. cooked
4 oz. (1½ to 2 c.) uncooked noodles	2 c. cooked
28 saltine crackers	1 c. crumbs
4 slices bread	1 c. crumbs
14 square graham crackers	1 c. crumbs
22 vanilla wafers	1 c. crumbs

SUBSTITUTIONS FOR A MISSING INGREDIENT

1 square **chocolate** (1 ounce) = 3 or 4 tablespoons cocoa plus ½ tablespoon fat
1 tablespoon **cornstarch** (for thickening) = 2 tablespoons flour
1 cup sifted **all-purpose flour** = 1 cup plus 2 tablespoons sifted cake flour
1 cup sifted **cake flour** = 1 cup minus 2 tablespoons sifted all-purpose flour
1 teaspoon **baking powder** = ¼ teaspoon baking soda plus ½ teaspoon cream of tartar
1 cup **sour milk** = 1 cup sweet milk into which 1 tablespoon vinegar or lemon juice has been stirred
1 cup **sweet milk** = 1 cup sour milk or buttermilk plus ½ teaspoon baking soda
¾ cup **cracker crumbs** = 1 cup bread crumbs
1 cup **cream, sour, heavy** = ⅓ cup butter and ⅔ cup milk in any sour milk recipe
1 teaspoon **dried herbs** = 1 tablespoon fresh herbs
1 cup **whole milk** = ½ cup evaporated milk and ½ cup water or 1 cup reconstituted nonfat dry milk and 1 tablespoon butter
2 ounces **compressed yeast** = 3 (¼ ounce) packets of dry yeast
1 tablespoon **instant minced onion, rehydrated** = 1 small fresh onion
1 tablespoon **prepared mustard** = 1 teaspoon dry mustard
⅛ teaspoon **garlic powder** = 1 small pressed clove of garlic
1 lb. **whole dates** = 1½ cups, pitted and cut
3 medium **bananas** = 1 cup mashed
3 cups **dry corn flakes** = 1 cup crushed
10 **miniature marshmallows** = 1 large marshmallow

GENERAL OVEN CHART

Very slow oven	250° to 300°F.
Slow oven	300° to 325°F.
Moderate oven	325° to 375°F.
Medium hot oven	375° to 400°F.
Hot oven	400° to 450°F.
Very hot oven	450° to 500°F.

CONTENTS OF CANS

Of the different sizes of cans used by commercial canners, the most common are:

Size:	Average Contents
8 oz.	1 cup
Picnic	1¼ cups
No. 300	1¾ cups
No. 1 tall	2 cups
No. 303	2 cups
No. 2	2½ cups
No. 2½	3½ cups
No. 3	4 cups
No. 10	12 to 13 cups

Copyright © 2011 by Cookbook Publishers, Inc.

Desserts

Frozen Chocolate Mousse

1 Tbsp. dry instant coffee
½ c. boiling water
1¼ c. granulated sugar, divided
12 oz. semisweet chocolate morsels
4 large eggs, separated
3 c. whipping cream
Pinch of salt
⅛ tsp. cream of tartar

Dissolve coffee in water. Add ½ cup sugar and stir over medium heat to dissolve. On low, add chocolate; stir until melted. Cool slightly. Add egg yolks one at a time, stirring with a whisk. Cool completely. Whip cream until it holds a shape but not until really stiff; set aside. With clean bowl and beaters, beat egg whites until foamy. Add salt and cream of tartar and beat until whites hold a soft shape. Reduce speed to moderate and gradually add ¾ cup of sugar, one spoonful at a time. Beat briefly between additions. Increase speed to high again and beat for a few minutes until meringue is quite firm, but not stiff or dry. Fold chocolate into egg whites, then fold in whipped cream. Pour into dessert cups and freeze, covered.

Carol Nieckarz
Albany/Capital Region, NY Chapter
Former Association Board Member

Pound Cake Tiramisu

1 c. heavy cream
4 oz. regular cream cheese, softened
3 Tbsp. confectioners' sugar
½ c. strong coffee or espresso, room temperature
2 Tbsp. dark rum or brandy
1 loaf pound cake, preferably marbled, cut into ½ inch thick slices
¼ c. shaved semisweet chocolate
Unsweetened cocoa powder for dusting the top

In a large bowl, using an electric mixer, beat the heavy cream, cream cheese, and confectioners sugar together until it is combined well. In a smaller bowl combine the coffee and rum/brandy. In a 2 quart baking dish, lay half the cake slices in a single layer, trimming to fit. Brush with half of the coffee mixture. Top with half the cream mixture and half the shaved chocolate. Repeat this layer and dust with cocoa powder. Cover and refrigerate at least 4 hours or overnight before serving.

Barbara McLaughlin
Naples, FL Chapter

Tiramisu

6 egg yolks
3 Tbsp. sugar
1 lb. mascarpone cheese
1½ c. strong espresso, cooled, divided
2 tsp. dark rum
24 packaged ladyfingers (hard, not spongy)
½ c. bittersweet chocolate shavings, for garnish

In a large bowl, using an electric mixer with whisk attachment, beat egg yolks and sugar until thick and pale, about 5 minutes. Add mascarpone cheese and beat until smooth. Add 1 tablespoon of espresso and mix until thoroughly combined. In a small shallow dish, add remaining espresso and rum. Dip each ladyfinger into espresso/rum mixture for only 5 seconds; letting the ladyfingers soak too long will cause them to fall apart. Place the soaked ladyfingers on the bottom of a 9x13 inch baking dish, breaking them in half if necessary in order to fit the bottom. Spread ½ of the mascarpone mixture evenly over the ladyfingers. Arrange another layer of soaked ladyfingers and top with remaining mascarpone mixture. Cover tiramisu with plastic wrap and refrigerate for at least 2 hours, up to 8 hours. Before serving, sprinkle with chocolate shavings.

Mary E. Kaster
Canton, OH Chapter

Desserts

Deep South Torte

Butter, for greasing pie pan
10 unsalted table crackers
   (such as Carr's Table
   Crackers, plain)
½ c. pecans, chopped small
¼ tsp. baking powder
4 egg whites
⅛ tsp. cream of tartar
1 c. sugar
½ tsp. vanilla extract

Preheat oven to 325°. Butter 9½ inch pie pan. Reduce crackers to a large crumb consistency (but not powder) with a food processor or rolling pin. In a medium bowl, combine cracker crumbs, pecans, and baking powder. Set aside. Beat egg whites in a second medium bowl, adding cream of tartar, then sugar (a tablespoon at a time). Beat until stiff peaks are formed. Add vanilla. Fold cracker mix into egg whites and spread mixture into pie pan. Bake for 30 to 35 minutes. Let cool completely; top with whipped cream.

Dori J. Smith
Palm Springs/Desert Cities, CA Chapter
Former Association and Foundation Board Member

New England Grape-Nuts Custard

6 eggs
6 c. low fat milk
½ c. sugar
1 tsp. cinnamon
1 tsp. vanilla extract (real is
   best)
¼ tsp. ground nutmeg
½ c. Grape-Nuts cereal

Slightly beat eggs using a fork or hand beater. Keep beating and add in all the ingredients except the Grape-Nuts cereal. Pour in 9x9 inch baking dish. Sprinkle the Grape-Nuts evenly over the mix. Bake for 40 to 45 minutes at 300°.

Caryn Jarvis and Ethel Jarvis
Port St. Lucie-Treasure Coast, FL Chapter, Palm Beach County
FL Chapter

Barton Creek Resort And Spa Signature Dessert

Bread Pudding:

6 c. whipping cream	15 egg yolks
2 c. milk	9 croissants, cut into 1 inch pieces
1 c. sugar	
20 oz. white chocolate, broken	9 flaky fruit Danishes, cut into 1 inch pieces
4 whole eggs	

Preheat oven to 350°. In a large saucepan, heat whipping cream, milk and sugar over medium heat. When hot, take off the heat and add white chocolate pieces. Stir until melted. Combine the whole eggs and egg yolks in a large bowl. Slowly pour the hot cream mixture into the eggs in a steady stream, continuously stirring eggs as you go (eggs will cook and "clump" if not vigorously stirred). Place the pieces of croissants and Danishes into a 9x12x2 inch pan. Pour ½ of bread pudding mix over bread, using your fingers to press the mix and bread together. Pour the remaining mix on top. Cover the pan with aluminum foil and bake for 1 hour. Take off the foil and bake for an additional 30 minutes, until set and brown.

Sauce:

½ c. whipping cream   8 oz. white chocolate, broken

Bring the cream to a boil in a saucepan. Take off the heat and add the white chocolate. Stir until completely smooth and melted. Spoon over bread pudding. Enjoy!

Karen Carlson
Northern Colorado Chapter
EWGA Chapter Development Representative

Eggnog Bread Pudding With Cherry Bourbon Sauce

Eggnog Bread Pudding:

- 1 loaf stale French bread, cut into 1 inch cubes
- 1 qt. eggnog (lite if desired)
- 3 eggs
- ½ tsp. cinnamon
- ½ tsp. nutmeg
- 2 Tbsp. vanilla
- ½ c. sugar

Preheat oven to 325°. Grease 9x13 inch pan. In large mixing bowl crumble the bread and pour eggnog over it, letting it stand until bread is soft. In smaller bowl, beat together the eggs, sugar, cinnamon, nutmeg, and vanilla and pour over bread and eggnog mixture. Bake for 1 hour and 10 minutes or until knife comes out clean. Let cool slightly before serving.

Cherry Bourbon Sauce:

- 1 (20 or 21 oz.) can cherry pie filling
- 1 stick margarine
- 4 Tbsp. bourbon

Combine all ingredients in a small saucepan over medium-low heat until margarine is melted and all mixed together and slightly bubbly. Spoon sauce over warm bread pudding.

Karen McIntosh
Genesee County, MI Chapter

Sweet Noodle Pudding

16 oz. broad egg noodles
8 beaten eggs
2 sticks butter, melted
1 lb. sour cream
1 lb. cottage cheese
3 Tbsp. vanilla extract
2 c. sugar
2 tsp. salt
1 Tbsp. cinnamon
1 pkg. slivered almonds
12 oz. raisins
2 c. cinnamon-nut corn flakes

Cook noodles in boiling water as package directs. Drain and rinse in cold water. In a large bowl, whisk the eggs with the melted butter. Fold in the sour cream, cottage cheese, vanilla and the rest of the dry ingredients, except for the corn flakes. Stir all and add the noodles until well mixed. Pour into a greased 9x13 inch pan. Pound corn flakes in plastic bag and spread over top. Bake for 1 hour at 350° until top is lightly browned and center is set, and knife comes out clean from center. Serve warm. Serves 8 to 10 people.

Michelle Florea
Ft. Lauderdale Area, FL Chapter

Easy Fruit Cobbler

1¼ c. self-rising flour
1 c. (2 sticks) butter, cold
1 c. white sugar
1 qt. sliced fruit, any kind

Blend butter and flour (use hands or fork) until it looks like cornmeal. Sprinkle butter and flour mixture plus sugar over fruit in an 8x8 inch baking dish (can be greased with butter for easier release). Bake at 350° for 35 minutes or until top is brown.

Theresa Stamey
Sacramento, CA Chapter

Microwave-Baked Apples

4 large Fuji or Gala apples
4 tsp. margarine or butter
4 Tbsp. dried cranberries or raisins
4 tsp. water or apple cider
1 tsp. sugar
¼ tsp. pumpkin pie spice
½ c. chopped walnuts or pecans

Core apples but do not cut through to bottoms. Beginning at stem end, peel apples ⅓ of the way down. Stand apples in 8x8 inch glass baking dish or 9 inch glass pie plate. Fill each apple with 1 teaspoon margarine, 1 tablespoon cranberries or raisins, and 1 teaspoon water or apple cider. In cup, combine sugar and pumpkin pie spice and sprinkle over apples. Cover with waxed paper and cook in microwave on medium-high (70 percent power) for 10 to 12 minutes or until apples are very tender. Let stand covered, 5 minutes. Sprinkle with nuts before serving.

Kathy Burns
Jacksonville, FL Chapter

No-Crust Apple Pie

⅔ c. flour
½ tsp. salt
½ tsp. cinnamon
1 tsp. baking powder
1 c. sugar
1 egg, beaten
1 apple, peeled and chopped
½ c. chopped pecans or walnuts

Sift together flour, salt, cinnamon, and baking powder. Add mixture to the rest of the ingredients and mix well. Place in greased 10 inch glass pie dish and bake at 350° for 25 minutes.

Lilliam Larson
Polk County, FL Chapter

Scottish Apple Pie

- 2 refrigerated pie crusts (one 15 oz. pkg.), room temperature
- 1½ lb. Granny Smith apples, peeled, cored, cut into ⅓ inch cubes
- 9 Tbsp. sugar, divided
- ½ c. gingersnap cookie crumbs
- ⅓ c. orange marmalade
- ⅓ c. golden raisins
- 1 tsp. grated orange peel
- 1 Tbsp. whipping cream

Preheat oven to 375°. Line 9 inch diameter glass pie dish with 1 pie crust. Mix apples, 8 tablespoons sugar, cookie crumbs, marmalade, raisins, and orange peel in large bowl. Spoon filling into crust-lined dish. Top with remaining crust. Press crust edges together to seal; crimp edge decoratively. Cut 1 inch hole in center. Blend cream and 1 tablespoon sugar in small bowl; brush over crust. Bake pie until crust is golden and filling bubbles thickly, about 45 minutes. Serve warm. Serves 8.

Kristen Skivington
Genesee County, MI Chapter

Key Lime Pie (No Bake) With Oreo Cookie Topping

- 8 oz. Philadelphia cream cheese, softened
- 1 (14 oz.) can sweetened condensed milk
- 4 oz. key lime juice (use only key lime juice)
- 1 ready-made pie crust (chocolate is great)
- 1 pkg. mini Oreo cookies

Mix cream cheese, milk, and juice in food processor until well blended. Pour into pie crust. Decorate top with mini Oreo cookies, or cookies can be crushed and crumbs sprinkled on pie. Instead of Oreo cookies, top with whipped cream. Chill until set. Recipe was given to me by a patient at Homestead Air Force Base 30 years ago! Still a great recipe!

Marlene Wolf, M.D.
Fort Lauderdale Area, FL Chapter

Pineapple Pie

1 (10.5 oz.) can crushed pineapple with juice
1 (16 oz.) container sour cream
1 (3.4 oz.) pkg. instant vanilla pudding
1 graham cracker pie crust
1 (12 oz.) container Cool Whip

Mix pineapple and sour cream. Add in vanilla pudding, stirring until thick. Pour into pie crust. Refrigerate 2 hours. Place Cool Whip on pie and serve.

Nancy Foran-Pinzon
Long Island, NY Chapter

Pumpkin Pie

1 pastry for a 9 inch pie
3 c. fresh or canned pumpkin puree
3/4 c. sugar
1/2 tsp. salt
1/2 tsp. grated nutmeg
1/4 tsp. ground cinnamon
1 tsp. fresh grated ginger root or 1/2 tsp. ground ginger
3 large eggs, lightly beaten
1 c. heavy cream

Preheat oven to 425°. Line a large pie dish with the pastry and build up a fluted edge. Chill. Combine the remaining ingredients in a mixing bowl and blend well. Pour mixture into the prepared shell and place in oven. Bake for 15 minutes. Reduce heat to 350°. Bake for 30 to 40 minutes longer, or until the filling is set. Serve, if desired, with sweetened and/or rum-flavored whipped cream.

Eva Valentine
Southern New Hampshire Chapter

Creamy Pumpkin Pie

1½ c. (15 oz. can) pumpkin puree
3 large eggs
6 oz. granulated sugar
½ tsp. salt
1 tsp. ground cinnamon
½ tsp. ground ginger
¼ tsp. ground cloves
1⅓ c. half and half
1 frozen deep dish pie crust (4 c. volume), thawed and baked

Place pumpkin puree in a bowl and stir in eggs with wire whisk one at a time. Stir all dry ingredients until well incorporated and add puree mixture. Stir until well blended. Stir in half and half (half at a time). Pour into prebaked pie crust shell and bake in a 350° to 375° oven for 30 to 45 minutes or until center does not wiggle when pie is tested. Cool. Top with whipped cream. Great for Thanksgiving!

Marlene Wolf, M.D.
Fort Lauderdale Area, FL Chapter

LBJ's Favorite Pecan Pie

1 unbaked 9 inch pie shell (can be store-bought or homemade)
1 c. white sugar
½ tsp. salt
1 c. dark corn syrup
3 eggs
1½ tsp. vanilla
2 c. broken pecans
½ c. butter, melted

Preheat oven to 325°. Combine sugar, salt, and syrup in a saucepan. Simmer until sugar dissolves; cool slightly. Beat eggs until foamy. Stir vanilla, pecans, butter, and eggs into sugar mixture. Pour into unbaked pie shell. Bake 40 minutes.

Roberta Ward Walsh
Naples, FL Chapter

Chocolate Peppermint Pie

18 to 20 Oreo chocolate cookies
1/3 c. butter or margarine, melted
1/2 gal. peppermint stick ice cream, softened
1/2 c. sugar
2 oz. chocolate, melted
1 (12 oz.) can evaporated milk
Peppermint stick candy, crushed

Crush cookies; mix with melted butter. Place crumb mixture into two 8 inch pie plates. Press on sides and bottom of pie plates and chill thoroughly. Spread half of ice cream in each shell. Cook sugar, melted chocolate, and milk until thick. Cool thoroughly. Spread over ice cream and store in freezer until ready to serve. Before serving, sprinkle with crushed candy. Each pie serves 8.

Mary Knueven
Des Moines, IA Chapter

Impossible Pie

2 c. milk
1 stick butter, room temperature
1/2 c. Bisquick mix
1 tsp. vanilla
1 c. shredded coconut
4 eggs
1 c. sugar
1 tsp. salt

Mix all ingredients thoroughly with mixer. Place in greased 10 inch glass pie dish. Bake at 350° for 45 minutes. Eat!

Lilliam Larson
Polk County, FL Chapter

Italian Ricotta Pie

¾ c. powdered sugar
3 large eggs
2 tsp. pure vanilla extract
1 Tbsp. orange zest
1 (15 oz.) container whole milk Ricotta cheese
½ c. cooked rice
⅓ c. toasted pine nuts
6 sheets thawed phyllo dough
¾ stick unsalted butter, melted

Preheat oven to 375°. Blend powdered sugar, eggs, vanilla, orange zest, and Ricotta in food processor until smooth (can also be done with a hand mixer). Stir in cooked rice and pine nuts. Set aside. Lightly butter 9 inch glass pie dish. Lay 1 phyllo sheet over the bottom and up sides of pan allowing phyllo to hang over the sides. Brush phyllo with melted butter. Top with second sheet, laying it in the opposite direction of the first and brush with butter. Continue layering remaining sheets, alternating after each one and buttering each sheet. Spoon the ricotta mixture into the pan. Fold the overhanging phyllo dough over the top of the filling to enclose it completely. Brush entire top with melted butter. Bake the pie until phyllo is golden brown and filling is set, approximately 35 to 40 minutes. Transfer the pan to a rack and cool completely. Sift powdered sugar over top of pie and serve.

Susan Tajalli
Palm Beach County, FL Chapter

Traditional Southern Chess Pie

1 ready to roll out pie crust (I like Pillsbury's.)
½ c. butter, room temperature
1 c. sugar
½ tsp. vanilla
3 eggs
1 tsp. corn meal
1 tsp. white vinegar

Roll out pie crust. Lightly flour both sides. Place into 9 inch pie dish. Cream butter with sugar and vanilla. Add 2 whole eggs plus yolk of a third egg. Beat well. Add corn meal and vinegar. Mix well and pour into pie crust. Bake at 400° for 15 minutes or until set. Cover edge of crust with foil. Lower heat to 325° and bake for 15 to 20 minutes.

Sara Hume
Palm Beach County, FL Chapter
Former EWGA Executive Director

Miss Peggy's Buttermilk Custard Pie

1 stick butter, softened
1½ c. sugar
3 eggs, separated
4 Tbsp. flour

1 pt. buttermilk
1 tsp. vanilla
1 deep dish unbaked pie shell

Preheat oven to 450°. Cream butter, sugar, and egg yolks well. Add flour and beat. Add buttermilk and vanilla, stir well. Add well-beaten egg whites and stir to mix. Place pie shell in a greased pie pan. Pour mixture on top. Bake at 450° for 10 minutes; then reduce heat to 350° and bake for 25 to 30 minutes longer or until a knife inserted in center comes out clean. Cool on wire rack to set.

This was my mother, Miss Peggy's, signature dessert. When she served it, my sister and I always hoped that when guests were in the house the situation was not "FHB" (family hold back) but that there was "MIK" (more in the kitchen). Enjoy!

Penny Hulbert
Tampa Bay, FL Chapter
Former Association Board President

Summer Fruit Tart

1 c. flour
¼ c. brown sugar
½ c. soft butter
½ c. chopped nuts
3 oz. cream cheese, softened
⅓ c. sugar

1 c. whipping cream
Assorted fresh fruit, sliced
  (strawberries, kiwi, peaches,
  nectarines, berries)
¼ c. melted apple jelly

For the crust, mix together flour, brown sugar, butter, and nuts. Press into the bottom of a 9 inch tart pan with removable bottom. Bake crust for 15 minutes at 375°. Cool. For filling, beat cream cheese until fluffy. Gradually add sugar then beat in whipping cream until soft peaks form. Spread topping onto crust; arrange fruit into concentric circles on top. Brush fruit with melted apple jelly. Refrigerate until serving time. Remove tart bottom from side ring. Place on serving platter and cut into wedges to serve.

Catherine Schiaffo
San Diego, CA Chapter

Butter Tarts

1 egg
1 c. brown sugar
3 Tbsp. butter, melted

Chopped raisins (optional)
12 muffin-size tart shells

Beat egg until thick; add brown sugar and beat well. Add melted butter; beat to combine. Fill unbaked tart shells two thirds full. Mix 1 teaspoon raisins in each. Bake in a hot 425° oven for 8 minutes. Reduce heat to 350° and bake 10 to 15 minutes longer. Makes 12 muffin-size tarts.

Cheryl Needham
Pittsburgh, PA Chapter

Gram's Apple Cake

4 eggs
1 tsp. vanilla
¼ c. orange juice
1 c. vegetable oil
2 c. sugar

3 c. flour
3 tsp. baking powder
5 apples, sliced, peeled or unpeeled, and mixed with cinnamon and sugar to taste

Mix all ingredients except apple mixture. Pour half the batter into a Bundt pan that has been greased or sprayed with PAM. Place apple slices on top of batter. Pour rest of the batter over apples. Bake at 350° for 35 minutes or until cake springs back with fingertip touch. Cool and serve. Add vanilla ice cream for a special touch.

Corinne Grandolfo
Westchester, NY Chapter

Nanny Anne Cone's Banana Cake

1¼ c. sugar
1 stick butter, room temperature
1 tsp. baking soda
4 Tbsp. sour cream

2 bananas, pureed
1½ c. flour
1 tsp. vanilla
¼ tsp. salt

Preheat oven to 350°. Blend all ingredients in a food processor. For muffins, bake about 18 minutes, and for a cake (9x9 inch pan, greased), bake 25 minutes. Check with a cake tester; it should come out clean.

Alice Osur
Northern New Jersey Chapter

Best Carrot Cake Ever

Cake:

1¼ c. salad oil
2 c. sugar
3 large eggs
2 tsp. vanilla
2 c. flour
2 tsp. baking powder
1 tsp. salt
2 tsp. cinnamon
⅛ c. chopped fresh coriander (or ¼ tsp. dried)
2 c. shredded carrots
1 c. crushed pineapple, drained
1 c. coconut
1 c. chopped nuts

Cream together oil, sugar, eggs, and vanilla. Sift together flour, baking powder, salt, cinnamon, and coriander and add to creamed mixture. Add carrots, pineapple, coconut, and nuts. Pour into one 9 x 13 inch or two 8 inch pans and bake at 350° about 30 minutes until toothpick inserted comes out clean.

Cream Cheese Frosting:

½ c. butter, room temperature
8 oz. Philadelphia cream cheese, room temperature
1 tsp. vanilla
2 to 3 c. powdered sugar

With an electric mixer, mix the butter and cream cheese together, about 3 minutes on medium speed until very smooth. Scrape down the sides and bottom of the bowl to ensure even mixing. Add the vanilla extract and mix. Slowly add the powdered sugar. Keep adding until you get to desired sweetness and thickness. Either spread on with a blunt knife or spatula, or spoon into a piping bag to decorate your cake or cupcakes.

Katharine Dyson
Golf and Travel Writer

Mandarin Orange Cake

1 box yellow cake mix (without pudding)
⅓ c. applesauce
2 eggs
1 (11 oz.) can mandarin oranges, undrained
1 (12 oz.) container Cool Whip (lite or fat free)
1 (3.4 oz.) pkg. fat free, sugar free instant vanilla pudding
1 (8 oz.) can crushed pineapple, undrained

Mix cake mix, applesauce, eggs and mandarin oranges thoroughly. Pour into a greased and floured 9x13 inch cake pan. Bake at 350° for 35 minutes or until done.

Mix Cool Whip, pudding and pineapple with a spoon. Spread on top of cooled cake and refrigerate. Cake is light and low calorie.

Kathy Thomas
Kansas City Metro and Tucson-Old Pueblo, AZ Chapters
Nancy Oliver Founder's Award Winner and
Former Association Board Member

Pineapple Delight Dessert

2 env. Knox gelatin
1 c. cold water
1 c. boiling water
¾ c. sugar
1 (20 oz.) can crushed pineapple, drained
1 pt. whipping cream
1 angel food cake, sliced 1 to 2 inches thick

In a large bowl, mix gelatin and cold water; let stand 5 minutes. Stir in boiling water, sugar and pineapple; let mixture stand until partially jelled. Whip cream and fold into gelled mixture. Butter a 9x11 inch cake pan; lay slices of cake to cover bottom. Pour half of the mixture over the cake. Repeat layers of cake and mixture. Refrigerate until served. Serves 12 to 15.

Shareen Howlett
Omaha, NE Chapter

Pumpkin Cake

1 box yellow cake mix
½ c. butter, softened
1 egg
½ tsp. cinnamon
1 (30 oz.) can Libby's pumpkin pie filling (plus ingredients for pumpkin pie listed on can)
1 c. whipping cream, whipped for topping

Mix first four ingredients together using a pastry blender until mixture is crumbly and the consistency of a pie crust. Press ⅔ of the mixture into the bottom of a 9x13 inch baking dish sprayed with Pam. Prepare the Libby's pumpkin, following the recipe on the can for a 9 inch pie. Pour the mixture over the pressed cake mix and then sprinkle the remaining cake mixture over the pie mix. Bake at 350° for 60 to 70 minutes or until the mixture is set in the middle; a toothpick inserted in the center should come out clean. Cut into squares and serve topped with whipping cream. Delicious! Better than pumpkin pie in my estimation.

BJ Hansen
Salt Lake City, UT Chapter

Pumpkin Squares

3 eggs
1 (16 oz.) pkg. Betty Crocker pound cake mix
2 Tbsp. butter or margarine
4 tsp. pumpkin pie spice, divided
1 (8 oz.) pkg. cream cheese
1 (14 oz.) can sweetened condensed milk
1 (15 oz.) can pumpkin pie filling

Mix 1 egg, pound cake mix, butter, and 2 teaspoons pumpkin pie spice until crumbly. Press into the bottom of a 9x11 inch baking dish. Mix 2 eggs, cream cheese, and sweetened condensed milk until combined. Add pumpkin pie filling and 2 teaspoons pumpkin pie spice and mix until smooth. Pour filling into baking pan. Bake at 350° for 35 to 40 minutes. Enjoy!

Jane Broderick, PGA, LPGA
Director of Golf Operations, PGA National Resort & Spa

Momma Smoot's Punkin Roll

Roll:

1 c. sugar
2/3 c. pumpkin
3/4 c. flour
3 eggs

1 tsp. salt
1 tsp. baking soda
1 tsp. cinnamon
1/2 c. chopped walnuts (optional)

Preheat oven to 350°. Mix dry ingredients in a medium size bowl. Add eggs and pumpkin and mix well until batter is smooth. Grease a jelly roll pan with Pam and line with wax paper. Sprinkle sheet with walnuts at this time. Pour batter into pan and bake for 15 minutes or until batter is cooked through. Before removing pan from oven, set a clean dish towel on kitchen table or counter and sprinkle with powdered sugar. Remove pan from oven and flip baked cake onto dish towel. Remove wax paper from baked cake while it is still warm and then roll the baked cake in the towel, beginning with the long side of the towel. Place rolled up cake, in the towel, in the refrigerator to cool for 10 minutes.

Filling:

8 oz. cream cheese
1 tsp. vanilla

1 c. powdered sugar

Combine ingredients for filling and mix well. Remove cooled cake from refrigerator and unroll. Spread filling evenly over cake and then re-roll without the towel. Wrap in aluminum foil and place in freezer for at least 30 minutes before serving. Slice and serve!

Marie Smoot
Greater Toledo, OH Chapter

Desserts

Summer Celebration Cake

1 box white cake mix
1 (3.4 oz.) pkg. strawberry gelatin
2/3 c. sour cream
2/3 c. powdered sugar
1 (8 oz.) container frozen whipped topping, thawed
1½ c. strawberries, sliced

Preheat oven to 350°. Grease two 8 or 9 inch round cake pans. Prepare cake batter as directed on package. Pour half of the batter into medium bowl. Add dry gelatin mix; stir until well blended. Spoon half of the pink batter and half of the white batter, side by side, into each prepared pan. Swirl batters together lightly, by pulling a teaspoon through the two batters. (Do not over swirl or the color of the cake will be all pink and not white and pink marbled.) Bake 30 minutes. Let pans cool 30 minutes. Next, remove cakes and let cool completely. Mix sour cream and powdered sugar in a medium bowl until well blended. Gently stir in whipped topping. With one cake layer on serving plate, spread top with 1 cup of whipped topping mixture. Top that with 1 cup of the strawberries. Place remaining layer of cake on top. Spread top and side of cake with remaining whipped topping mixture. Top with ½ cup strawberries just before serving. Store leftover cake in refrigerator.

Karen McIntosh
Genesee County, MI Chapter

Tropical Fruit Cake

1 (21 oz.) can cherry pie filling
1 box white cake mix
1½ sticks margarine, melted
1 (20 oz.) can crushed pineapple with juice
1½ c. coconut
½ c. chopped pecans

Pour pie filling into 13x9 inch ungreased baking sheet pan. Sprinkle ½ of cake mix over the pie filling, drizzle with melted margarine. Spread pineapple over mixture and cover with remaining cake mix. Cover with coconut and drizzle with remaining margarine. Sprinkle nuts on top. Bake 40 minutes at 350°.

Linda Keaton
Huntsville, AL Chapter

Pound Cake

3 sticks butter or margarine, softened
3 c. sugar
5 eggs
3⅓ c. cake flour
½ tsp. salt
½ tsp. baking powder
1 c. milk
2 tsp. vanilla or lemon extract

Cream butter or margarine and sugar. Add eggs one at a time until creamy. Mix flour, salt and baking powder in a separate bowl. Add flour mixture and milk to butter and eggs (approximately ⅓ at a time). Add lemon or vanilla and mix well. Bake in greased Bundt or tube pan 1½ hours at 300°.

Linda Keaton
Huntsville, AL Chapter

Double Chocolate Chip Pound Cake

1 box yellow cake mix
1 (5.9 ounce) box instant chocolate pudding mix
½ c. sugar
⅔ c. water
½ c. vegetable oil
4 large eggs
1 (8 oz.) container sour cream
1 (12 oz.) bag mini chocolate morsels
Confectioners sugar

Preheat oven to 350°. Grease and flour 10 cup Bundt pan. Combine cake mix, pudding mix, and sugar. Add water, oil, and eggs. Beat with electric mixer at medium speed until smooth. Stir in sour cream and morsels. Pour batter into pan and bake for 1 hour. Let cool in pan 10 minutes. Remove from pan and allow cake to cool completely. Sprinkle with powdered sugar and enjoy!

Carolyn Schmidt
Polk County, FL Chapter

Chocolate Angel Food Cake

3/4 c. sifted flour
3/4 c. plus 2 Tbsp. sugar
1/4 c. cocoa
1 1/2 tsp. vanilla
1 1/2 c. egg whites (about 12 eggs)
1 1/2 tsp. cream of tartar
1/4 tsp. salt
3/4 c. sugar
Favorite frosting or Cool Whip (optional)

Sift flour, sugar (3/4 cup plus 2 tablespoons), and cocoa three times and set aside. Separately, put vanilla, egg whites, cream of tartar and salt in a bowl. Gradually add sugar (3/4 cup) to egg whites and beat until stiff peaks. Then gradually fold in sifted flour-sugar-cocoa mixture. Pour into angel food pan. Bake at 375° for 30 to 35 minutes. If desired, can ice with favorite frosting or top with Cool Whip.

Kathy Thomas
Kansas City Metro and Tucson-Old Pueblo, AZ Chapters
Nancy Oliver Founder's Award Winner and
Former Association Board Member

Black Bottom Cupcakes

8 oz. cream cheese, room temperature
1 egg
1 1/3 c. sugar, divided
1/8 tsp. salt
1 c. chocolate bits
1 1/2 c. flour
2 (1 oz.) squares chocolate, melted
1 tsp. baking soda
1/2 tsp. salt
1 c. water
1/3 c. oil
1 Tbsp. vinegar
1/8 tsp. vanilla

Mix cream cheese, egg, 1/3 cup sugar, and 1/8 teaspoon salt. Beat well and stir in chocolate bits; set aside. In another bowl, mix flour, 1 cup sugar, melted chocolate, baking soda, and 1/2 teaspoon salt. Make a well in the mixture and add in water, oil, vinegar, and vanilla. Beat well. Fill mini paper cups (2 inch) 1/2 full and top with cream cheese mixture (1 teaspoon). Bake at 350° for 20 to 25 minutes. Makes 36 plus cupcakes.

Lisa Lifer
Northern New Jersey Chapter
Association Board President and Foundation Board Member

Desserts

Better Than Sex Cake

1 box Duncan Hines yellow cake mix
½ c. Crisco oil
½ c. water
1 (3.4 oz.) pkg. instant vanilla pudding mix
4 eggs
1 c. sour cream
6 oz. sweetened chocolate, grated
8 oz. chocolate chips
1 c. chopped pecans
1 c. shredded coconut (optional)

Stir together cake mix, oil, water, and pudding mix. Add eggs one at a time, stirring after each one. Add sour cream, grated chocolate, chocolate chips, pecans, and coconut. Mix thoroughly. Bake in greased Bundt pan or tube pan at 350° for 55 minutes. Frost with your favorite cream cheese icing. This is a very "Southern" recipe. It can vary from place to place. This one is from Monroe, LA and Atlanta, GA.

Judith R. Shepp
Orlando, FL Chapter

"Study the rules so that you won't beat yourself by not knowing something."

-Babe Didrikson Zaharias

Desserts

The Birdie Cake

Cake:

1 box white cake mix
1 (3.4 oz.) pkg. vanilla instant pudding mix
1⅓ c. water
4 eggs
¼ c. oil
1⅓ c. angel flake coconut
1½ c. chopped nuts

Preheat oven to 325°. Combine cake mix, pudding mix, water, eggs, and oil. Blend until mixed, then beat on medium speed 4 minutes. Stir in coconut and nuts and pour into greased and floured 10 inch tube pan. Bake 1 hour. Cool in pan 15 minutes. Remove and cool completely on wire rack.

Frosting:

2 (3 oz.) pkgs. cream cheese, softened
⅓ c. butter, softened
1 (16 oz.) pkg. powdered sugar
4 tsp. milk
½ tsp. vanilla extract
2 c. flaked coconut

Beat cream cheese and butter until well blended. Add powdered sugar alternately with milk, blending well after each addition. Add vanilla. Spread frosting over top and sides of cake. Sprinkle coconut over frosting.

Judy Lacko
Charlotte, NC Chapter

Twinkie Cake

1 box yellow cake mix (plus added ingredients listed on pkg.)
5 Tbsp. flour
1 c. milk
1 c. sugar
½ c. Crisco
½ c. margarine
½ tsp. salt
½ tsp. vanilla

Prepare and bake cake in a 9x13 inch pan lined with waxed paper according to instructions. Turn out cake and let cool. Mix and cook flour and milk over moderate heat until thick. Set aside and let cool. Beat sugar, Crisco, margarine, salt, and vanilla until fluffy. When fluffy, add the cooled flour and milk mixture; beat all together until light and fluffy. Cut cooled cake horizontally through the center, making two cakes. Spread desired amount of cream mixture on one layer; place the second layer on top. Recipe makes a lot of filling, so you can also frost cake if desired. Store in Tupperware container and keep cool. A family favorite!

Darlene 'Babe' Lamb
Kansas City Metro Chapter

"It's great to win, but it's also great fun to be in the thick of any truly well and hard fought contest against opponents you respect, whatever the outcome."

-Jack Nicklaus

Tres Leches Cake (Three Milk Cake)

Cake:

1½ c. all purpose flour
2 tsp. baking powder
4 eggs, separated

1½ c. sugar
½ c. milk

Preheat oven to 350°. Grease and flour a 9x13 inch baking pan. Sift flour with baking powder. In large bowl with clean electric beaters, beat egg whites until fluffy. Add sugar gradually, beating to form stiff peaks. Add yolks one at a time. Fold in flour mixture and milk; mix well but do not beat. Pour batter into prepared pan and bake until edges are golden brown about 30 to 35 minutes. Remove from oven; let pan cool on a rack.

Three Milk Mixture:

1 (12 oz.) can evaporated milk (can use low fat version)
1 (14 oz.) can sweetened condensed milk (can use low fat version)

1 c. sour cream (can use fat-free)
1 c. milk (can use fat-free)

Combine milks and sour cream (do not beat). Use a toothpick to punch small holes all around the top of the prepared cake to help absorb the three milk mixture. Pour mixture over cooled cake and let sit until all mixture is absorbed, about 30 minutes. Best if refrigerated overnight.

Whipped Cream Topping:

2 c. whipping cream
1 Tbsp. sugar

1 tsp. vanilla or almond extract

Chill the cream and bowl (to be really precise, also chill the beaters). Beat the cream with electric mixer until it begins to thicken. Gradually add sugar and vanilla and beat until stiff peaks form. Using a spatula, cover top and sides of cake with whipped cream.

Alicia Jansen
Houston, TX Chapter
Nancy Oliver Founder's Award Winner and
Former Association Board President

Desserts

Harvey Wallbanger Cake

Cake:

1 box orange/lemon cake mix (or plain as a last resort)	4 eggs
	½ c. cooking oil
1 (3.4 oz.) pkg. vanilla instant pudding (still add even if cake mix already has pudding in it)	¾ c. orange juice
	2 oz. vodka
	2 oz. Galliano

Mix all ingredients. Bake in a greased tube (Bundt) pan at 350° for 45 to 50 minutes.

Frosting:

1 c. confectioners sugar	1 Tbsp. vodka
1 Tbsp. orange juice	1 Tbsp. Galliano

Mix ingredients thoroughly and drizzle over cake while still warm.

Nancy Foran-Pinzon
Long Island, NY Chapter

"The more you practice, the better. But in any case, practice more than you play."

-Babe Didrikson Zaharias

Welsh Cakes

2 c. all purpose flour
1/3 c. granulated white sugar
2 1/4 tsp. baking powder
1/4 tsp. salt
1/4 tsp. ground cinnamon

1/4 tsp. ground mace
1/2 c. unsalted butter, cold
1/3 c. currants or raisins
1 large egg (lightly beaten)
2 to 4 Tbsp. milk

In a large bowl, whisk together the flour, sugar, baking powder, salt, ground cinnamon, and mace. Cut the butter into small pieces and blend into the flour mixture with a pastry blender or two knives. The mixture should look like coarse crumbs. Stir in the currants. Add the beaten egg and enough milk to form a light dough. Knead the dough gently on a lightly floured surface and roll to a thickness of 1/4 inch (5 mm). Cut into rounds using a 2 1/2 inch (6 cm) cookie cutter. Traditional Cooking Method: Lightly butter a bake stone (griddle, heavy frying pan, or electric frying pan) and heat to medium hot. Cook the Welsh cakes for about 5 minutes per side, or until they are golden brown, but still soft in the middle. Alternate Baking Method: Welsh Cakes can also be baked in a 350° F (177° C) oven. Place on a parchment paper lined baking sheet and bake for about 7 to 9 minutes on each side or until set and very lightly browned yet still soft inside (they will not get as brown as when you cook them on a griddle). Immediately after baking, sprinkle with additional granulated white sugar (optional). Serve warm or at room temperature. Welsh cakes can also be eaten buttered or split in half and spread with jam. Makes about 20, 2 1/2 inch cakes.

Robin Aurelius
Palm Beach County, FL Chapter
EWGA Systems Manager

Ginger Molasses Cookies

2¼ c. all-purpose flour
2 tsp. baking soda
½ tsp. salt
1 tsp. ground cinnamon
1 tsp. ground ginger
¾ c. unsalted butter, softened

1 c. dark brown sugar
1 egg
¼ c. unsulphured molasses
   (Grandma's brand works well)
Turbinado sugar (for coating
   cookies before baking)

Preheat oven to 350°. Line baking sheets with parchment paper or Silpats. Combine flour, baking soda, salt, cinnamon, and ginger in a medium bowl. Cream the butter and brown sugar in a large mixing bowl with mixer on high speed until light and fluffy, about a minute. With mixer on medium speed, beat in the egg and molasses, increase to high speed and beat 1 minute longer, until mixture no longer looks curdled. Mix in the flour mixture on low speed. The cookie dough will be stiff. Place Turbinado sugar on a small plate. Use a small or medium ice cream scoop to form cookie dough portions. Roll each portion into a ball, then roll each ball in the Turbinado sugar. Place sugared balls on baking sheet evenly. They will spread during baking. Dampen fingers with water and press down lightly on each cookie to flatten a little. Bake for 12 minutes or until cookies have spread and are slightly firm to the touch. Remove from oven and let cool on baking sheet. Makes 24 to 30 cookies.

Shelia Sampolesi
Seattle, WA Chapter
Former Association Board Member

Desserts

Whoopie Pies

Cake:

2 c. unsifted flour
1 tsp. baking soda
¼ tsp. salt
⅓ c. cocoa
1 c. sugar

1 egg
⅓ c. Crisco oil
1 tsp. vanilla
¾ c. milk

Mix together flour, baking soda, salt, cocoa, and sugar. Add remaining ingredients. Beat all together. Drop by tablespoon on a greased cookie sheet, leave room between dough for spreading. Bake at 350° for 12 minutes.

Filling:

1 stick margarine
1 c. powdered sugar
1 heaping tablespoon marshmallow fluff (may need more)

1 tsp. vanilla

Mix all ingredients and put cooled cakes together with filling in between.

Pam Swensen
Palm Beach County, FL Chapter
EWGA Chief Executive Officer

Ice Cream Cookies

6 Tbsp. butter, softened
6 Tbsp. confectioners sugar
1 egg yolk

1 tsp. vanilla extract
1 c. sifted flour

Using a hand mixer, cream butter and sugar together thoroughly. Add egg yolk and vanilla and beat well. Next, add flour and beat well. Drop by teaspoon onto ungreased cookie sheet (can shape into 24 small cookie balls). Press each cookie gently with a fork. Bake at 350° for 15 to 20 minutes. After baking and cooling, can decorate with icing, sparkling sugar, etc. The cookies taste like ice cream, hence the name!

Marilyn E. Gambill
Cincinnati, OH Chapter

Fig Newtons

Filling:

1 lb. dried figs (or 2 pounds fresh figs)
1 c. sugar
½ or 1 c. water (½ c. if using dried figs, 1 c. if using fresh figs)

Dice figs, soak in water 1 hour. Add sugar and cook on medium heat until thin jam consistency.

Pastry:

1 c. sugar
½ c. butter, room temperature
1 egg
1 Tbsp. cream or milk
½ tsp. vanilla
½ tsp. salt
1 tsp. baking powder
1¾ c. flour

Beat sugar, butter, egg, milk, and vanilla until well blended. Add dry ingredients and mix well; refrigerate for 1 hour. Place ½ dough on well floured dough cloth and knead about 6 times. Roll out to ¼ inch thick. Line 9x13 inch glass dish with dough. Cover dough with figs. Roll remaining dough, cover figs, and cut off any excess dough. Cook at 350° for 30 minutes. Let cool and cut into squares.

Jeanne Hoffman
Stockton/San Joaquin, CA Chapter

Chocolate Graham Crackers

12 graham crackers (your choice)
1½ sticks unsalted butter, cold and cut into pieces
½ c. light brown sugar, packed
⅛ tsp. salt
1½ c. semisweet chocolate chips
1 c. walnuts, pecans or almonds, chopped

Preheat oven to 375°. Line a 15x10x1 inch baking pan with foil, leaving a 2 inch overhang at each end. Line bottom of pan with graham crackers (it will be a tight fit). Melt butter in a 1½ to 2 quart heavy saucepan over moderately low heat, then add brown sugar and salt and cook, whisking, until mixture is smooth and combined well, about 1 minute. Pour over crackers, spreading evenly, and bake in middle of oven until golden brown and bubbling, about 10 minutes. May vary with oven temperature, remove once it bubbles. Scatter chocolate chips evenly over crackers and bake in oven until chocolate is soft, about 1 minute. Remove pan from oven and gently spread chocolate evenly over crackers with offset spatula. Sprinkle nuts evenly over chocolate and cool crackers in pan on a rack 30 minutes. Freeze until chocolate is firm, 10 to 15 minutes. Carefully lift crackers from pan by grasping both ends of foil, then peel foil from crackers. Break crackers into serving pieces. Best kept in freezer in an airtight container for up to 2 weeks.

Chin Oh
Kalamazoo/Battle Creek, MI Chapter

Graham Cracker Holiday Cookies

1 (14 oz.) can sweetened condensed milk
1½ c. finely crushed graham crackers
1⅓ c. flaked coconut
½ c. semisweet chocolate chips

Preheat oven to 350°. Mix all ingredients. Grease and flour an 8x8 inch baking pan. Spread batter evenly into prepared pan. Bake for 30 minutes. Cool for 10 minutes. Remove from pan. Allow to cool thoroughly and then cut into squares.

Cindy McGeever
Greater Philadelphia, PA Chapter
Nancy Oliver Founder's Award Winner and Former Association Board President

Pecan Shortbread Cookies

3 sticks unsalted butter, room temperature
1 c. sugar
1 tsp. pure almond extract
1 tsp. pure vanilla extract
3½ c. flour
¼ tsp. salt
1½ c. small diced pecans

Combine butter and sugar, add vanilla and almond extracts. Sift together flour and salt and add to butter mixture. Add pecans and mix on low. Dump onto a floured surface and form into a flat disk. Wrap in plastic wrap and chill 30 minutes. Roll out to ½ inch thick and cut with plain or fluted cookie cutter. Place on parchment lined cookie sheet. Bake at 350° for 19 minutes until edges begin to brown.

Barbara McLaughlin
Naples, FL Chapter

Best Ever Biscotti

¼ c. light olive oil
¾ c. white sugar
2 tsp. vanilla extract
¼ tsp. almond extract
2 eggs
2 c. all purpose flour
¼ tsp. salt
1 tsp. baking powder
½ c. dried cranberries
1 c. pistachio nuts

Preheat oven to 300°. In large bowl, mix oil and sugar until well blended. Mix in vanilla extract, almond extract, and beat in eggs. In another bowl, combine flour, salt, and baking powder; stir flour mixture into egg mixture. Mix in cranberries and nuts. Divide dough in half. Wet hands and form two logs (12x2 inch) on cookie sheet sprayed with cooking spray. Dough will be sticky; keep hands wet. Bake for 45 minutes in preheated oven. Remove from oven and cool 10 minutes. Use sharp knife to cut logs on diagonal into ¾ inch thick slices. Cool completely and store in airtight container.

Nancy Lobby, D.O.
Palm Beach County, FL Chapter

Biscotti

6 eggs
1 c. canola oil
1 Tbsp. vanilla, almond, or anise extract
2 tsp. baking powder
Pinch of salt

4½ to 5 c. flour
1 c. sugar
1 c. chopped walnuts, almonds, or pecans
1 c. chocolate chips (optional)

Beat together with a mixer the eggs, oil, and sugar. Add the vanilla. Mix the baking powder, salt, and 4½ cups of flour together and gradually add to the egg mixture. Add in the nuts and chocolate chips, and add more flour if necessary. Consistency should be a little sticky but manageable. Put on a floured board or towel and work until it is one smooth ball (just a few minutes). Add flour to the board if necessary. Cut into four equal parts and form into logs about 2x12 inches. Place on a lightly greased cookie sheet. Sprinkle with a cinnamon-sugar mixture if desired. Bake for 35 minutes at 350°. Cool cookie logs on cookie sheet for 10 minutes, then cut on a diagonal about 1 inch wide. Put biscotti back on the cookie sheet on their sides so they can brown. Put back into a 375° oven for 10 minutes. Cool and enjoy. You can also drizzle melted chocolate on them (adds a few calories).

Barbara McLaughlin
Naples, FL Chapter

Four Star Fudge Bars

¾ c. margarine
2 c. brown sugar
2 eggs
2 tsp. vanilla
3 c. uncooked oatmeal
2½ c. Bisquick

12 oz. chocolate chips
1 c. sweetened condensed milk
½ tsp. salt
1 c. chopped nuts
2 tsp. vanilla (yes, twice)

Mix together margarine, brown sugar, eggs, 2 teaspoons vanilla, oatmeal, and Bisquick. Press ⅔ of the mixture on the bottom of a 9x13 inch pan. Smooth with a knife. Combine chocolate chips, condensed milk, salt, and nuts over low heat, stirring until the chocolate chips are melted. Stir in 2 teaspoons vanilla. Spread the chocolate mixture in the pan over the oatmeal mixture. Drop the remaining dough in small pieces on top of the chocolate mixture. Bake at 350° for 30 minutes. Let cool.

Sandy Cross
Palm Beach County, FL Chapter
Association and Foundation Board Member

Special K Bars

1 c. sugar
1 c. white Karo syrup
1 c. peanut butter
½ tsp. vanilla extract
6 c. Special K cereal

1 (12 oz.) pkg. semi-sweet chocolate chips
½ (12 oz.) pkg. butterscotch chips

Mix sugar, syrup, and peanut butter over low heat. Add vanilla extract to mixture. Add Special K cereal and press into greased 9x13 inch pan until flat. Cool. For the topping, melt chocolate chips and butterscotch chips in microwave or double boiler and spread over bars.

Le Ann Finger, PGA, LPGA
Palm Beach County, FL Chapter
National Promotions Specialist, PGA of America

Aunt Edna's Bars

Graham crackers, approx. 9
1 c. butter
1 c. brown sugar
1 c. sugar
1 c. chopped almonds
8 Hershey chocolate bars

Line 11x15 inch cookie sheet with foil, butter foil lightly or spray with Pam. Arrange graham crackers to cover bottom of cookie sheet. Boil butter and brown sugar together for 2 minutes. Pour boiled mixture over graham cracker layer; spread to cover. Sprinkle with chopped almonds. Bake for 7 minutes at 400°. Remove from oven, and while hot, lay Hershey bars on top. When melted, spread to cover. Cool and cut into single serving pieces.

Patty Evans
Northern Nevada Chapter

Gooey Butter Bars

1 box yellow cake mix
3 eggs
1 stick butter, room temperature
8 oz. cream cheese, room temperature
1 lb. powdered sugar

Mix cake mix, 1 egg, and butter until moist. Press in a 9x13 inch pan. Mix cream cheese and remaining two eggs thoroughly, and add powdered sugar slowly. Mix for 1 minute after all the sugar is added. Pour on top of cake mixture. Bake at 350° for 30 to 40 minutes until golden brown. Let stand 30 to 40 minutes. Refrigerate at least 4 hours before serving.

Darlene 'Babe' Lamb
Kansas City Metro Chapter

Desserts

Blueberry Swirl Cheesecake Bars

1 c. graham cracker crumbs
1 c. plus 3 Tbsp. sugar, divided
3 Tbsp. margarine or butter, melted
4 (8 oz.) pkgs. cream cheese, softened
1 tsp. vanilla
1 c. sour cream
4 eggs
2 c. fresh or thawed frozen blueberries

Preheat oven to 325°. Mix crumbs, 3 tablespoons sugar and butter. Press firmly onto bottom of foil lined 9x13 inch baking pan. Bake 10 minutes. Meanwhile, beat cream cheese, remaining 1 cup sugar and vanilla in large bowl with mixer on medium speed until well blended. Add sour cream; mix well. Add eggs, one at a time, beating on low speed after adding each egg, just until blended. Pour over crust. Puree the blueberries in a blender or processor. Gently drop spoonfuls of the blueberry puree over batter; cut through batter several times with knife for marbled effect. Bake for 45 minutes or until center is almost set; cool. Cover and refrigerate for at least 4 hours before serving. Makes 16 servings.

Karen McIntosh
Genesee County MI, Chapter

No-Bake Blueberry Cheesecake Bars

16 graham cracker squares (or 8 whole crackers), crushed
¼ c. ground pecans or walnuts (optional)
3 Tbsp. butter, melted
1 (8 oz.) pkg. cream cheese, room temperature
1 c. Ricotta cheese
2 Tbsp. honey (or to taste)
Rind of lemon, freshly grated
Pinch of salt
About 1½ c. blueberries

Combine crushed graham crackers, nuts (if using), and melted butter. Press evenly into the bottom of an 8 or 9 inch square pan (glass is good) to form a crust about ¼ inch thick. Put in refrigerator until ready to use. Using a standing or hand mixer, or a whisk, combine cream cheese, Ricotta, honey, lemon rind, and salt. Blend until smooth. Spread cream cheese mixture evenly over crust, using a spatula or butter knife to smooth top. Cover with fresh blueberries and chill for at least an hour, or until set. Cut into squares or bars and serve. Makes 8 to 12 servings. Recipe attributed to Evan Sung, The New York Times.

Betsy Clark, LPGA
President, dbc Consulting

Carrot Bars

2 eggs, beaten
1 c. sugar
1 tsp. cinnamon
½ tsp. salt
1 tsp. baking soda
¾ c. vegetable oil
1 c. flour

1 (8 oz.) jar carrot baby food
1¾ c. powdered sugar
¼ c. butter, room temperature
3 to 4 oz. cream cheese, softened
¼ tsp. vanilla
1 c. chopped pecans

Mix beaten eggs, sugar, cinnamon, salt, baking soda, oil, flour, and baby food. Pour mixture into a 9x13 inch greased pan and bake at 350° for 15 to 20 minutes. Cool. While carrot bars are cooling, beat powdered sugar, butter, cream cheese, and vanilla until creamy. Spread over cooled bars and topped with chopped pecans.

Mary Knueven
Des Moines, IA Chapter

Fat Free Zucchini Brownies

½ c. applesauce
1½ c. white sugar
2 tsp. vanilla extract
2 c. flour
½ c. unsweetened cocoa

1½ tsp. baking soda
1 tsp. salt
2 c. shredded zucchini
½ c. chopped walnuts (optional)

Preheat oven to 350°. Spray 9x13 inch pan with non-stick spray. In large bowl mix applesauce, sugar and vanilla until well blended. In another bowl combine flour, cocoa, baking soda and salt. Stir dry ingredients into wet ingredients. Fold in zucchini and, if desired, nuts. Batter will appear dry but will moisten. Spread into prepared pan. Bake 25 to 30 minutes until tester comes out dry. You may sprinkle with powdered sugar before serving.

Karen McIntosh
Genesee County, MI Chapter

Juanita's Brownies

½ c. melted butter
1 c. sugar
2 eggs
1 tsp. vanilla
1 c. flour
2 Tbsp. cocoa

½ c. chopped nuts
¼ c. melted butter
2 Tbsp. cocoa
½ tsp. vanilla
2 c. powdered sugar
¼ c. milk

Stir together melted butter and sugar; blend in eggs one at a time. Add vanilla. In a separate bowl, stir together flour, cocoa, and nuts. Add flour mix to butter mixture and mix well. Spread in greased 8x8 inch pan. Bake at 350° for 30 minutes. Be careful not to overbake. Cool.

Frosting: Cream together ¼ cup melted butter, 2 tablespoons cocoa, and ½ teaspoon vanilla. Slowly beat in powdered sugar; add enough milk to make spreading consistency. Spread over cooled brownies and cut into squares.

Danita Bounds
Kansas City Metro Chapter
EWGA Women Who Lead Award Winner

Peanut Butter-Toffee Cheesecake Brownies

1 pkg. Pillsbury chocolate fudge brownie mix
½ c. Crisco pure vegetable oil
¼ c. water
8 oz. cream cheese, softened
2 eggs
1 (14 oz.) can sweetened condensed milk
½ c. creamy peanut butter
8 oz. Heath milk chocolate toffee bits
1 c. Hershey's milk chocolate baking chips
3 Tbsp. whipping cream

Preheat oven to 350°. Lightly spray 9x13 inch pan with non-stick cooking spray. In medium bowl, stir brownie mix, oil, water and eggs; 50 strokes with spoon. Spread batter in pan; set aside. In large bowl, beat cream cheese with electric mixer on medium speed until fluffy. Add milk and peanut butter; beat until smooth. Stir in 1 cup of the toffee bits. Spoon mixture over batter; spread evenly. Bake 30 to 40 minutes or until cheesecake layer is set and edges are light golden brown. Cool on cooling rack 30 minutes. Refrigerate 40 minutes. In small microwaveable bowl, microwave chocolate chips and cream uncovered on high 40 to 60 seconds or until chips are melted; stir until smooth. Spread over cheesecake layer. Sprinkle with remaining toffee bits. Cool completely, about 1 hour. Cut into 6 rows by 6 rows. Store covered in refrigerator. Makes 36 brownies.

Joyce Vanatter
Manatee, FL Chapter
EWGA Recruiter of the Year Award Winner

Microwave Caramels

½ c. butter
2¼ c. brown sugar (best if you use a name brand like C&H)
1 (12 oz.) can sweetened condensed milk
1 c. white Karo syrup
1 tsp. vanilla

Melt butter and add brown sugar. Gradually add milk and syrup to butter and sugar mix; place in a microwaveable bowl. Cook on high 18 to 19 minutes. Stir every 2 minutes. Looks like bubbling lava when done. Add vanilla at end of cooking. Pour into buttered 9x13 inch pan; cool, cut, and wrap with wax paper squares.

Darlene 'Babe' Lamb
Kansas City Metro Chapter

Peanut Butter Buckeyes

1½ c. creamy peanut butter
6 c. confectioners sugar
1 c. (2 sticks) butter, softened
½ tsp. vanilla extract
4 c. semisweet chocolate chips

Line a cookie sheet with waxed paper; set it aside. Using a wooden spoon, mix together the peanut butter, sugar, butter, and vanilla extract in a large bowl (the dough will look dry; add more confectioners sugar if batter is too liquid). Roll the dough into 1 inch balls. Set them on the prepared cookie sheet and insert a toothpick into each ball. Chill them in the freezer until hard, about 30 minutes. Melt the chocolate chips in a heatproof bowl set atop a pot of simmering water over medium-high heat (double boiler). Stir continuously until smooth. Remove the pan from the heat. Using the toothpick as a handle, dip the balls into the melted chocolate, leaving a small circle at the top uncovered. Place the dipped candies back on the cookie sheet and refrigerate until the chocolate is set, about 2 hours. Store in an airtight container in the refrigerator. Kids will have a ball making these rich treats. Although the centers are traditionally creamy, you can add graham crackers to the mix if you prefer crunchy.

Stephanie Jennings, PGA
Palm Beach County, FL Chapter
EWGA Director of Golf Programs

Butterscotch Haystacks

2 (10 oz.) pkgs. butterscotch chips
1 c. peanut butter
6 oz. chow mien noodles
1 c. mini-marshmallows

Melt chips in a big pot over medium heat, stirring constantly. Stir in peanut butter. Remove from heat. Stir in chow mien noodles and marshmallows. Spoon onto waxed paper. Let cool. Makes about 4 or 5 dozen (depends on size).

Judy Hillhouse
Charlotte, NC Chapter

"It's not enough just to swing at the ball. You've got to loosen your girdle and let 'er fly."

-Babe Didrikson Zaharias

Notes

Golf Games for Fun & Profit

Games for the Course

Golf Etiquette Guidelines
Published by the USGA

On the Tee
- Always be on time and prepared to play.
- Choose a tee that best matches your ability.
- Avoid taking divots with practice swings.
- Remain silent as other players hit their shots.
- Always be aware of your safety and the safety of others – wait until the group ahead is out of range, be sure you are well away from others before taking practice swings, and stand on the same side as the ball when watching someone hit.

Through the Green
- Replace your divots or fill with soil/seed mixture.
- Smooth footprints and displaced sand after playing from bunkers.
- Avoid taking divots with practice swings.
- Follow the daily rules for golf cart regulations and access.
- Estimate yardage and select several golf clubs before walking to your ball.
- Shout a warning if your ball may hit someone.

Greens
- Keep golf carts at least 30 yards away and parked in direction of next hole.
- Learn how to repair a ball mark. When time allows, repair other players' marks.
- Keep golf bags off the putting surface.
- Remove golf balls from the hole with your hand, not the head of a putter.
- Stay off other player's line of putt.
- Be careful not to damage the hole when removing or placing a flagstick.
- Avoid dropping clubs on the putting green or leaning on your putter.

Avoid Slow Play
- Play ready golf, especially on the putting greens.
- Walk to your own ball unless another player needs help in locating their ball.
- Limit or eliminate practice swings.
- Play a provisional ball when it is likely yours is lost.
- Park golf carts and bags in direction of next hole.
- Know yardage for the course and plan the next shot before you arrive at the ball.
- Keep a brisk pace. Do not allow your group to fall more than a hole behind the players in front of you. Know the course's pace rating for total expected playing time.
- Have players pick up their ball on any hole for which they have exceeded their stroke allowance, except when playing tournaments.
- Record scores on the next tee while others are playing or after you have played your tee shot.

Ball Mark Tips
- Repair a ball mark by inserting a repair tool or tee at the edges of the ball mark and bring the edges to the center. Do not lift the center of the ball mark. Try not to tear the grass.
- A repaired ball mark will heal in two to three days whereas an unrepaired ball mark will take three weeks to heal.

Games For The Course

30 & In

30 & In is a great challenge for improving your short game and raising money for your favorite charity. Here is how it works.........when you are 30 yards or closer to the flag, your goal is to get the ball in the hole in 2 strokes or less; either with a chip in or a chip and a putt. If it takes you more than 2 strokes, you owe your charity kitty a quarter. Depending how your kitty grows, you choose when to make a donation to your favorite charity and start your kitty over. Good Luck!

Individual Game
EWGA Cookbook Committee

Bag Raid

Bag Raid is a match play game between two players. Every time a player wins a hole, her opponent gets to choose one club from her bag and remove that club from play. For example, after player 1 wins the first hole, player 2 removes player 1's pitching wedge from play. For the rest of the round, player 1 cannot use that pitching wedge. Immunity is normally given to the putter.

Two Player Game
Genesee County, MI Chapter

One Putt Challenge

One Putt Challenge is an individual putting game which requires players to focus on their putting. Prior to playing the first hole, each player antes $1.00 into the Putt Pot. For each green a player 3-putts on the putting surface, they add a quarter to the Putt Pot. The last player to 1-putt a green during the 18 holes where all other players have 2 or more putts wins the Putt Pot. This could be a hole early in the game or on the 18th hole. However, if a player chips-in on any hole, they automatically win the Putt Pot. At that point, the group may choose to start another Putt Pot.

Two to Four Player Game
EWGA Cookbook Committee

Accuracy Challenge

Accuracy Challenge is an individual stroke play game where a penalty awaits the wild hitters and a reward awaits those who are accurate. On each hole, a player records their score plus adds the following penalty strokes: 1 penalty stroke for each shot made from the rough, 1 penalty stroke for each shot made from a bunker, and 1 penalty stroke for each putt made after two putts on the putting green.

It is easiest if you keep two lines per player on the score card, one line for the players score on the hole and one line for the number of penalty strokes on the hole. After all 18 holes are played, you add the players score and their penalty strokes together and subtract their full handicap. The player with the lowest score wins the challenge and of course, any wager the group agreed to prior to playing the first hole.

Four Player Game
EWGA Cookbook Committee

Bingo-Bango-Bongo

Bingo-Bango-Bongo is an individual stroke play game where there are three points possible on each hole. One point to the golfer whose ball first comes to rest on the putting surface (Bingo), a second point to the golfer whose ball is nearest the cup after all players are on the putting surface (Bango), and the third point goes to the golfer who first sinks their putt (Bongo). On short holes, where it is possible to reach the putting surface from the tee, no point is awarded for the first golfer on the putting surface, since the player with the teeing honor has too great an edge. Instead, this point goes to the golfer whose ball is second nearest to the flag after all balls are on the putting surface. The player who is furthest away always plays first. This is critical for the Bongo point.

In settling up, each golfer wins the difference between her total points and the total points of each golfer with fewer points. The group must determine the wager prior to playing the first hole.

Four Player Game
EWGA Cookbook Committee

Fairways And Putts

Fairways and Putts is an individual stroke play game where a player receives five points for their ball coming to rest in the fairway or on the green off the tee and loses points for their number of putts on the putting surface. For example, if player #1's ball comes to rest on the fairway off the tee (5 points awarded) and then they take 3 putts on the putting surface to hole the ball (3 points deducted), player #1 records 2 points for that hole (5-3). If player #1's ball had not come to rest on the fairway off the tee, zero points would have been awarded and with the 3 putts, player #1 would have recorded -3 points for that hole (0-3). The player with the most points wins the game and of course, any wager the group agreed to prior to playing the first hole.

Four Player Game
EWGA Cookbook Committee

Games For The Course

Honey Pot

Honey Pot is an individual stroke play game where players ante an agreed to amount into the Honey Pot and play for low net. The wager can be for the entire 18 holes or it can be broken into the first nine, second nine and the eighteen. After all 18 holes are played, each player subtracts their 18-hole handicap from their 18-hole gross score to determine the low net winner of the Honey Pot. If you choose to wager by nines and total eighteen, each player will subtract their 9-hole handicap from each 9-hole gross score to determine the low net winners who will share the Honey Pot for each nine holes and total eighteen.

Four Player Game
EWGA Cookbook Committee

Cod - Carts, Opposites & Drivers

COD is a low-net match play game where two players in a foursome partner for six holes against the other two. The first 6-hole teams are determined by the two players riding in the same cart, the second 6-hole teams are determined by the driver of one cart paired with the rider of the other cart, and finally, the third 6-hole teams are determined by the drivers of each cart and the riders of each cart. If your group is walkers, you may toss tees or balls to see who will be the first 6-hole teams. Each player is given their handicap strokes by hole. For each hole, the partner with the low-net score wins the hole for their team. If the teams tie low-net scores, each team receives ½ point. After the 6 holes have been played, the winning team is determined by the most points won. Yes......you may have a tie in which case there is no winning team for those 6 holes. The same scoring process is used for the second and third set of 6-hole matches.

In settling up, each player determines how many matches (None, 1, 2 or 3) they won with their partners. The players with more wins than any of the others collect on the difference between the number of matches won based on the agreed to wager prior to playing the first hole. For example, if the wager is $1.00 per match and player #1 wins no matches, player #2 wins 1 match, player #3 wins 3 matches, and player #4 wins 1 match, then: Player #1 owes player #2 - $1.00, player #3 - $3.00, and player #4 - $1.00..........Player #2 owes player #3 - $2.00...........Player #4 owes player #3 - $2.00..........And....Player #3 owes no one and is the "Big Winner"!

Four Player Game
EWGA Cookbook Committee

Wolf

Wolf is a stroke play game where players receive their full handicap on each hole and win points based on net scores. Players rotate being the "Wolf". The player designated as the Wolf gets to choose whether to play the hole 1 against 3 (herself against the other three players in the group) or 2 on 2 (with a partner). If the Wolf chooses to play 2 on 2, she must choose her partner immediately following that player's drive. For example: Player A is the Wolf. Player B hits a bad drive, Player C hits a pretty good drive. If the Wolf wants C as a partner, she must claim her partner before Player D hits her tee ball. The side with the lowest net score wins the hole or a point. If it's 2 on 2, then the winning side wins the point. If it's 1 on 3, the Wolf wins double or loses double points. There's also Lone Wolf, in which the Wolf announces before anyone tees off - including herself - that she is going it alone. On a Lone Wolf hole, the Wolf wins triple or loses triple points.

In settling up, the player with the most points wins and collects the wager agreed to prior to playing the first hole based on the difference between their points and the points won by each player.

Four Player Game
EWGA Cookbook Committee

Fairways & Greens

Fairways & Greens is a betting game best for groups of golfers with similar handicaps. The object as always is to hit fairways and greens. The catch is that you have to be the only player to hit the fairway (off the tee) to win the bet, or the only player to hit the green to win the bet. Before the round determine the value of each fairway and each green. Each hole (exclude the par 3's) has two bets - one for the fairway and one for the green. If you're the only player in the fairway off the tee, you win the designated points. If two or more players find the fairway, or two or more players are on the green, then that bet carries over to the following hole.

Four Player Game
Genesee County, MI Chapter

Rabbit

In Rabbit, the object is to achieve the low score on a hole, and to still have that honor after the 9th and 18th holes. When the round begins, the first player to singly have the low score on a hole captures the Rabbit. If two players tie for low score, no one captures the Rabbit. If on a following hole someone other than the holder of the Rabbit is the low scorer, the Rabbit is set free. And then the Rabbit can be won back by the next player to singly achieve a low score on a hole. So before another player can get the Rabbit, the Rabbit must first be set free. The player who holes the Rabbit on the 9th hole and on the 18th hole wins. They can be different players. Sometimes no one will win either instance because the Rabbit will be free. If you want to make sure someone captures the Rabbit, then eliminate setting the Rabbit free. Then, when a different player achieves a low score, the Rabbit changes hands at that point.

Four Player Game
Genesee County, MI Chapter

Shazam

Shazam is a putting game, where players bet that an opponent will three-putt a green. Once a player has reached the green and before she putts, one or more of the other players in the group may call out "Shazam." This forces a bet on the player with each person who calls out Shazam. If the player three-putts the green, she loses the bet (stakes agreed upon before the game, usually any amount up to $1). If she four-putts, she loses double the bet. If she sinks the putt, she wins double the bet. If she two-putts, no wager changes hands. A player may also Shazam herself if she is outside one flagstick-length from the hole, thereby forcing a bet with all other members of the group. If she sinks the putt, she wins the bet, but loses double if she three putts. Since handicaps do not factor into the betting, this game is appropriate for players with similar skill.

Four Player Game
Genesee County, MI Chapter

Games For The Course

Putt For Dough

Putt for Dough is a points game that can be played between four players, or as a side game for any group of golfers. In Putt for Dough, the object is to make putts, but the key is to 1-putt. The amount of points is determined by the distance of the putt. Point values are 4, 3, 2 and 1. The player who is farthest from the cup, once all players are on the green, gets 4 points if she 1-putts. The next player up gets 3 points for a 1-putt, the next player gets 2 points for a 1-putt and the player closest to the hole gets 1 point for a 1-putt. Anyone who holes out from off the green with something other than a putter gets a 5-point bonus. Play it for bragging rights or give a prize to the person with most points.

Four Player Game
Genesee County, MI Chapter

Point Game (Stableford Format)

The Point Game or Stableford Format is an individual stroke play game where each player receives their full handicap by hole and is awarded the following points for their net score on each hole: 4 points for an eagle, 3 points for a birdie, 2 points for a par, 1 point for a bogie, and 0 points for any other score. The player with the most points wins the game and of course, any wager the group agreed to prior to playing the first hole. If the game is used for an event, the players may be divided into flights by handicap and prizes can be awarded by flight.

Four Player or Event Individual Game
EWGA Cookbook Committee

Flag Tournament

Flag Tournament is an individual stroke play game that can be played with or without handicap. For either format, each player is given a small flag on a stick with their name on it. Without handicap, once the player's total gross score reaches par for the course, the player places their flag at that spot on the course. The player whose flag is closest to the hole on the 18th green is declared the winner. For a large field of players with a wide range of handicaps, the players could be flighted by handicap and winners for each flight could be awarded prizes.

With handicap, each player is given a game score by adding their handicap to the par for the course (e.g. course par is 72, player's handicap is 18, their game score is 72 + 18 = 90). When a player's total gross score equals their game score (e.g. 90), the player places their flag at that spot on the course. The player whose flag is closest to the hole on the 18th green or beyond the 18th hole (Note: players may need to play more than 18 holes to reach their game score.). For a large field of players with a wide range of handicaps, the players could be flighted by handicap and winners for each flight could be awarded prizes.

Event Individual Game
EWGA Cookbook Committee

3 Club Monte

3 Club Monte is a golf format that requires the players to pick just three clubs to use during their round. All players are allowed their putters in addition to the three other clubs they choose. The choice of clubs cannot be changed during the round.

Event Individual Game
Genesee County, MI Chapter

Red, White And Blue Tournament

Red, White and Blue tournament makes reference to the color of the tee markers. If your course uses different colors, or has more than three tee boxes, think of it as the Forward, Middle and Back Tournament. All women golfers tee off from the red (forward) tees on their first hole. After that, the tee used depends on the golfer's score on the previous hole. Golfers who make a par, tee off from the blue (back) tees on the next hole; golfers who make bogey, from the white (middle) tees; golfers who score double bogey or higher, from the red (forward) tees. A Red, White and Blue Tournament can be played with or without handicaps.

Event Individual Game
Genesee County, MI Chapter

Five Of Clubs

Five of Clubs is a tournament in which each golfer has to choose only five of her clubs to use during the tournament. In most cases, the putter counts as one of those five.

Event Individual Game
Genesee County, MI Chapter

Disaster

Disaster is a points game in which the winner at the end of the round is the player (or team) that has collected the LEAST number of points. Points are assigned for bad shots. Hit a ball out of bounds, that's a point. Points can be given any value, and what earns a point can vary. An example follows: Water ball = 1 point, Out of bounds = 1 point, In a bunker = 1 point, Failing to get ball out of bunker = 1 point, 3-putt = 1 point, Hitting a tree = 1 point, 4-putt = 2 points, Hitting from one bunker into another = 2 points, and Whiff = 2 points.

Event Individual or Team Game
Genesee County, MI Chapter

Three Blind Mice

Three Blind Mice is a tournament format that requires the winner to not only have golf skills but also a bit of luck. In Three Blind Mice, after the scorecards are turned in, the tournament organizer randomly draws three holes just played. Everyone's scores on those three holes are eliminated. The scorecards are retabulated and the winner is crowned. Three Blind Mice can be played by individuals or teams, gross or net.

Event Individual or Team Game
Genesee County, MI Chapter

Everything But Putts

Everything But Putts is the opposite of Low Putts. Rather than the winner being determined by fewest putts, the winner is determined by all strokes other than putts. At the end of the round, subtract the number of putts from the total strokes; the player or group with the fewest remaining strokes is the winner. This is one time putts do not count.

Event Individual or Team Game
Genesee County, MI Chapter

Low Putts

Low Putts is a popular tournament format or bet. It is very simple. Keep track of your putts throughout the round. At the end of the round, total up the putts. The low individual or low group in total number of putts is the winner.

Event Individual or Team Game
Genesee County, MI Chapter

Take Out The Trash

Take Out the Trash is an individual or team event game where a player or a team gets to drop their worst score or 'the trash' on each nine giving them a 16-hole score. The 16-hole score is used to determine the individual or team winners. If using net scores, any handicap strokes on the holes with 'the trash' scores will also be void.

Event Individual or Team Game
Palm Beach County, FL Chapter

"It's Your Turn" Tournament

It's Your Turn Tournament is where a three person team hits alternate shots. The first person hits the drive, the next person then hits from the resulting drive and the third person hits from there. Alternate shots until the ball is in the cup.

Event Three Player Team Game
Genesee County, MI Chapter

Florida Scramble

The Florida Scramble uses the traditional scramble format where players in the group hit off the tee and the best shot is selected by the group. All players then pick up their balls and move to the position of the best shot, placing their ball within a club length (not changing the cut of grass). All players then hit again from this selected spot and continue this process until the ball is holed. However, in the Florida Scramble, the player whose shot is selected doesn't get to play the next shot. For example, with teams of four, all four players tee off, the best shot is selected, then only three players hit their second shots. The best of the second shots is selected - and the player who hit that shot sits out on the third shots; and so on until the ball is holed.

Event Team Game
EWGA Cookbook Committee

"Clue" Murder Mystery

Please reference the following two pages for this game's instructions.

Event Team Game
Catherine Schiaffo
San Diego, CA Chapter

Herewith the Clues –
A Murder Mystery in 18 Holes

Deputy Inspector Divot shook his head in disbelief as he watched the coroner's van head down the driveway at the Hazard Center Golf Course. "Who in the world would have wanted to kill Kim Teebox"? The D.I. knew that the EWGA was occasionally a competitive group, and that Kim was an up-and-coming golfer who could play her way into the tournament and steal the $1 million purse. Still, he was dismayed to think that one of the world's top EWGA golfers could have done it. He knew a long drawn out investigation – not to mention the scandal itself – could be enough to sink the group's reputation as easily as a 3-foot putt. Thus, D.I. Divot decided to not wait for the autopsy results and forged ahead to solve the case.

First, he studied the six EWGA players who made up the invitational field at Hazard Center, one of who would prove to be the killer of poor Kim Teebox. It was a stellar field consisting of Frieda Fairway, Greta Green, Betty Bunker, Hannah Hazard, Patty Putter and Debbie Driver. Next, he gathered what he believed could be the murder weapon: a rake, a 5-iron, a red hazard stake, a flagstick, a ball washer, or a lawn mower. Finally, he traversed the golf course and deduced that one of the following was likely the scene of the dastardly crime: a green side bunker, the cart barn, the water hazard, the golf shop, the parking lot, the snack shack, the driving range, the ladies locker room, or the practice putting green.

D.I. Divot's solution to the crime – the identity of the murderer, the weapon used and the location – have been placed in a sealed envelope to be revealed at the end of today's round. You, too, can try to solve the crime by picking up clues that have been left on each green **provided that you or your partner score a net par or better on the hole**. Failure to score net par or better means you do not get to look at the clue.

Each team will be given an investigation report form so they can keep track of the clues they have earned the right to view. At the end of the round, the team must make an accusation that identifies their best guess as to the killer, the means, and the murder location, using the process of elimination from the clues they gathered – or just dumb luck.

Games For The Course

Herewith the Clues – A Murder Mystery in 18 Holes

Investigation Report Form:

SUSPECTS	
Frieda Fairway	
Greta Green	
Betty Bunker	
Hannah Hazard	
Patty Putter	
Debbie Driver	
WEAPONS	
Rake	
5-iron	
Red hazard stake	
Flagstick	
Ball washer	
Lawn mower	
CRIME SCENE	
Green side bunker	
Cart barn	
Water hazard	
Golf shop	
Parking lot	
Driving range	
Snack shack	
Ladies locker room	
Practice putting green	

Notes

Index of Recipes

Appetizers, Snacks & Beverages

Baked Chestnuts 16
Bear Catcher Drink 29
Beer Cheese 18
Black Bean Salsa 25
Black Bean Salsa 25
Blue Inlet Wild Roasted Red Pepper "Love" Dip 22
Brook's Shrimp Shooters 3
Buffalo Chicken Dip 20
Caramelized Sweet Onion And Goat Cheese Tartlets 8
Chicken Wing Dip 21
Chicken Wings 13
Chip And A Putt Appetizer 24
Chipped Beef Tailgate Dip 23
Chutney Topped Cream Cheese 14
Cowboy Caviar 17
Crab Triangles 1
Crunchy Orange Spice Snack Mix ... 28
Curried Fruit 16
Dilly Dip 19
Dried Beef & Dill Pickle Spread .. 23
Easy Sassy Salsa 26
Fiesta Veggie Dip 21
Gorgonzola Torte 9
Hummus 17
Ikra (Ukrainian Eggplant Appetizer) 10
Irish Cream 30
Jalapeno Shrimp Wraps With Bacon 3
Jalapeno Smoked Oyster Appetizer 4
Jezebel Sauce 27
Kahlua (Get Your Bottles Ready!) . 31
Katherine's Blue Inlet Wild Salsa. 26
KPJ's Back Nine Energy Squares ... 27
Lemon And Garlic Hummus 18
Lite Iced Coffee Beverage 30
Marinated Shrimp 2
Meatballs 6
Mexican Caviar/Avocado Salad 16
Mississippi Spiced Pecans 29
Mouth-Watering Meatballs 4
My Granny's Favorite Clam Dip 24
19th Hole Root-Beer Martini 29
PB & J Martini 31
Persian Melon With Prosciutto, Mint, And Balsamic Reduction 12
Quick Cheesy Ro-Tel Dip 19
Rachael Ray's Red Pepper Hummus 18
Raspberry Liqueur 31
Reuben Dip 22
Sausage Crescent Wrap 7
Sausage In Puff Pastry 6
Shoa Mai Dumplings 9
Shrimp Butter 2
Slush 32
Small Pizza For Lunch 15
Spanekopita 11
Spiced Apple Cider 30
Stuffed Belgian Endive Appetizer . 10
Sugared Wine Nuts 28
Sweet & Sour Meatballs 5
Sweet Cranberry Crockpot Meatballs 5
Swiss-Bacon Dip 19
Toasted Rye Rounds 13
Vegetable Pizza 14
Veggie Pizza 15
Vodka Shake 32
Zesty Buffalo Chicken Dip 20

Soups & Salads

Angel Hair Pasta Salad 44
Ann Liguori's Holiday Jello Delight 42
Asian Slaw 50
Asian Vinaigrette Dressing 58
Bacon And Raisin Broccoli Salad .. 47
Black Bean Salad 46
Blueberry Salad 42
Broccoli Blue Cheese Salad 47
Broccoli Slaw 49
Cabbage Salad For 8 50
Caesar Salad Dressing 58
Cherry Salad 43
Chicken Almond-Pear Salad 58
Chicken Soup Ala Alice Osur 41
Coleslaw 49
Company Tuna Salad 45
Confetti Soup 34
Corn, Black Bean, And Avocado Salad 48
Cream Of Cauliflower-Crab Soup ... 37
Crunchy Romaine Toss 48
Dot's Turkey Chili 37
Fiesta Lime Salad 55
French Market Soup 40
Frozen Tropical Salad 43
Grandma Vivi's Potato Salad 52
Height Of Summer Salad 55

Kale Salad.......................... 54
Mango Gazpacho 36
Mimi's Cranberry Apple Salad....... 44
Minestrone Soup................... 33
Mixed Citrus Green Salad 56
Onion Soup........................ 35
Orange Fluff 43
Oriental Salad 51
Orzo Salad 57
Salad Olivia (Persian Potato
   Salad).......................... 52
Simple Summer Fish Chowder....... 36
Sliced Tomato With Balsamic
   Vinaigrette..................... 54
Southern Cornbread Salad 51
Spinach Salad Dressing 59
Strawberry & Spinach Salad........ 56
Taco Salad 57
Taco Soup......................... 38
Tomato Caprese Salad With An "Extra
   Slice" And A "Hook"............. 53
Tortellini Salad.................... 46
Tortilla Soup...................... 39
Tuna Macaroni Salad............... 45
Waldorf Salad 44
White Bean Chili 38

Vegetables

Best In The West Baked Beans..... 62
Broccoli Puff...................... 62
Carrot Pudding 63
Carrot Souffle 64
Cheese-Frosted Cauliflower 64
Corn Pudding 65
Corn Pudding 65
Corn With Bruschetta.............. 64
Eggplant Parmesan 66
Eggs Florentine.................... 70
Greek Tomatoes 72
Green Bean Casserole.............. 68
Grilled Asparagus.................. 61
Grilled Zucchini Sandwich........... 74
Haricots Verts With Mustard Seeds
   And Toasted Coconut 68
Mixed Vegetable Casserole...........73
Roasted Brussels Sprouts 63
Root Vegetable Apple Gratin 72
Spinach Casserole 69
Spinach Squares................... 69
Squash Casserole.................. 71
Squash Casserole Supreme.......... 71
The Best Eggplant Parmesan 67
Vegetable Medley...................73
Zucchini Quiche 74

Pasta, Rice & Potatoes

Annika's Bolognese Pasta 77
Baked Noodles And Vegetables 85
Beans And Rice Southwestern...... 85
Bow Ties With Sausage, Tomatoes, And
   Cream.......................... 81
Caribbean Rice.................... 86
Chicken Pasta Primavera........... 80
Easy Potatoes..................... 88
Fabulous And Easy Wild Mushroom
   Ravioli......................... 82
Garlic White Lasagna 78
Grilled Fingerling Potatoes With
   Tarragon Vinaigrette............ 87
Hash Brown Party Potatoes 89
Holiday Wild Rice.................. 87
Luau Rice......................... 86
Marinara Sauce....................75
Mexican Lasagna 79
Orzo Mushroom Casserole.......... 81
Party Potatoes 89
Pasta Carbonara................... 77
Pesto Pasta 79
Rotini With Spinach And Asiago
   Cheese 83
Scalloped Potatoes 88
Spicy Bacon Mac And Cheese 84
Sweet Potato Casserole............ 90
Thursday Sauce 76

Meat & Poultry

Babyback Ribs 103
Barbecue Sloppy Joe............... 92
Barbequed Beef.................... 96
Basil Burger With Bacon Chutney ... 92
Breakfast Casserole 138
Cajun Stew 116
Chicken And Cheese Enchiladas.....133
Chicken And Wild Rice Casserole 115
Chicken Breast Hot Dish 117
Chicken Cacciatore................ 122
Chicken Casserole................. 119
Chicken Cassoulet 114
Chicken Empanada................. 120
Chicken Enchiladas................ 137
Chicken Enchiladas With Mexican
   Rice.......................... 136
Chicken Golf Balls..................117
Chicken In Wine Sauce............. 127
Chicken Pot Pie 121
Chicken Pot Pie 121
Chicken Stew With Cornmeal
   Dumplings 118

Chicken Tetrazzini 123
Chicken With Chocolate 129
Chili Egg Puff 139
Corned Beef And Cabbage 99
Crock Pot Chicken Tortilla/Tacos..... 133
Crock Pot Italian Beef 102
Crockpot Chicken Enchilada
    Casserole 120
Dad's Barbeque Sauce 91
Dinner-In-A-Dish Casserole 96
Easy Low Fat Chicken Parm 126
Easy Oven Barbecued Ribs 103
Enchiladas 95
Fast Fettuccine Cacciatore 124
Goat Cheese, Artichoke, And Smoked
    Ham Strata 108
Green Chicken Enchiladas 135
Grilled Chicken Ala Rosie 130
Grilled Tri Tip With Citrus Garlic
    Marinade 102
Hot Chicken And Chips Retro 119
King Ranch Casserole 116
Lamb Curry With Condiments 111
Mango BBQ Chicken With Mango
    Salsa 132
Marinated Flank Steak 100
Mexican Albondigas 134
Michaela's Authentic Swedish
    Meatballs 93
Mom's Meatballs 94
Mozzarella Chicken 126
Nancy's Mom Mim Bennett's
    Brisket 98
No Peek Mushroom Brisket 97
Pastel De Montezuma 137
Petto Di Pollo Farcito With Formaggio Di
    Capra E Peperoni Rossi
    Arrostiti 124
Pine Nut And Feta Stuffed
    Chicken 128
Pork Chop Stew 107
Pork Chops Al Tamarindo With Cannellini
    Beans And Tomatoes 106
Pork Medallions With Mustard Cream
    Sauce 105
Pulled Pork Sandwiches 107
Quiche With Hash Brown Crust 138
Quick Chicken Pot Pie 122
Quick Coq Au Vin 131
Rack Of Lamb For Two 112
Rita's Rump Roast 101
Rosemary Chicken 125
San Antonio Brisket - Slow
    Cooker 99
Sausage & Fruit Stuffed Acorn
    Squash 109

Sausage & Squash Casserole 110
Sausage Strata 109
Sauteed Chicken Breast With Mustard
    Sage Sauce 125
Slow Cooker Pork Ribs 104
Southwestern Tamale Pie 94
Swedish Meatballs 93
Taco Pizza 95
Tasty Pork Tenderloin 104
Texas Steak Rub 91
Turkey Meatloaf Apricot 113
Vermouth Flank Steak 100
Walt's Roast & Gravy 101

Seafood

Baked Fish Fillets 143
Basil-Crusted Salmon 146
Bouillabaisse 141
Crab Quesadillas 142
Easy But Delicious Crawfish
    Etouffee 143
Fish Florentine 144
Flounder Galliano 145
Fried Fish Fillets With Nut Crust ... 144
Grilled Lemon Garlic Shrimp 151
Grilled Salmon With East-West Spice
    Rub 147
Grilled Salmon With Spice
    Blends 148
Honey-Mustard Glazed Salmon
    Steaks 150
Layer Up Salmon Pizza 150
Mahi Mahi Fish Tacos With Slaw.... 145
Roasted Salmon Platter 149
Salmon Loaf 150
Salmon With Basil And Champagne
    Sauce 146
Sesame Seed And Cracked Black Pepper
    Crusted Tuna Steaks 153
Shrimp Quinoa 152
Shrimp Santorini 152
Shrimp Scampi 153
Spicy Baked Shrimp 151
Steamers On The Grill 142

Breads & Rolls

Banana Bread/Cake 158
Banana Bread 157
Basic Muffin Recipe 161
Beer Bread 163
Beer-Cheese Triangles 164
Blueberry Pound Cake 158
Brioche 155

Creme Brulee French Toast	167
Easy French Toast Strata	168
Easy Moist Cornbread	163
Green Tomato Breakfast Cake	166
Hutterite Corn Bread	163
Kitty's French Bread Melt	165
Lemon Bread	159
Mashed Potato Rolls	157
Monkey Bread	159
Night Before French Toast	169
Pineapple Stuffing	165
Prosciutto Muffins	164
Pumpkin Bread	160
Pumpkin Spice Muffins	162
Sally Lunn Bread	156
Ski Team Buttermilk Pancakes	170
Sour Cream Coffee Cake	166
Special Occasion French Toast	169
Swedish Pancakes	170
Walnut Muffins	162
Zucchini Bread	160
Zucchini Bread	161

Desserts

Aunt Edna's Bars	205
Barton Creek Resort And Spa Signature Dessert	174
Best Carrot Cake Ever	185
Best Ever Biscotti	202
Better Than Sex Cake	192
Biscotti	203
Black Bottom Cupcakes	191
Blueberry Swirl Cheesecake Bars	206
Butterscotch Haystacks	211
Butter Tarts	184
Carrot Bars	207
Chocolate Angel Food Cake	191
Chocolate Graham Crackers	201
Chocolate Peppermint Pie	181
Creamy Pumpkin Pie	180
Deep South Torte	173
Double Chocolate Chip Pound Cake	190
Easy Fruit Cobbler	176
Eggnog Bread Pudding With Cherry Bourbon Sauce	175
Fat Free Zucchini Brownies	207
Fig Newtons	200
Four Star Fudge Bars	204
Frozen Chocolate Mousse	171
Ginger Molasses Cookies	198
Gooey Butter Bars	205
Graham Cracker Holiday Cookies	201
Gram's Apple Cake	184
Harvey Wallbanger Cake	196
Ice Cream Cookies	199
Impossible Pie	181
Italian Ricotta Pie	182
Juanita's Brownies	208
Key Lime Pie (No Bake) With Oreo Cookie Topping	178
LBJ's Favorite Pecan Pie	180
Mandarin Orange Cake	186
Microwave-Baked Apples	177
Microwave Caramels	210
Miss Peggy's Buttermilk Custard Pie	183
Momma Smoot's Punkin Roll	188
Nanny Anne Cone's Banana Cake	184
New England Grape-Nuts Custard	173
No-Bake Blueberry Cheesecake Bars	206
No-Crust Apple Pie	177
Peanut Butter Buckeyes	210
Peanut Butter-Toffee Cheesecake Brownies	209
Pecan Shortbread Cookies	202
Pineapple Delight Dessert	186
Pineapple Pie	179
Pound Cake	190
Pound Cake Tiramisu	172
Pumpkin Cake	187
Pumpkin Pie	179
Pumpkin Squares	187
Scottish Apple Pie	178
Special K Bars	204
Summer Celebration Cake	189
Summer Fruit Tart	183
Sweet Noodle Pudding	176
The Birdie Cake	193
Tiramisu	172
Traditional Southern Chess Pie	182
Tres Leches Cake (Three Milk Cake)	195
Tropical Fruit Cake	189
Twinkie Cake	194
Welsh Cakes	197
Whoopie Pies	199

Games For The Course

Accuracy Challenge	214
Bag Raid	213
Bingo-Bango-Bongo	215
"Clue" Murder Mystery	223
Cod - Carts, Opposites & Drivers	216

Disaster 221	Point Game (Stableford Format).... 219
Everything But Putts 222	Putt For Dough 219
Fairways & Greens................. 217	Rabbit............................. 218
Fairways And Putts................ 215	Red, White And Blue Tournament ... 221
Five Of Clubs 221	Shazam 218
Flag Tournament................... 220	Take Out The Trash 222
Florida Scramble.................. 223	30 & In 213
Honey Pot 216	3 Club Monte...................... 220
"It's Your Turn" Tournament........ 223	Three Blind Mice 222
Low Putts 222	Wolf............................... 217
One Putt Challenge................. 214	

Index of Contributors

Abrams, Betty 51
Adler, Barbie 158
Alesch, Karen 29,121
Anderson, Robin K. 40,135,162
Argall, Lori 48
Aurelius, Robin 197
Ayres, Pat 58
Baltzer, Carol 36
Barr, Patti 56,90
Bartlett, Christy 100,137
Bel Jan, Jan 44,58
Bessette, Ava (A.J.) 31,61,91
 109,125
Bettman, Barbara 9,17
Birklund, Renee 26,168
Black, Jayne 147
Blalock, Jane 112
Blanchette, Cyndi 115
Bounds, Danita 73,75,208
Brammann, Pam 4
Braun, Maggi 71,149,157
Broderick, Jane 187
Brothers, Ellen 16,18,19,45,
 50,101,136
Bryant, Gigi Edwards 150
Burdi, Vita Anne 70
Burke, Mary Jo 13
Burns, Kathy 56,64,146,148,162
 163,177
Butkus, Linda 95
Camens, Denise 150
Campioni, Virginia 142
Caplan, Carolyn 170
Carlson, Karen 120,138,174
Carter, Kristie M. 5
Caruso, Susan 8
Cavanaugh, Joan 35
Choiniere, Joan 110
Clark, Betsy 36,206
Clinkscales, Carolyn 47
Coil, Kathie 50
Cook, Kim 43
Corbett, Bobbie 27
Cortese, Joanne 79
Cox, Donna 118
Cross, Sandy 204
Dahan, Tiss 64,116
Davis, Cindy 24
Dean, Paula 23,30,48,54
Dixon, Jo-Ann 3,29,63,107,164
Dickinson, Judy 6
Donahue, Sandra 122
Dowell, Valoree 55
Downey, Margaret 62

Dugan, Lisa 20
Dupree, Everette 161
Dushenski, Diane 44
Dyson, Katharine 185
Eader, Linda 103,122
Eldridge, Connie 52,66
Evans, Nancy Bennett 98
Evans, Patty 80,88,145,205
Ferguson, Chris 16
Finger, Le Ann 2,109,117,204
Fleming, Trina 117
Florea, Michelle 82,176
Footz, Nona 131
Foran-Pinzon, Nancy 57,179,196
Fraser, Kathy 85
French, Shelley 10
Furtado, Karen 44
Gambill, Marilyn E. 199
Goddu, Marlene 72
Grandolfo, Corinne 184
Grant, Kelly 19
Greene, Sherry 151
Gross, Deborah 112
Hall, Sharon 24
Hansen, BJ 17,19,187
Harvey, Sheri 64,89,144,164
Hendrix, Sue 38
Hillhouse, Judy 15,211
Hoffman, Jeanne 200
Howlett, Shareen 186
Huff, Darla 133
Hulbert, Penny 183
Hume, Sara 182
Jansen, Alicia 195
Jarvis, Caryn 173
Jarvis, Ethel 173
Jarvis, Tyra 11,167
Jeffers, Dawn 94
Jenkins, Paula 34
Jennings, Stephanie 25,210
Jesse, Sue 159
Johnson, Diana 37
Johnson, Rita Kathryn 39
Jones, Luanne 68,72,86,142,153
Jones, Rosie 130
Joyce, Patricia L. 13
Kang, Stephanie Sook 15
Kaster, Mary E. 172
Keaton, Linda 42,121,189,190
Kerler, Hollis 54,87
Knueven, Mary 181,207
Koenig, Kerstin 29
Kravitz, Rebecca 21
Kuehn Sr., George 31,153

Kulik, Rosalyn Franta 47
Lacko, Judy 193
Lamb, Darlene 'Babe' 22,28,32,95,
                        102,194,205,210
Landa, Lisa 134
Landman, Linda 57
Larson, Lilliam 177,181
Lenegan, Marylou 126
Lemon-Steiner, Linda 12
Lifer, Lisa 191
Liguori, Ann 42
Lobby, D.O., Nancy 202
Macaluso, Becky..... 45,62,65,69,143,
                              159,163,165
Malysz, Carol..................... 129
Marriott, Lynn.................... 141
Marshall, Terrie 30,31
Martin, Sue 21
Mattox, Marlene 125,144
Matus, Nancy 14
McArthur, Barbara 127
McGeever, Cindy 1,58,59,165,201
McIntosh, Karen 25,30,38,51,71,124,
                          175,189,206,207
McLaughlin, Barbara 161,172,202,
                                     203
Meli-Rizzo, Jackie 76
Miller, Alice 79
Moraghan, Karen 139,166
Morzella, Cathy.................... 73
Moseley, Linda.................. 85,96
Murphy, Linda C................... 158
Murray, Del 119
Naugle, Susan 23,88,94,101,104
Needham, Cheryl 184
Nieckarz, Carol 171
Niehoff, Angie 6,96
Nilsson, Pia 141
North, Lori Cook 14
Ogden, Bonnie 152
Oh, Chin...................... 83,201
Oliver, Nancy 91
Orender, MG 67,128
Orfanos, M.D., Jackie 152
Osur, Alice 18,41,84
Oswald, Barb 7
Palacios-Jansen, Karen 27
Pearce, Terri 3
Pecuch, Renee 160
Peterson, Brenda 99
Pierson, Kay...................... 28
Powell, Renee 99
Rabinowitz, Esther 63,68,81,150
Rader, Dana 100
Rahman, Penelope 'Penny' 9,146
Reich, Sharon 49

Reid, Linda 138
Reynolds, Jennifer 84,92,113
Ricco, Ronna Jo 163
Richards, Nune 16
Riggs, Teresa 133
Rinehold, Elizabeth 4,74
Roberts, Katherine 22,26
Rooney, Dorothy 33,37
Sampolesi, Shelia 104,156,198
Schiaffo, Catherine 87,102,105,151
                                     183
Schmidt, Carolyn 190
Schutte-Reed, Jan 55
Shaeffer, Susan 20
Shepp, Judith R. 58,192
Shivers, Jean 49
Silverman, Debbie 126
Skivington, Kristen 108,178
Slobidsky, Lucy Doroshenko 10
Smith, Dori J. 173
Smith, Gordon 92
Smith, Jen 5
Smoot, Marie 188
Snyder, Clarise 106
Sorenstam, Annika 77
Stamey, Theresa 176
Stelter, Gretchen ... 31,32,145,153,170
Stelter, Hugh 170
Stelter, Ruth 32
Sternberg, Stina 93
Swensen, Pam 199
Tajalli, Susan 52,78,114,120,182
Talese, Paula 124
Taylor, Molly 46
Thomas, Kathy 43,89,157,186,191
Thomas, Kim 53
Thompson, Meg 137
Tobin, Liz 132
Trahan, Zona 103,143,169
Unknown, Contributor 123,166
Valentine, Eva 179
Vallee, Shirley 119
Vanatter, Joyce 209
Van Divender, Lisa 2,46
Voll, Patricia 74,169
Vollstedt, Linda 107
Votaw, Ty M. 77
Walsh, Roberta Ward 180
Washinko, Carla 86
Weistart, Lisa 156
West, Hollie 65
Whitworth, Kathy 116
Wilson, Michaela 93

Wolf, M.D., Marlene 63,68,69,81, 92,97,150,159,160,178,180
Young, Janet 43
Zaffuto, Vivian 81

Suggestions for Lowering Fat Content in Your Diet

FOOD CATEGORY	CHOOSE	DECREASE
Meat Fish Poultry	Lean cuts of meat with fat trimmed, such as: beef-round, sirloin, rump steak, loin Poultry without skin Pork tenderloin	"Prime" grade meats Fatty cuts, like: corned beef, brisket, short ribs, spareribs Goose, duck, organ meats, sausage, bacon, hot dogs, regular luncheon meats
Dairy Products	Skim milk, lowfat buttermilk, lowfat evaporated or nonfat milk Lowfat or nonfat yogurts and cheeses	Whole milk, cream, half & half, nondairy creamers, real or nondairy whipped cream, cream cheese, sour cream, ice cream, custard-style yogurt High-fat cheese, like: Brie, Swiss, American, Cheddar
Eggs	Egg whites, cholesterol and fat-free egg substitutes	Egg yolks (substitute 2 egg whites for 1 egg)
Fats Oils	Unsaturated vegetable oils (in limited quantities): corn, olive, peanut, canola, safflower, sesame, soybean Fat-free mayonnaise, cream cheese, and salad dressings Mustard and flavored vinegars (when cooking, use spray oils or nonstick pans and decrease amount of fat in recipe by 1/3 or substitute applesauce for fat)	Butter, coconut oil, palm kernel oil, palm oil, lard, bacon fat
Breads Cereals Pasta	Breads like whole wheat, pumpernickel, rye, pita, bagels, English muffins, rice cakes Lowfat crackers and bread sticks Plain cereals (hot and cold) Spaghetti and macaroni Any grain Dried peas and beans	Croissants, butter rolls, sweet rolls, pastries, doughnuts, most snack crackers, granola-type cereals made with saturated fats, egg noodles, pasta and rice prepared with cream, butter, or cheese sauces
Vegetables Fruits	Fresh, frozen, canned (no salt added)	Vegetables prepared in butter, cream, or sauce Fruits served in glazes

Copyright © 2011 Cookbook Publishers, Inc.

Fat Facts

Reducing fat in the diet is a major focus in America today, and for good reason. A high fat diet can contribute to elevated blood cholesterol levels, a risk factor for heart disease. Excess dietary fat has also been linked to obesity and cancer. As a result, lower fat intake has become a priority for many.

Cholesterol is a fat-type substance found in all animal tissues. In adults, a blood cholesterol level below 200 milligrams per deciliter is desirable. A level above 240 milligrams is considered high. Blood cholesterol can also be broken into two categories: "good" and "bad" cholesterol. High density lipoproteins (HDL) are known as "good" cholesterol because of their high protein content and low cholesterol content, and because people with higher HDL levels have a lower incidence of heart disease. Low density lipoproteins (LDL) contain more cholesterol than HDL and are responsible for cholesterol build-up on artery walls, thus earning the label "bad" cholesterol. A lowfat, low cholesterol diet, as well as exercise and being at a desirable weight, can help lower blood cholesterol levels and raise HDL levels.

Dietary fat can be divided into three different types: saturated, polyunsaturated, and monounsaturated. Foods we eat contain a mixture of these fats.

- **SATURATED FATS** are generally solid at room temperature. They have been shown to increase blood cholesterol levels. Saturated fats are primarily found in animal products such as butter, milk, cream, and lard. Some plant foods, such as palm oil, coconut oil, vegetable shortening, and some peanut butters also contain large amounts of saturated fats.

- **POLYUNSATURATED FATS** tend to lower blood cholesterol levels. These fats are found in high concentrations in vegetable oils, and are usually liquid at room temperature. Fats such as sunflower oil, corn oil, and soft margarines have large amounts of polyunsaturated fats.

- **MONOUNSATURATED FATS** have also been shown to decrease cholesterol levels in the blood. They can be liquid or solid at room temperature, and can be from plant or animal sources. Olive, peanut, and canola oils are high in monounsaturated fats.

- **DIETARY CHOLESTEROL** comes from animal sources such as meat, poultry, fish and other seafood, and dairy products. Egg yolks and organ meats contain high amounts of dietary cholesterol.

- **HYDROGENATION** is a chemical process in which hydrogen is added to unsaturated oils to make them firmer at room temperature. Hydrogenated fats such as shortening or margarine are more saturated than the oil from which they are made. When choosing a margarine, pick one with 2 grams or less saturated fat per tablespoon.

Heart Healthy guidelines include: (1) Limit total fat intake to 30% or less of total calories. (2) Of these calories, up to one-third can be saturated fat, and the remaining two-thirds should come from polyunsaturated and monounsaturated sources. (3) Limit daily cholesterol intake to 300 milligrams or less.

Copyright © 2011 Cookbook Publishers, Inc.

Calculating Percent Fat

To achieve a desirable percentage of total calories from fat, it is helpful to know how much fat is in individual foods. To determine the percentage of a food's total calories that come from fat, you can use the following formula. In order to calculate this percentage, you need to know the total calories and the grams of fat per serving, both of which are usually listed on the food label.

$$\frac{\text{grams of fat} \times 9^*}{\text{total calories}} \times 100 = \% \text{ of total calories from fat}$$

* Each gram of fat contains 9 calories. Multiplying grams of fat by 9 gives the total calories from fat. On food labels, this number has already been calculated, and is listed on the same line as total calories.

When reading a food package, the front of the label may not tell the whole story. For instance, a package of boiled ham might claim to be 96% fat free. From this information, the consumer might assume that the food contains 4% fat, which is well within the recommended guideline of eating foods with 30% or less of total calories from fat. Although the 96% fat free claim is truthful, it refers to the amount of fat by weight rather than by the food's total calories. To get a clearer picture, use the above calculation. The label of the boiled ham shows 60 calories and 2.5 grams of fat per serving.

$$\frac{2.5 \text{ grams of fat} \times 9}{60 \text{ total calories}} \times 100 = 37\% \text{ of total calories from fat}$$

By calculating the percentage of total calories from fat, you can make more informed decisions about the nutritional qualities of foods. In this case, the ham may be lower in fat than other ham products, but it is still above the 30% guideline. If you are trying to follow a lowfat diet, you should eat this food in moderation.

Copyright © 2011 Cookbook Publishers, Inc.

"Heart Healthy" Recipe Substitutions

ORIGINAL INGREDIENT	ALTERNATIVE	REDUCES: TF	SF	C
1 pound ground beef	• 1 pound ground turkey	✔	✔	✔
1 ounce Cheddar, Swiss, or American cheese	• 1 ounce lowfat cheese • 1 ounce part-skim cheese (Mozzarella)	✔ ✔	✔ ✔	✔ ✔
1 egg	• 2 egg whites • ¼ c. low cholesterol egg substitute	✔ ✔	✔ ✔	✔ ✔
1 c. whole milk	• 1 c. skim milk	✔	✔	✔
1 c. cream	• 1 c. evaporated skim milk	✔	✔	✔
1 c. sour cream	• 1 c. nonfat sour cream • 1 c. plain nonfat yogurt • 1 c. lowfat cottage cheese plus 1 to 2 tsp. lemon juice, blended smooth	✔ ✔ ✔	✔ ✔ ✔	✔ ✔ ✔
1 ounce cream cheese	• 1 ounce nonfat cream cheese • 1 ounce Neufchatel cheese	✔ ✔	✔ ✔	✔ ✔
1 c. butter	• 1 c. margarine • 1 c. vegetable oil		✔ ✔	✔ ✔
1 c. shortening	• 7 fluid oz. vegetable oil		✔	
1 ounce baking chocolate	• 3 Tbsp. cocoa powder plus 1 Tbsp. vegetable oil		✔	
roux: 1 part fat 1 part starch	• ½ part fat to 1 part starch	✔		
1 can condensed cream soup	• Mix together: ½ c. nonfat dry milk 2 Tbsp. cornstarch 2 tsp. low sodium chicken bouillon ¼ tsp. onion powder ⅛ tsp. garlic powder ¼ tsp. basil ¼ tsp. thyme ¼ tsp. white pepper 9 oz. cold water Add the following if desired: ¼ c. chopped celery or ½ c. sliced mushrooms Heat to a boil; stir frequently. Per "can": 215 calories, 1g fat, 8mg cholesterol, 200mg sodium	✔	✔	✔

KEY:
TF = total fat
SF = saturated fat
C = Cholesterol

Copyright © 2011 Cookbook Publishers, Inc.

Food Labeling Definitions

Government regulations give specific guidelines as to what words can be used on a food label to describe the product. Here is a list of these descriptive terms.

FREE A product must contain no amount or only an insignificant amount of one or more of the following: fat, saturated fat, cholesterol, sodium, sugar, and calories. The terms *no, without,* and *zero* can also be used.

Calorie-free: less than 5 calories per serving
Sugar-free or Fat-free: less than 0.5g per serving
Sodium-free: less than 5mg per serving

LOW This term can be used when referring to one or more of the following: fat, cholesterol, sodium, and calories. The terms *little, few,* and *low source of* can also be used.

Low calorie: 40 calories or less per serving
Lowfat: 3g or less per serving
Low saturated fat: 1g or less per serving
Low cholesterol: less than 20mg per serving
Low sodium: less than 140mg per serving
Very low sodium: less than 35mg per serving

LEAN Meat, poultry, and seafood containing less than 10g of fat, less than 4g saturated fat, and less than 95g of cholesterol per 3.5 oz. serving.

EXTRA LEAN Meat, poultry, and seafood containing less than 5g of fat, less than 2g saturated fat, and less than 95g of cholesterol per 3.5 oz. serving.

HIGH One serving of a product must contain 20% or more of the *Daily Value* (recommended daily intake of a nutrient).

GOOD SOURCE One serving must contain 10% to 19% of the Daily Value.

REDUCED A nutritionally altered product containing 25% less of a nutrient or of calories than the regular product. If the regular product already meets the criteria for *low,* a *reduced* claim cannot be made.

LESS A food that contains 25% less of a nutrient or of calories than a similar food. Cream cheeses that have 25% less fat than butter could use the term *less* or *fewer.*

LIGHT This term can still be used to describe food characteristics such as color and texture if the label makes the meaning clear; for example, *light brown sugar.* The term also carries two other meanings:

✦ A nutritionally altered product that contains one-third less calories or half the fat of the original food
✦ A food's sodium content has been cut by 50% or more

MORE A food using this claim must contain 10% more of the Daily Value of a nutrient than the reference food. To use the words *fortified, enriched,* or *added,* this standard must also be met.

UNSALTED, NO SALT ADDED, or WITHOUT ADDED SALT The sodium naturally found in the product is still there, but it has been prepared without the salt that is normally added.

Copyright © 2011 Cookbook Publishers, Inc.

Sodium

Sodium is a mineral used by the body to maintain a proper balance of water in the blood. Although it is a vital nutrient, the body needs very little sodium to stay healthy. Because it is found naturally in some foods and is added to many other foods, getting too little sodium is usually not a problem. A high sodium diet, on the other hand, can contribute to high blood pressure in some people. Reducing sodium intake in the diet may help prevent or control high blood pressure. It is hard to know who will develop high blood pressure, or who might benefit from eating less sodium. For these reasons, and because most individuals consume much more sodium than needed, it is generally suggested that we reduce sodium intake.

Table salt is the major source of sodium in our diet. It is made up of about half sodium and half chloride. An adult diet containing between 1,100mg and 3,300mg of sodium per day is considered adequate. One teaspoon of salt contains 2,000mg of sodium.

WAYS TO REDUCE DIETARY SODIUM

- Taste food before salting. Salt food only sparingly at the table.

- Cut back on sodium slowly to give the body time to adjust to less salty flavors. *Salt-craving* taste buds will eventually be replaced by new ones that do not have an affinity for salt.

- Choose foods that have little or no sodium added. In general, the more processed the food, the more sodium it contains. For example, processed turkey breast purchased at a deli has considerably more sodium than fresh turkey breast.

- In many recipes, the salt can be cut back or even eliminated without greatly affecting the taste. Experiment with recipes at home, using less salt each time and using low sodium substitutes for high sodium ingredients.

- Read labels on food packages. Compare the sodium content to similar items and to the recommended sodium intake for an entire day.

- Limit intake of high sodium foods such as cheeses, processed meats, soups, broths, snack foods, canned vegetables and vegetable juices, pickled vegetables, gravies, sauces, commercial casserole mixes, frozen dinners, and condiments. In many cases, lower sodium alternatives are available.

- When eating in restaurants, ask for foods to be prepared without added salt and request to have sauces, gravies, dressings, and condiments served on the side.

- Use herbs and spices instead of salt to enhance the flavor of foods. Check the label of seasonings to be sure they do not contain sodium. Use onion powder rather than onion salt, garlic powder instead of garlic salt. In place of seasoning salt, try commercially prepared herb and spice blends or make your own.

Copyright © 2011 Cookbook Publishers, Inc.

Low Sodium Seasoning Suggestions

	Allspice	Basil	Bay Leaves	Caraway Seed	Celery Seed	Chives	Curry Powder	Dill	Garlic	Ginger	Dry Mustard	Onion Powder	Oregano	Rosemary	Sage	Tarragon	Thyme
Beef	✓								✓	✓					✓	✓	
Pork				✓					✓						✓		✓
Veal			✓				✓			✓				✓			✓
Ground Meat	✓	✓		✓					✓		✓						
Poultry		✓					✓			✓				✓		✓	
Fish						✓	✓	✓								✓	
Eggs				✓		✓						✓	✓				
Soups/Stews	✓	✓	✓	✓	✓			✓				✓					✓
Sauces		✓											✓			✓	
Pasta				✓													
Rice		✓							✓			✓					
Popcorn							✓										
Asparagus				✓													
Beets				✓													
Broccoli										✓		✓					
Cabbage				✓			✓										
Carrots			✓	✓													
Cauliflower							✓									✓	
Green Beans								✓		✓							
Lima Beans					✓	✓								✓			
Potatoes										✓				✓			✓
Tomatoes		✓				✓		✓					✓				
Salads				✓		✓						✓					

Try this low sodium spice blend in your shaker instead of salt:

1 Tbsp. dry mustard
1 tsp. garlic powder
1½ Tbsp. onion powder
½ Tbsp. ground pepper
½ Tbsp. thyme, crushed
1 tsp. sage
½ tsp. marjoram, crushed
1 Tbsp. paprika
½ tsp. basil, crushed
½ tsp. ground oregano

Copyright © 2011 Cookbook Publishers, Inc.

Food Safety Guidelines

Food safety is an important part of food preparation. Bacteria that cause food-borne illnesses are present in many foods. Fortunately, with proper handling and cooking of foods, the danger from these bacteria and the toxins they may produce can be greatly reduced.

Follow these safety guidelines to help protect against food-borne illnesses:

Keep the temperature in the refrigerator between 35° F. and 40° F. A freezer should be at 0° F. or below.

Thaw all meat, fish, or poultry in the refrigerator. Do not thaw on the kitchen counter. For faster thawing, a microwave can be used, but meat should be cooked immediately after thawing.

Cook all meat and poultry thoroughly. The following chart is a guide.

FOOD	MINIMAL INTERNAL TEMPERATURE
Ground Meat	160° F.
Ground Poultry	165° F.
Beef, Veal, Lamb	145° F.
Pork	160° F.
Poultry	170° F.

Cook fish until it is opaque, firm, and flakes easily with a fork.

Cook eggs until the white is set and the yolk is starting to thicken. Do not eat raw eggs or those with cracks in the shell. Separate the egg white from the yolk by using an egg separator or a slotted spoon rather than by using the shell.

Once cooked, hold food at temperature below 40° F. or above 140° F. Do not allow perishable food to sit between these temperatures for more than two hours. This is considered the *danger zone* at which bacteria can readily grow or produce toxins.

Cool foods such as soups, sauces, and gravies in shallow pans no more than two inches deep.

Keep raw animal products and their juices separate from other foods.

+ Place raw meat on a plate or pan in the refrigerator to keep juices from dripping on other foods.
+ Wash kitchen surfaces, utensils, and hands after they have been exposed to raw meat, poultry, fish, and eggs.
+ Thoroughly clean cutting boards used for raw meat before using them for cooked foods or foods to be eaten raw, such as salad greens.
+ Use a clean container to hold cooked meat. Do not reuse the container that held the raw meat without cleaning it first.

When roasting a turkey or chicken with stuffing, it is best to cook the stuffing in a separate pan instead of in the cavity of the bird. If you choose to stuff the bird, however, do so just prior to putting it in the oven. When checking for doneness, make sure a thermometer placed into the center of the stuffing reads at least 165° F.

Copyright © 2011 Cookbook Publishers, Inc.

Basic Guidelines for Losing Weight

There are many diets and weight loss products available for those struggling to lose weight. The sad reality, however, is that most diets do not work. In the long run, people often regain even more weight than they originally lost. There is hope for those who want to shed some extra pounds. The key to long-term weight reduction is gradual and permanent changes in lifestyle habits.

Decrease the amount of total fat eaten. Fat has more than twice the calories of carbohydrates or protein. Thus, even small amounts of high fat items such as butter, margarine, oil, sauces, and gravies can contain large amounts of calories. Dietary fat is also the nutrient most easily converted into body fat. Much of the carbohydrates and protein we eat are burned up before they can be stored as fat.

Eat a variety of foods and do not restrict certain foods from the diet. In general, it is not the occasional food that keeps someone from achieving a desirable weight; it is what is eaten on a daily basis. For example, limit dessert to one or two times per week instead of after each meal. Forbidding foods often makes them more desirable, and may undermine weight loss efforts.

Eat breakfast. People who eat breakfast are generally more successful at losing weight.

Try not to eat before going to bed. Food eaten at this time of day is often not burned up and is more likely to be stored as fat.

Eat single portions of food and give the body time to signal that it is full. Often we eat so fast that the second portion of food is almost gone before the body can signal that it was satisfied after the first.

Eat foods high in complex carbohydrates. This includes breads, cereals, pasta, rice and other grains, fruits, and vegetables. Although many weight loss diets in the past have limited starchy foods, it is the high fat items that often accompany these foods that inhibit weight loss efforts, not the starchy foods themselves.

Exercise. Aerobic exercise is an excellent way to achieve and maintain a desirable weight. Walking, jogging, biking, and rowing are examples of aerobic activities. Before beginning any exercise program, it is a good idea to consult a physician.

Do not starve yourself. Low calorie diets may slow a body's metabolism, making weight loss more difficult.

Lose weight slowly, 1 to 2 pounds per week is desirable. Most people who need to lose weight need to lose excess fat. The body cannot burn off more than a few pounds of fat per week. Faster weight loss is probably due to muscle breakdown.

Set reasonable weight goals. Despite our society's obsession with thinness, it is not practical for most of us to expect to have the body of a model. Instead, setting a goal which is achievable and maintainable may, over time, result in greater physical and psychological health benefits.

Copyright © 2011 Cookbook Publishers, Inc.

Anatomy of MyPyramid

One size doesn't fit all
USDA's new MyPyramid symbolizes a personalized approach to healthy eating and physical activity. The symbol has been designed to be simple. It has been developed to remind consumers to make healthy food choices and to be active every day. The different parts of the symbol are described below.

Proportionality
Proportionality is shown by the different widths of the food group bands. The widths suggest how much food a person should choose from each group. The widths are just a general guide, not exact proportions. Check the Web site for how much is right for you.

MyPyramid.gov
STEPS TO A HEALTHIER YOU

Activity
Activity is represented by the steps and the person climbing them, as a reminder of the importance of daily physical activity.

Moderation
Moderation is represented by the narrowing of each food group from bottom to top. The wider base stands for foods with little or no solid fats or added sugars. These should be selected more often. The narrower top area stands for foods containing more added sugars and solid fats. The more active you are, the more of these foods can fit into your diet.

Personalization
Personalization is shown by the person on the steps, the slogan, and the URL. Find the kinds and amounts of food to eat each day at MyPyramid.gov.

Variety
Variety is symbolized by the 6 shaded bands representing the 5 food groups of the Pyramid and oils. This illustrates that foods from all groups are needed each day for good health.

Gradual Improvement
Gradual improvement is encouraged by the slogan. It suggests that individuals can benefit from taking small steps to improve their diet and lifestyle each day.

Inside the Pyramid

Grain
Make half your grains whole
- Eat at least 3 ounces of whole grain bread, cereal, crackers, rice, or pasta every day.
- Look for "whole" before the grain name on the list of ingredients.

Vegetable
Vary your veggies
- Eat more dark green veggies
- Eat more orange veggies
- Eat more dry beans and peas

Fruit
Focus on fruits
- Eat a variety of fruit
- Choose fresh, frozen, canned, or dried fruit
- Go easy on fruit juices

Oil
Know your fats
- Make most of your fat sources from fish, nuts, and vegetable oils
- Limit solid fats like butter, stick margarine, shortening, and lard

Milk
Get your calcium-rich foods
- Go low-fat or fat-free
- If you don't or can't consume milk, choose lactose-free products or other calcium sources

Meat & Beans
Go lean on protein
- Choose low-fat or lean meats and poultry
- Bake it, broil it, or grill it
- Vary your choices – with more fish, beans, peas, nuts, and seeds

Physical Activity *(Find your balance between food and physical activity.)*
- Be physically active for at least 30 minutes most days of the week.
- Children and teenagers should be physically active for 60 minutes every day, or most days.

Understanding the Nutrition Facts Food Label

The **Nutrition Facts** food label is designed to help the consumer make nutritious choices when selecting foods. It can be found on most packaged products in the grocery store. Information about serving size, calories, and several nutrients help to give an overall picture of the nutritional qualities of each food. The label on the following page is a typical example, although some labels list additional nutrients.

Serving Sizes have been set at an amount that people would typically eat. If your normal serving is smaller or larger, adjust the nutrient values accordingly. Serving sizes are in standard household and metric measures. Metric abbreviations used on the label include:

g: grams - 28g = 1 ounce
mg: milligrams - 1,000mg = 1g
ml: milliliters - 30ml = 1 fluid ounce

Nutrients listed are those considered to be important to today's health conscious consumer. These include total fat, saturated fat, cholesterol, sodium, and fiber.

The **Percent of Daily Value** tells you if the food is high or low in a particular nutrient. It also shows how that food fits into an entire day's diet. Percent of Daily Values are based on a 2,000 calorie diet and on current dietary guidelines. An individual's daily values may be higher or lower depending on calorie needs. As a rule of thumb, if the Daily Value is 5% or less, the food contains only a small amount of that nutrient. For total fat, saturated fat, cholesterol, and sodium, foods with a low Percent of Daily Value are good choices.

Terms used on the label to describe the food's nutritional content have strict definitions set by the government. Eleven **Descriptive Terms** have been identified: *free, low, lean, extra lean, less, reduced, light, fewer, high, more,* and *good source*. Because precise guidelines must be met for a food to use one of these terms, you can be assured that the claim is believable. For example, if a food claims to be sodium free, it must have less than 5ml of sodium per serving.

Claims regarding a food's relationship to various health-related conditions must also meet specific guidelines. To make a health claim about fats and heart disease, a food must be low in total fat, saturated fat, and cholesterol. A food making a statement regarding blood pressure and sodium must be low in sodium.

The **Ingredients List** is located in a separate location on the label. Ingredients are listed in descending order by weight; thus, if the first ingredient is sugar, there is more sugar in that product than anything else.

Nutrition Facts	
Serving Size 1 cup (228g)	
Servings Per Container 2	
Amount Per Serving	
Calories 260	Calories from Fat 120
	% Daily Value*
Total Fat 13g	20%
Saturated Fat 5g	25%
Cholesterol 30mg	10%
Sodium 660mg	28%
Total Carbohydrate 31g	10%
Dietary Fiber 0g	0%
Sugars 5g	
Protein 5g	
Vitamin A 4% •	Vitamin C 2%
Calcium 15% •	Iron 4%

* Percent Daily Values are based on a 2,000 calorie diet. Your daily values may be higher or lower depending on your calorie needs:

		Calories:	2,000	2,500
Total Fat	Less than		65g	80g
Sat Fat	Less than		20g	25g
Cholesterol	Less than		300mg	300mg
Sodium	Less than		2,400mg	2,400mg
Total Carbohydrate			300g	375g
Dietary Fiber			25g	30g

Calories per gram:
Fat 9 • Carbohydrate 4 • Protein 4

Copyright © 2011 Cookbook Publishers, Inc.

TABLE SETTING

Buffet Setting

A buffet makes it easy to serve a large group in a small dining area. This setting can be used for any meal by just placing the food in the order of your menu, plates first and eating utensils last.

1. Plates; 2. Main dish;
3. Gravy boat on liner plate;
4. Vegetable dish;
5. Other side dish; 6. Salad bowl;
7. Relish tray; 8. Basket of rolls; 9. Napkins with knives, forks and spoons;
10. Salt and pepper;
11. Centerpiece and candles.

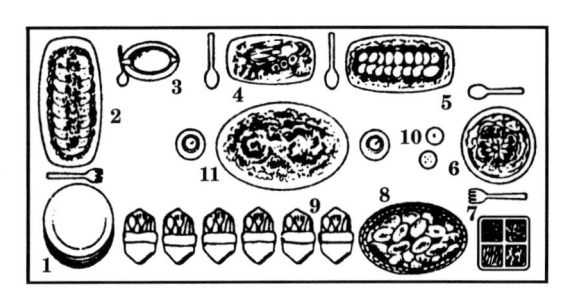

Luncheon

A luncheon can be great fun no matter what size the crowd. An optional fruit or soup first course could be followed by:
1. Hot casserole or omelet, bread and a light dessert.
2. Cold combination salad, bread and a rich dessert.
3. Small salad, hot main dish and dessert.

1. Bread and butter plate and knife; 2. Water glass; 3. Optional drink glass; 4. Napkin; 5. Luncheon fork; 6. Dessert fork; 7. First course bowl and liner plate; 8. Luncheon plate; 9. Knife; 10. Teaspoon; 11. Soup spoon.

Dinner

You don't have to wait for a special occasion to have a formal dinner party. Sunday dinners with family and friends is a wonderful reason to celebrate by serving a formal dinner and it will almost guarantee help with the extra dishes!

1. Salad plate; 2. Water glass; 3. Optional drink glass; 4. Napkin; 5. Salad fork; 6. Dinner fork; 7. Dessert fork; 8. First-course bowl and liner plate; 9. Dinner plate; 10. Dinner knife; 11. Teaspoon; 12. Soup spoon.

NAPKIN FOLDING

Add a final decorative touch to your dinner table by folding napkins into any of the shapes below. Napkins may also be placed on the dinner plates.

BUTTERFLY

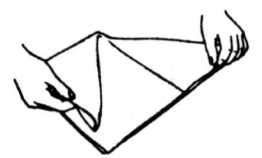

Form a triangle from an open napkin. Fold the right corner to the center.

Take the left corner up to center, making a diamond. Keeping the loose points at the top, turn the napkin over, then fold upward, to form a triangle.

Tuck the left corner into the right. Stand up napkin; turn it round, then turn the petals down; it's now a butterfly.

ARTICHOKE

Place all 4 points to the center of an opened napkin.

Fold the 4 points to the center of the napkin once more.

Repeat a third time; turn napkin over and fold points to the center once more.

Holding finger firmly at center, unfold 1 petal first from underneath each corner.

Pull out 4 more from between the petals. Then pull out the next 4 under the petals.

The artichoke now has 12 points.

SILVER BUFFET

Fold the napkin over twice to form a square. Hold the square in a diamond shape.

Take the top 2 flaps and roll them halfway down the napkin.

Fold under the right and left points at the sides. There is now a pocket into which you can place the knife, fork and spoon.

About the EWGA Foundation

On a warm July afternoon in 1991, a group of 28 women gathered at the Emerald Dunes Golf Course in West Palm Beach, Florida to learn to play golf. The women were from many professions and most were interested in using golf for business. They saw their male counterparts in the office taking clients out to the golf course and playing in company and charity outings. They wanted to be able to play, too.

Yet, what happened during those golf lessons led to so much more. Everyone had so much fun getting to know each other as they learned the game that they asked Nancy Oliver, the golf marketing executive who organized the gathering, to put together more events so they could keep playing together. And that is the beginning of what we know today as the EWGA (Executive Women's Golf Association).

In 2003, the EWGA established the EWGA Foundation, a 501(c)(3) tax exempt organization that exists to create and fund education and leadership programs for women of all ages. Its initiatives include:

Fundraising support of LPGA-USGA Girls Golf, a developmental junior golf program for girls ages 7-17. To date, EWGA Chapters and the EWGA Foundation have donated almost $500,000 to Girls Golf, making EWGA one of the largest single contributors to this program, aside from the USGA.

Women On Par® Scholarship Program to provide financial support to women ages 30 and older who are interested in beginning or completing their undergraduate college education to get 'on par' with their peers and better themselves both personally and professionally.

Drive for Dreams outreach program to share our good fortune with those less fortunate by means of contributing golf equipment and other resources needed to give the gift of golf.

Financial support to develop the EWGA Golf Education curriculum and bring speakers with expertise in leadership development training and facilitation to EWGA meetings and gatherings.

Since EWGA's inception, more than 100,000 women's lives have been enriched through the game of golf.

Learn more at www.ewga.com.

Make A Contribution to the EWGA Foundation Today!

Copy this page and send your contribution to:

EWGA Foundation
300 Avenue of the Champions, Suite 140
Palm Beach Gardens, FL 33418-3615
Or visit us online at www.ewga.com
All donations are tax deductible as allowable by law.

EWGA Foundation Contribution Amount: $ _____

Please Designate my Gift for:

☐ ____ General ☐ ____ *Drive for Dreams* Campaign

☐ ____ *Women On Par*® Scholarship Program

☐ ____ Christy Bartlett *Women On Par*® Scholarship

Name _____ Phone ( ) _____

Billing Address _____

City _____ State _____ Zip _____

Email Address _____

Checks payable to: **EWGA Foundation**

OR

Charge: ☐ American Express ☐ Visa ☐ MasterCard ☐ Discover

Cardholder Name _____

Signature _____

Card# ☐☐☐☐☐☐☐☐☐☐☐☐☐☐☐☐ CCID# ☐☐☐☐

Expiration date (mm/yy) ☐☐/☐☐

*Did you know that many employers sponsor matching gift programs and will match charitable contributions made by their employees? These matches are often dollar for dollar, which doubles your charitable donation power. To find out if your company has a matching gift policy, check with your company's human resources/payroll department, or visit www.matchinggifts.com to conduct a search based on your company's name.
EWGA Foundatin Federal EIN: 11-3695416*

This Cookbook is a perfect gift for Special Occasions and Chapter Recognition!

To order additional copies, please use Order Form on reverse side of this page or order online at www.ewga.com.

"Recipes for Success – On and Off the Course"
Order Form

Use this order form to obtain additional copies
or order online at www.ewga.com.
Pricing includes Shipping & Handling
You may order additional copies at a rate of $19.50 USD (1-4 copies)
or at a bulk rate of $17.50 USD (5 or more copies) per book ordered.

Complete and Return To:

EWGA Foundation
300 Avenue of the Champions, Suite 140
Palm Beach Gardens, FL 33418-3615
Fax: (561) 691-0012
foundation@myewga.com

Send me _____ copies of your Cookbook (1-4 copies) @ $ 19.50 ea.
OR:
I'm placing a bulk order (5 or more books).
Send me _____ copies of your Cookbook (5 or more) @ $ 17.50 ea.

Ship books to:

Name_____

Address_____

City, State, Zip_____

Total Amount: $ _____   ☐ Check enclosed, payable
                                                                  to EWGA Foundation
OR:
Charge: ☐ American Express ☐ Visa/MasterCard ☐ Discover

Cardholder Name: _____

Cardholder Signature: _____

Billing Address (if different from shipping address):

Address: _____

City: _____ State _____ Zip _____

Card # ☐☐☐☐☐☐☐☐☐☐☐☐☐☐☐☐

CCID # ☐☐☐☐   Exp. (mm/yy) ☐☐/☐☐